Qualitative Research in Arts and Mental Health

Contexts, meanings and evidence

Editor

Theo Stickley

PCCS Books
Monmouth

First published in 2012

PCCS Books Ltd
Wyastone Business Park
Wyastone Leys
Monmouth
NP25 3SR
UK
Tel +44 (0)1600 891 509
www.pccs-books.co.uk

This selection © Theo Stickley, 2012
The chapters © the authors, 2012

All rights reserved.
No part of this publication may be reproduced, stored in a retrieval system, transmitted or utilised in any form by any means, electronic, mechanical, photocopying or recording or otherwise without permission in writing
from the publishers. The authors have asserted their rights to be identified as the authors of this work in accordance with the Copyright, Designs and Patents Act 1988.

Qualitative Research in Arts and Mental Health: Contexts, meanings and evidence

A CIP catalogue record for this book is available from the British Library

ISBN 978 1 906254 39 1

Cover image 'Release' © Charissa Borroff, 2012
Cover design by Old Dog Graphics
Printed by ImprintDigital, Exeter, UK

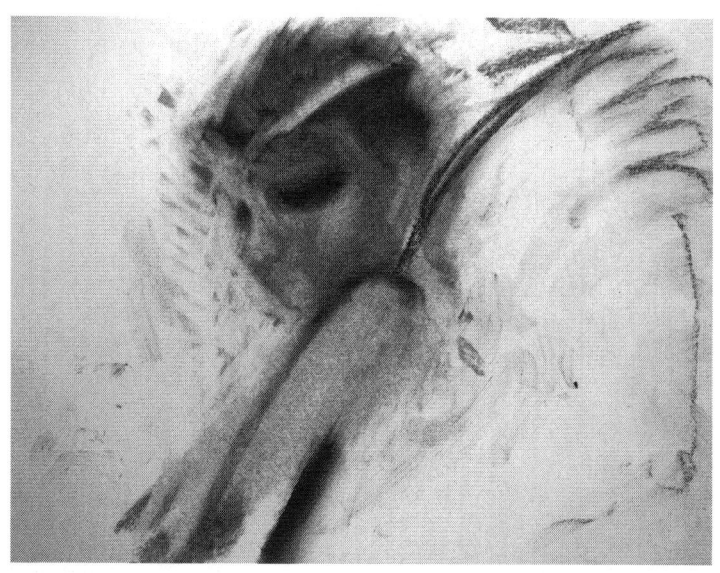

Contents

Introduction
Theo Stickley   vii

1. **The Arts and Mental Health: Creativity and inclusion**
   Hester Parr   1

2. **Is Art Therapy?**
   Langley Brown   22

3. **Innovation, Arts and Mental Health: An evaluation of four innovative arts-based mental health projects**
   Helen Brooks & David Pilgrim   42

4. **Creating Something Beautiful: Art in Mind**
   Theo Stickley   58

5. **Social Identity and Belonging: The Lost Artists Club**
   Theo Stickley   75

6. **Interview as Generative Practice in Arts and Wellbeing Partnership Work**
   Julie Hanna & Polly Moseley   98

7. **Movies, Movements and Moving Moments: Connecting film, user involvement and student learning**
   Mick McKeown, Russell Hogarth, Fiona Jones, Mark Edwards, Keith Holt, Sarah Traill, Jane Priestley, Garry Watkins, Michael Hellawell, John Lunt & Lisa Malihi-Shoja   118

8. **Working with Artists to Promote Mental Health and Wellbeing in Schools: An evaluation of processes and outcomes at four schools**
   Edward Sellman with Alma Cunliffe   140

9. **Art, Autoethnography, and the Use of Self**
   Brendan Stone   170

10. **Film, Fractals, and Emergent Themes**
    Shaun & Marian Naidoo   185

11. **Catching Life: The contribution of arts initiatives to recovery approaches in mental health**
    Helen Spandler, Jenny Secker, Lyn Kent, Suzanne Hacking & Jo Shenton   199

    Final Thoughts
    Theo Stickley   213

    Contributors   217

    Index   219

This book is dedicated to my Guiding Lights in life, Pat and Ray Stickley. They met on the stage (quite literally) about 60 years ago and have performed sublimely ever since.

List of Illustrations*

Angel Susan Hammami	ii
'Don't look at me' Susan Hammami	vii
Flying or Falling Willow Merryweather	1
Derby Road Melvyn William James	22
Paranoia Mark Foster	42
IOWA Cathy Eddamri	58
Mental Breakdown Nicola Oliver	75
Trapped Anthony Garriff	98
Space Willow Merryweather	118
What Lies Beneath Simon Wragg	140
Untitled Emma Constable	170
Wild Woman Fiona Adams	185
Anthropometry Rob Van Beek	199
Longsufferer Brick	213
Darkness on the Edge of Town Paine Proffitt	217

---

* The editor and publisher wish to thank the artists for their kind permission to use their work.

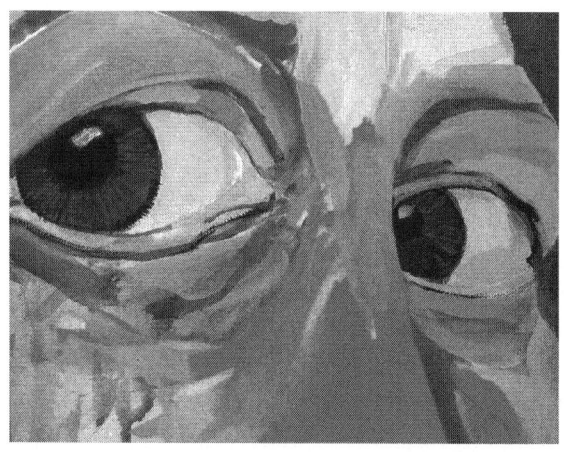

Introduction

Theo Stickley

There are thousands of books published on the subject of mental health, possibly hundreds devoted to qualitative research, and a small number about participatory arts, but this may be the one and only book that brings the three together. Hopefully, this book will inspire and show the value of participatory arts for people's mental health and wellbeing in the future.

In recent years, arts practitioners working in healthcare environments have been ardently seeking to provide research and evaluation evidence to support their initiatives. Every journal article or book devoted to the wide subject of Arts and Health is welcome as it provides further evidence for the effectiveness of the work. In that sense, this book makes a small contribution to the theory and therefore the evidence base on the subject.

This is not, however, a purely theoretical book, but one that speaks about real-life practice which has been going on in the UK in recent years. It is hoped that this book will be used as a textbook by researchers, practitioners and students for years to come. It is by no means exhaustive; there are many arts and mental health projects around the country that get no mention here. What is presented is perhaps a snapshot of typical examples of good practice. There is little here that relates to art therapy. This is the one area of arts and mental health practice that is better established in terms of research output. The kinds of 'arts' talked about in this book are more participatory than art therapy (the subject of 'Is art therapy?' is theoretically engaged with in Chapter 2).

Because this book is about 'qualitative' research, it does not imply that quantitative approaches are not needed in Arts and Health research. On the contrary, where it is appropriate to do so, quantitative research can make a very important contribution; for example, Clift and Hancox (2001), Hacking et al. (2008). It is my view however that qualitative research suits arts activities more than quantitative research. Qualitative research can be made creative, non-intrusive and fun. Furthermore, some qualitative approaches are artistic themselves, as examples in this book demonstrate.

One of the problems in presenting a book of this nature is that the three concepts that unite the book (arts, mental health, and qualitative research) are each contested concepts. The arts are very difficult to define as they are inseparable from culture and everyday life; mental health can also be culturally and subjectively determined; and qualitative research is diverse and often regarded as the poor relation to scientific research.

The evidence base for Arts and Health work is growing. In her review of the Arts and Health literature, Staricoff (2004) examined health and medical literature published between 1990 and 2004 in order to explore the relationship of the arts to healthcare, and the influence and effects of the arts on health. She identified approximately 264 studies in the 14-year period to inform the discussion of the subject. There has been no subsequent study on this scale, but it is clear that the growth in published research has been enormous. There are now two journals devoted to the topic (*Arts & Health: An International Journal for Research, Policy and Practice,* and *Journal of Applied Arts and Health*) as well as many other journals publishing this kind of research.

There is therefore much evidence continually being produced that supports Arts and Health practice. However, what constitutes evidence in terms of scientific inquiry is often beyond the reach of Arts and Health projects and researchers (e.g., randomised controlled trials). There is, however, plenty of evidence for the efficacy of participatory arts in terms of personal and social outcomes, but until the right kind of evidence is produced for the National Health Service, the evidence that is produced often remains marginalised and will continue to be subject to criticism within the scientifically dominated healthcare arena.

Arts practitioners may become easily discouraged when the evidence they produce is dismissed by healthcare budget holders because this evidence does not meet the acceptable standards. It is at this point I would like to call upon the common-sense argument. Let's imagine Dr Bloggs, a successful medical consultant who holds a £10 million NHS budget. Before he will fund an Arts on Prescription programme he demands to see the evidence of its effectiveness and is given a qualitative research report. There is much of what he considers to be 'anecdotal' evidence – stories of how people enjoy it and appear to 'get something' from it. He looks for the 'hard' evidence – the cost savings to GPs, the recovery rates and hospital bed-use reductions. He dismisses the evidence he has been given because it is not a double-blind trial. He will then drive home in his car listening to music. He arrives home and is welcomed by the paintings on his walls. He and his wife visit the ballet in the evening; he reads from a novel before sleeping. If questioned about his engagement with art and culture, he would inevitably greatly value what he almost takes for granted. By his choices in life, Dr Bloggs provides evidence of the value of engaging with arts and culture. He doesn't first measure the effect of the arts on his life before he engages with something; he knows, by *common sense* that the arts are good for him.

Ultimately, we are unlikely to win the common-sense argument in terms of being able to see the arts mainstreamed in healthcare. So, we continue to research the Arts and Health and document the findings from this research in journals and books such as this in the hope that one day, common sense will prevail and creative approaches in mental health will become more valued and embedded in practice. This does not mean that we should not research and evaluate our practice; on the contrary, the more we document Arts and Health work, the more the evidence grows.

When you read through the chapters of this book, I think you will find a good deal of common sense. This is not a scientific book, it is an artistic book. You will find first-person accounts (autoethnography) and stories that researchers have accrued (narratives). At times, the authors' voices become poetic. The researchers are inevitably sympathetic to the arts and believe in the projects that they are researching. Does this therefore invalidate the research because of the researchers' bias? The truth is that all research is biased in one way or another, because all research is conducted by human beings, not robots. The important thing in qualitative research is to acknowledge that bias exists; this transparency in the research process is what gives the research validity. The authors in this book are not silent, anonymous data-gatherers; they are fully functioning human beings, each with their own emotional and psychological processes. This is therefore a book of real-life arts and mental health research and not a purely academic book.

The book commences with a chapter from Hester Parr who introduces an essential discussion about the relationship between art and mental health with reference to its historical positioning as both therapeutic and outsider art. Hester reports the findings from her research based upon two arts projects in Scotland with various 'outcomes' such as: inclusion, outsiderness, artistry, senses of belonging and communality. Chapter Two offers something of a contrast as Langley Brown takes the reader on an autoethnographic journey. The chapter delineates the two approaches to creativity in mental healthcare: art therapy, where the emphasis is placed on healing, with the client as patient-to-be-cured; and non-clinical arts activity, where the emphasis is placed on art, with the participant as artist-in-the-making. The study describes the history and modes of practice of each approach, identifies areas of contention, and lays foundations for collaborative development in pursuit of a continuum of creative opportunities for people experiencing mental health problems. Chapter Three is authored by Helen Brooks and David Pilgrim. They discuss the findings from an evaluation of eleven innovative mental health projects throughout the UK, with a particular focus on four arts-based projects: one with homeless people, another includes filmmaking with vulnerable adults, the third based upon work in a medium-secure psychiatric unit, where users were the audience of cabaret evenings, poetry readings and so on. The fourth area is animation for vulnerable children and families.

I have authored both Chapters Four and Five; the first is what I consider to be an unusual chapter focusing on narrative interviews with people who worked together to set up a programme of work promoting mental health through participatory arts. The chapter also includes personal reflection of my roles in both strategic development and as a researcher. In Chapter Five I present the findings from my research with members of the Lost Artists Club, a community development led by the residents of one inner-city community. Julie Hanna and Polly Moseley authored Chapter Six and focus on two research projects with which they have been individually involved. They also draw on evolving arts and wellbeing practice in Liverpool, where significant investment has been made in a city-wide programme over the last nine years. Mick McKeown authored Chapter Seven with a number of people he has worked with in a university department on *Movies, Movements and Moving Moments: Connecting film, user involvement and student learning*. The chapter develops thinking about participation in different but connected initiatives concerned with mental health, the arts and humanities. Chapter Eight is authored by Edward Sellman and Alma Cunliffe. The focus is on how collaboration between artists and schools can promote mental wellbeing and the ways in which such approaches can be evaluated. Research undertaken with groups of students at four schools is shared, showing how working with an artist on a group project for 8 to 12 weeks helped develop friendships, social skills, increased confidence and resilience.

Chapter Nine, by Brendan Stone, includes the author's own autoethnographic work and shows why artistic endeavour must inform not only therapeutic interventions in the treatment of severe distress, but also that research in this field should itself be open to employing creative methods of inquiry and dissemination. Shaun and Marian Naidoo present Chapter Ten: *Film, Fractals, and Emergent Themes*. The chapter discusses how their use of film and video in qualitative research has developed from the initial recognition of the importance of video as a data collection tool. Film is a valuable asset to qualitative researchers. On an individual level it can record the richness of the individual story and across a larger project it can be used to evidence emergent themes and patterns while remaining authentic to its primary source. The final chapter by Helen Spandler and colleagues draws on qualitative research that was undertaken as part of a national study to assess the impact of participatory arts provision for people with mental health needs. It explores how arts and mental health projects may facilitate some of the key elements of what has been termed a 'recovery approach' in mental health. It is argued that it is precisely these elements – the fostering of hope, creating a sense of meaning and purpose, developing new coping mechanisms and rebuilding identities – which are hard to standardise and measure, yet may be the most profound and significant outcomes of participation in such projects.

As I have already said, there are thankfully many arts and mental health projects and programmes of work throughout the UK and these are only a few examples. I hope though that you will feel inspired and enriched from reading these varied accounts to continue to develop practice as well as experiment with ways to evaluate and research in the future.

Finally in this introduction I would like to thank Helen Spandler for her help in the preparation of this book. Helen suggested a number of the contributors as well as the title for the book! The entire project may not have come to fruition without her help.

References

Clift, S & Hancox, G (2001) The perceived benefits of singing: Findings from preliminary surveys of a university college choral society. *Perspectives in Public Health, 121*(4), 248–56.

Hacking, S, Secker, J, Spandler, H & Kent, L (2008) Evaluating the impact of participatory art projects for people with mental health needs. *Health & Social Care in the Community, 16*(6), 638–48.

Staricoff, R (2004) Arts in health: A review of the medical literature. *Research Report 36.* London: Arts Council England.

CHAPTER ONE

The Arts and Mental Health: Creativity and inclusion

Hester Parr

Introduction

Recent research suggests that participation in the arts by people with mental health problems might facilitate versions of inclusivity and 'insiderness' in both mainstream and interest communities for this often stigmatised grouping. This chapter seeks to complicate and critique this basic assumption, while still bearing witness to the extraordinary social and artistic journeying that arts participation can bring about. I am writing as a geographer and so my attention is on how arts participation occurs through different spaces: spaces of artistic process itself, spaces of artistic networks and spaces of the city in particular. Attention to these 'topographies' allows us nuanced insights into how arts participation actually works for vulnerable people, and at a variety of scales.

In the first part of the chapter the relationship between art and mental health is discussed with reference to its historical positioning as both therapeutic and outsider art. I then go on to introduce a contemporary case study to complicate these two positions, attempting to show how arts-for-mental-health is a fragile and contingent process of engagement – with various 'outcomes' regarding mental health, inclusion, outsiderness, artistry, senses of belonging and communality.

Locating the arts and outsider 'madness'

There is evidence that people with mental health problems have been representing their own complex experiences through art for a long time (Haywood Gallery, 1996). Whether as a result of therapeutic art work in asylums or through the 'discovery' of innate 'talents' (Laing, 2000), there is a recognisable history of 'outsider art' in the mental health field.

'Outsider art' or 'art brut', to use the original term advanced by the French painter Jean Dubuffet (1901–1985), is 'a catch-all phrase for everything that is ostensibly raw, untutored and irrational in art' (Rexer, 2005: 6). Outsider artists are primarily self-taught, idiosyncratic and unusually self-expressive, and in addition 'outsider art is not an art movement recognised by its practitioners' (ibid.: 12). As Rhodes (2000) argues, artist-outsiders are, by definition, different to their audience and are often conceived as being dysfunctional in respect of the parameters set by the dominant culture. Outsider art and artists were originally often located and identified in the context of institutions, and indeed psychiatric patients were a key group at the heart of early definitions of outsider art (see also Carter Park et al., 1994). 'Insane art', as it is also known, is primarily a 20th century phenomenon, although artistic expression by patients did exist before that, but was often thought to be valueless beyond its selective use for clinical teaching (Philo, 2006). The early collectors of insane art were psychiatrists, with some using work to illustrate different forms of pathology (see Lombroso, 1911/1972), while others, famously the likes of Hans Prinzhorn (1886–1933), amassed a large collection of insane art where the works considered were taken to have some kind of aesthetic value, if only as supposed rare access points into the confused schizophrenic psyche and the assumed pure, developmental stages of artistic expression and growth (Haywood Gallery, 1996). Patients' own representations were thus subsumed into a clinical framing of disorder, one that resonated with the difference-making of other medicalised visualisations.

Insane outsider art was mainly produced in psychiatric asylums and was sometimes even exhibited by these institutions, such as the early landmark exhibitions of 'psychotic art' organised by the Bethlem Royal Hospital in 1900 and 1913 (Rhodes, 2000). The location of outsider artists and their art in closed-off asylum spaces arguably signified their 'not belonging' – not to mainstream society but nor to its mainstream cultural logics and productions. In contemporary times, outsider art *still* attracts great cultural interest, and many exhibitions and collections orientate themselves around this loose and problematic category: for example, 'The Scottish Collection of Extraordinary

Art' in Pittenweem, Fife, which draws in part on the art work of present and discharged psychiatric patients, proving the *continuing* influence of the genre for this group, albeit sometimes at a distance from psychiatric institutions and diagnostic power (e.g., Laing, 2000).

Although artists and artistry in all their forms are *not* always rationalist endeavours, institutionalised artists with severe and enduring mental health problems have nonetheless been rendered different in ways that have particular and profound social and spatial dimensions. Indeed, there is little evidence to suggest that the (institutionalised) psychiatric patients who have produced 'outsider art' have ever individually benefited from artistic attention and critique, or participated in any social life with other (outsider) artists, and so arguably their positions have remained firmly marginal with respect to both mainstream and also avant-garde culture.

Art and insiderness

There are arguably two main relevant contexts to why the relationship between art and outsiderness has been disrupted: the first being the development of art therapy within mental healthcare. Popular since the middle of the 20th century, this is, alongside therapeutic drug use, credited with the demise of the category of 'pure' outsider art/artists, since both therapeutic mediums have supposedly contributed to a 'quietening' of raw insanity and its artistic expression (Rhodes, 2000). Art therapy originated (and has partially remained within) the closed-off spaces of the asylum/hospital, but it has *also* become more prominent in the context of deinstitutionalisation: the spatial move of patients 'back' from the institution (and outsider positions) into everyday community life (and insider positions). In terms of the success of this 'new' insiderness, art therapy might be argued to work in particular ways. There is a common (arguably mistaken) assumption, for example, that art comes second to therapy in this and other similar rehabilitative practices, which therefore risks being merely a tool for the rehabilitation of the damaged or pathological self rather than specifically facilitating transferable artistic skills and identities (Malchiodi, 1999; Hogan, 2001; Willis, 2002). Overall, though, reconfiguring the differentness of insane art through therapeutic intervention has potentially contributed to the possibility of cultural insiderness, enabling psychiatric patient-artists to be released from the specific (exclusionary) category of outsider art(ists). Indeed, art therapy may exist as a 'limit case' example in relation to outsider art, in that it seeks to achieve exactly the opposite outcome in helping with the attainment of states of insiderness.

The second context that is relevant relates to the supposed benefits of community and public art whereby marginalised people and places are (not unproblematically) considered to gain access to empowering forms of representation and expression that somehow help a project of centring and insiderness (Rose, 1997).

In this view, marginalised psychiatric patients subject to stereotyping and stigmatisation might also be drawn in to a newly inclusive cultural city by participation in public and community arts projects. Whilst examples must abound of cases where precisely this has happened for specific individuals with mental health difficulties, the participation of people with severe and enduring mental health problems *as a group* in community arts is more likely to have occurred as a result of specific mental health and arts projects in community settings. While certainly helping to disrupt the historic association between mental health and art in institutional space, these arts-for-health projects may engender experiences of what has been termed *bonding* and not necessarily *bridging* social capital for participants.[1] If so, this outcome has implications for senses of insiderness, integration and, indeed, wider 'belongings' (White, 2003), questioning the success of what has been called an inclusive 'arts advocacy' approach that often underlies such initiatives (Maddern & Bloom, 2004). Despite this caveat, these two broad contexts have arguably contributed to a disruption of the association between mental health, arts and outsiderness or not-belonging, although there is a need to understand in more detail what *precisely* constitutes a relationship between art, insiderness and belonging in community settings.

The arts for mental health?

In attending to questions of insiderness and outsiderness associated with arts practices, the idea of 'belonging' has been flagged above as one possible outcome of artistic engagement. In order to explore this claim further, and drawing on artist voices from arts-for-mental-health projects in the Scottish cities of Dundee and Glasgow, *experiential* accounts of artistic endeavour and the different kinds of belonging that it can engender are foregrounded.

Reading the creation of situated and unstable belongings through artistic

---

1. This refers to the fact that arts projects may involve the accumulation of 'bonding' social capital *amongst* its members (leading to increased self-understanding and esteem, friendship and social networks, skills and peer-support and learning), but that such benefits may not always occur as a result of wider community networking, whereas 'bridging' social capital is created between art project participants and all manner of other (non-project-based) community members.

experiences and voices is therefore pursued below in relation to a range of social geographies, including interior creative spaces, the spaces of arts projects themselves, and the collective place of art and artists associated with mental health in the cultural city. One key purpose is to elaborate arts work as a complex and not straightforwardly celebratory practice for the creation of inclusionary belonging.

Experiencing artistic geographies for mental health

By highlighting the voices of people who participate in mental health and arts projects, consideration is given to how and whether artistic practice facilitates senses of belonging and insiderness in ways that disrupt trajectories of both outsider art and art therapy, as well as allowing us to better elaborate current discourses of cultural inclusivity at different scales. I am drawing on research carried out between 2003 and 2007 with two city-wide mental health and arts projects in central Glasgow (Trongate Studios, now called Trongate 103) and Dundee (Art Angel), chosen because of their relative high profiles in their respective locations. In both projects participants had a mix of arts-related experience ranging from none at all to degree-level training in fine art. Neither project required that participants had such experience or training, and both held outreach workshops and operated phased introductory access to art work and group workshops. Of the 35 artists who were interviewed,[2] only five had formal training, although all professed a long-standing interest in visual art (predominantly), writing or performance, which for some began in hospital settings. They were hence largely a self-selecting group, which may have implications for how artistic emotional geographies are experienced.

At the time of the research, Art Angel in Dundee was operating in Dudhope Arts Centre, a largely abandoned building just north-west of the city centre, and was core-funded by the National Health Service (NHS) and

---

2. This research involved 40 interviews with paid staff and working artists who made up the client base of the projects, as well as substantial ethnographic engagement in 2003–2007. In addition, cultural officers of Glasgow and Dundee City Councils and relevant NHS personnel were also interviewed. In both projects the artists were predominantly working class and of white British origin. As in many community projects orientated around mental health issues, the numbers of women were smaller than that of men (8 out of 35 artist interviews were with women), and participants were referred to the projects from a range of access points (including GPs, community psychiatric nurses, psychiatrists, hospital wards, outreach project work and friendship networks). Interviews with artists covered a range of topics, but broadly addressed the benefits and difficulties of engaging in the practice of art work and community art projects for mental health. These were transcribed and coded with the NVivo software package using over 100 emic and etic codes.

the City Council's Regeneration Fund, with 60 people registered as using its city-wide service. For six years prior to this, the project was known as Arts Advocacy and located in the Dundee Rep Theatre in the prestigious cultural quarter of the city. A combination of funding difficulties and local politics led to the project having to move from this site, a point revisited below. Art Angel ran a weekly arts group in Liff Hospital (a former asylum) and several community group arts workshops in visual art, photography and writing. LUNA, a next-step arts organisation (originally based in Liff), was also hosted by Art Angel and run by people with mental health problems themselves, who engage in a range of activities from filmmaking to performance to writing projects. See the Art Angel website for more information about their current activities: http://artangeldundee.org.uk/

Trongate Studios, for people with mental health problems in Glasgow's city centre, was part of Project Ability between 2003 and 2007, and at its core sat an arts project for a permanent group of learning-disabled artists, although work with ethnic minorities, children and youth also featured strongly in their programmes. The Trongate Studio initiative was distinct from these programmes, and was partially supported by Project Ability's funding from the Scottish Arts Council and the City Council's Arts development budgets, in addition to being directly core-funded by the NHS. Seventy studio artists were registered with the Trongate Studios at the time of research, and shared or individually occupied a small studio space in an open plan arrangement (see Figure 1.2). They have since relocated to a large purpose-built and high-profile arts centre (http://www.trongate103.com/). The Studios ran introductory group workshops for prospective members, although there had been up to a three-year waiting list to access the project in the past. The main activity of the studios was visual arts work and, unlike Art Angel, the Trongate Studios had gallery space, which was open to the public.

Interior creative spaces

The activities of the Trongate Studios and Art Angel involved work across a range of artistic mediums, including visual art, craft-making, sculpture, writing, filmmaking and performance (termed 'art' or 'arts' here, although there are important embodied, social and material differences between the artistic mediums used[3]). In interviews and in everyday conversation with artists,

---

3. For example, filmmaking is often constructed as a collective, very social form of participation in the arts, whereby visual arts work or writing can be (although not necessarily) a more individualised experience (see Parr, 2007).

they discussed their participation in the arts in many ways, but often, significantly, as a non-clinical practice that involved experiences of stability and wellbeing. Experiences of stability, arguably an important precursor for sensing belonging in proximate social networks and physical places (Parr, 1999), were represented as emerging from different dimensions of what might be called artistic geographies involving different psychological, social and material properties. In discussing the spatiality of creativity and wellbeing in particular, many artists evoked a complex fusion of thoughts, materials, movements and imagination in the production of art work. This embodied fusion – viscerally experienced in the creative process of painting, making, writing and filmmaking – was perceived as a beneficial and sometimes therapeutic interiority (see also Crouch, 2005 and Figure 1.1). Artistic practice facilitated a sense of psychological locatedness, enabling a temporarily all-consuming occupational space that distracted from negative and disruptive thoughts and affects:

> *It sounds corny, but it's like a kind of magic, [you] go into a sort of trance and I think it's a fantastic thing when it happens. It doesn't always happen ... but for me it was a way of getting out of the depression. (Ben, artist, Glasgow)*

> *Art is therapeutic because it's so absorbing and you can go to this place that is not you and it's not world, and it's safe because it's a sort of mediation ... and you're not going into it forever. (Tina, artist, Glasgow)*

Although not always the case by any means (see below), such comments demonstrate individual artists encountering interior creative space as a predominantly calm, safe 'location' that can be accessed as part of a strategy for recovery.[4] For many participants, the creative space between hands, thought, canvas, imagination and practice was difficult to articulate, but usually entailed a sense of temporary escape, reconciliation and challenge that assisted with the recovering self. Such practices are difficult to understand and translate, particularly as objective evidence of beneficial outcomes, especially in the context of mental health problems where creative space that is 'trance-like' and 'not world' could be misread as symptomatic of mental instability.[5]

---

4. Not all artists understood themselves as in recovery, although all interviewees understood art as a potentially therapeutic practice that assisted in coping with the effects of mental health problems.
5. Although such experiential spaces are not only accessed by artists with serious mental health problems.

Figure 1.1 Spaces of creative practice: author photograph

As artists nonetheless go on to explain, experiencing art work as a stabilising practice is an important 'stepping stone' for reinsertion into wider social geographies outside of clinical or artistic spaces. Embodied spaces of art-making, for example, enabled participants to learn about themselves, and to experiment with communicating feelings or work through difficulties encountered in other aspects of their everyday lives. A strong sense of art work as a relational practice – one that might help participants to sense belonging in mainstream social spaces – therefore also emerged from artists who previously had had difficulties communicating aspects of themselves, particularly during periods of illness:

> *It [art] was another form of communication, because I couldn't talk very well. Actually I [just] couldn't talk sometimes and I wasn't being understood, so I used painting and writing as other forms of trying to communicate with people ... [and so] for me it was vital. (Peter, artist, Dundee)*

It is debatable, of course, how effectively such art work does communicate the intentions and messages of its authors, even if these are clearly known, as interviewees went on to acknowledge. Even so, the tentative engagement in relational processes as part of the production of art is what is of most importance here. In terms of belonging, increased individual psychological stability (feeling connected to oneself) and collective inclusion (the capacity to be connected to others) are clearly relevant. Whilst art works can thus be relational in these terms and also act as a catalyst for more fluid social selves, helping artists to enter into a greater diversity of social relations (see below), the emotional geographies of art-making are *also* characterised by sensing boundaries:

> *I think art was ... it contains ... so if you are feeling really really bad and anxious, then, yes, you are making a bad anxious, messy picture, but you are somehow or other, it's like a bit of shit you get out .... (Tina, artist, Glasgow)*
>
> *I started on paper maché balls, because it was trying to bind myself to something. So it would be, if I felt I was losing the place, I could do paper maché balls because one ball has a finishing you know? It's a finished object ... a boundary. (Cath, artist, Dundee)*

For these artists, negative feelings can be 'contained' in art, or offer ways of binding senses of self to finished art objects in order not to 'lose the place'. Some commentators on the characteristic forms of outsider art note that intensive attempts to imprint aspects of the inner self onto paper or canvas are common: 'a consistent ... solution that allows them to concretise their interior world [in which] a kind of equilibrium emerges' (Jadi, 1996: 24, but see also Rhodes, 2000). While not interpreting the interviewees above as outsider artists, and thus implying their ultimate differencing, their search for psychological boundaries through artistic practice is tangible.

This reveals a partial picture of the therapeutic dimensions to art practice, about which there is, of course, a substantial and nuanced literature, primarily influenced by clinical psychotherapeutic tropes (Edwards, 2004). Yet, the people and the projects represented here are clear that they do *not practice nor participate in art therapy* as a clinical discipline. Rather, they recognise that artistic practice can be experienced as therapeutic and involve profound and sometimes spatialised senses of relationality, coherence, recovery, trauma, emotional conflict and resolution (see also Bondi with Fewell, 2003). Many artists also used their work to self-evaluate both artistic and personal development:

> *I would draw a picture of myself each day. Not from looking in the mirror, but from how I felt ... and I'd learned something from those drawings, learned strongly about how people influence me. (Cath, artist, Dundee)*
>
> *It helps give you an insight into your own struggle. (Kip, artist, Glasgow)*

The yearning for insight is tangible in these quotations, and, indeed, understanding of both self and illness through artistic work was a dominant theme for many artists (albeit one gradually replaced for some by a development of other artistic agendas with subsequent implications for identity, see below). Artists also discussed the range of emotions evoked when engaging in artistic activity, including excitement, frustration, attaining a creative 'high' and being challenged: all examples of positive outcomes. Notwithstanding the difficulties of art work and embodying creative spaces when experiencing severe and enduring mental health problems – and these were significant, a fact often underplayed in popular and policy accounts of arts for health – the majority of artists experienced creative processes as psychologically and socially stabilising, and therefore as having positive impacts upon other aspects of everyday life in terms of behaviour and emotions with regards to family and friends.

Art project spaces and feeling 'belonging'

Beyond the positive experience of art-making itself for the (precarious) creation of psychological stability, the daily or weekly attendance at and in art project spaces arguably provides structure, routine and opportunities for expanding social networks for project participants. While many forms of what might be called 'daycare' offer such opportunities (Parr, 2000), there are *particularities* associated with bonding social capital in arts-for-mental-health project spaces that go beyond the usual dimensions to mental health community-making. Opportunities for specific kinds of art talk, peer-advice giving, acts of reciprocity, facilitation of workshops and participation in cultural events like exhibitions within and beyond art project space: all of these were dimensions that artists identified as ones fostering both self-esteem and a range of positive emotions that might arguably contribute to senses of belonging:

> *Coming here and doing the work, the art work, makes you feel as though you've become more stable, because you've been doing it, participating in the project. (Ron, artist, Glasgow)*
>
> *I'm like an apprentice with them, learning to do things. And ... in the space up from me there is a guy attends and that guy's got a master's degree in Art from the Royal College of Art in London. (Mick, artist, Glasgow)*

Participation in these community arts projects hence enabled instances of learning, with possibilities for the development of previously ascribed 'static' or stigmatised identities. In explaining this, some artists compared art project spaces with experiences of art work in hospital settings. In the case of the former, a sense of choice in the development of art work, materials and skills helped in the assertion of positive forms of post-hospital or post-clinical self-identification:

> *In Liff you get a palette in front of you, specific colours in front of you, pick up a brush ... you don't get to choose your own colours and here you can do what you want, work with your own colours or whatever ... it's a kind of individual thing in here ... and there's no psychiatrist saying this means that feeling and that kind of crap ... in Liff we would get a set of materials and be told what to do with it, and in here we get a set of choices. (Mal, artist, Dundee)*

A crucial point is that art work is not open to clinical interpretation in community arts project spaces, and so a fundamental difference exists between these social spaces and therapeutic sessions in older institutional sites. However, despite advancing a strong sense of the importance of moving on from hospital-based arts experience, working alongside other people with mental health problems who are being creative and working positively for recovery is also valuable to many:

> *Most people feed off each other ... we have people that work alongside each other and it's not a competition thing ... that's not what the project is about. (Sam, artist, Glasgow)*

A distinctive theme is also the sense of shared illness experience between artists, one that may not necessarily be expressed as part of a collective visual representation of mental health, for example, but one that is quietly present and expressed through daily and weekly project participation (see also Philo et al., 2005). For many artists a politics of mental health[6] as advocated through the arts is not a core concern, although various individual projects and exhibitions may have been orientated towards this in the past. Both project staff and artists argue that it is important to move beyond representations of illness and treatment in order to fulfil artistic development, and also to maximise opportunities for social inclusion beyond project spaces:

---

6. In this case a politics of mental health references diverse challenges to bio-medical and psychiatric orthodoxies.

It's a vehicle at certain times to write about our problems and it flavours our writing, or painting, it flavours everything, but ... there is an ordinary enjoyment of art that comes in, slowly, but surely, you know, and particularly once you get to trust what is happening ... [that] is being done by us. (Jack, writer, Dundee)

To begin with most people are looking for a wee bit of catharsis, a wee bit of therapy ... but as time goes by and people become aware of their developing abilities and find skills they didn't know they had, there is a real kind of hunger in them, and to get their work out there. (Ona, artist, Dundee)

Figure 1.2 Collective art project spaces: author photograph

Interestingly, some artists also discuss the possibility of 'reading' their own art work and that of others as bearing witness to daily psychological difficulties. In other words, working with particular colours, how progress is made on a particular piece, and how materials are handled are all markers of wellbeing for some artists, which are then read by others as clues for how to relate and to socialise non-prescriptively with the person in the next studio space:

You can see just looking at people's work, you can mostly tell when they've gone down a way, just by looking ... you just know, I recognise it, it could be with form or colour, it depends [but] I would often say 'what's worrying you?', 'what's been through your mind?' and then it's vice versa, people will say to me and I've opened up to them. (Rene, artist, Glasgow)

This interpretation of artists and their work allows these arts projects to be envisaged as protective *non-clinical* social spaces within which people cultivate positive versions of self-identity, further enabled by an inclusive sociability with others around them. For many, these are spaces primarily for artistic development in a non-pressurised environment that combines different ways in which to experience art work. Interviewees discussed the development of their artistic and personal identities by charting a progression from a tentative entry to arts projects when engagement with people, art talk, materials and creative ideas seems daunting or impossible, to current positions where individual artists may have built up portfolios, be developing new directions or even advocating for others:

> *When I first joined the project, I just used to go along to the writing group, but then I became more involved in the running of projects and different projects as well. I know how to go from someone sitting, having an idea, because plenty of people do, they think wouldn't that be a great idea for a film, or I'd really like to publish a book, or I'd like to have my music recorded. I know how to go from there to having a film on the screen or having a book that you can hold in your hand and show to someone. I know how to do that ... and that's the main thing that I've learnt ... (Peter, artist, Dundee)*

By and large these artists eschewed the notion that they are engaged in art therapy, and simultaneously signalled how they embody a progressive, self-conscious artistic development process, not representative of (typical constructions of) the innate (non-taught) expressiveness of outsider artists. Cultivating a sense of belonging within these 'in-between' art project spaces is thus partly dependent on the development of independent artistic identities (see p. 17), the ability to participate with others on specific projects, and the development of a range of art-related skills and talk, amongst other things.

The positive depiction of the arts and art projects above belies how they can also be difficult social geographies. Notwithstanding individual struggles for creative expression in times of illness, nor the individual risk of creative 'excitement' being the *cause* of ill health, arts projects can also be characterised as tense, risky collective spaces in which good mental health cannot always be assured:

> *When you have all these conditions in one community, sometimes, if someone kicks off, it can wave through the whole studio and that can have a dark, a kind of dark atmosphere, because you are talking about people who are very sensitive. (Sam, artist, Glasgow)*

> *There's no question that LUNA in particular takes things a step further and for people who have the confidence ... [and] there are certain aspects of that which are not therapeutic ... it's not just turning up and going to an art group in the afternoon ... [you] have to be prepared to do things which aren't always fun. (Peter, artist, Dundee)*

Not only does art work create challenging risks, then, but collective art and mental health project spaces are also occasionally characterised by competitiveness, jealousies and critical judgements, as in any working environment, but with particular sensitivities and intensities as connected to the participants' psychological health. These are *particular* social and artistic spaces, although not isolated and exclusive ones, as shall be elaborated below.

Inside and outside in the cultural city

In her writing on community arts in Edinburgh, Rose (1997) argued that using a language of inside and outside to describe community arts projects relative to wider geographies of power does not necessarily have to rely on essentialising definitions of identity or location. Indeed, she argued that community arts workers have nuanced understandings of the spatialities of the communities in which they work, noting that 'community' is 'both partial and mobile, changing its form as the particular individuals, groups and activities that constitute it change' (Rose, 1997: 12), and likewise that spatialities within creative communities are dynamic: 'people "move on", they "get from there to there", they reach "the next step", [and] projects are described as "stepping stones"' (ibid.). Such movement is not unidirectional, zonal or hierarchically structured, and thus community, in the context of community arts, is therefore best conceived as a complex and uncertain spatiality. Rose's ideas resonate with the experiences of artists from mental health and arts projects in Glasgow and Dundee, as we see below, although for them questions of inside and outside remain pertinent when considering their place in artistic communities of interest.

It is difficult to place both art work and artists within mental health projects relative to mainstream artistic and cultural communities, logics and productions. As already indicated, there is some evidence still of the special status and special spaces of mentally ill artists and their productions, albeit perhaps differently conceived from the early outsider art forms.[7] Work and

---

7. For example, in a UK context, see http://www.outsiderart.co.uk/, as well as specific sites such as 'The Art Extraordinary Gallery' Pittenweem, Scotland (www.artextraordinarytrust.co.uk/).

exhibition spaces today vary in whether or not they use an 'outsider' signifier to categorise the artists and their work, but a common theme often remains that such art work provides an access point for the wider public to understand more about mental health issues, illness experiences and the disrupted psyche. Media and other representational discourses about such work, its value and connection with wider cultural forms may still highlight the fundamental *difference* of mentally ill art and artists, therefore, but a more common focus may become the therapeutic potential of art work for disordered selves. In terms of a discussion of belongings, however, I want to move beyond such rhetoric and 'placings' of difference to focus more on the everyday experiences of mental health project artists in wider communities of artists and other cultural workers.

Certainly it is the case that the arts bring with them the possibility for centring marginalised voices, experiences and locations. In Dundee, for example, there was a sense of a legitimate, if radical and disruptive occupation of mainstream cultural city spaces, with representations of asylum life and mental illness forming a major exhibition at the city's McManus Galleries:

Figure 1.3 'Restraint' by Pat Donnelly, exhibited at the Life at Liff Exhibition, McManus Galleries, Dundee. Reproduced here with the permission of Art Angel.

> *One of the most incredible events was the Liff exhibition which was held in the premier public exhibition space in Dundee, and from being in this place [Royal Dundee Liff Hospital] regarded with suspicion seven miles out of Dundee, we took it right into the middle of the city and said 'we are here, this is us'. We are not hiding in the country anymore in a big Victorian building, we are right in the middle of town now. That was an incredible experience, it was one of the largest collections of work by local people in Dundee, an absolutely major collection and I felt hugely part of the city and its history. (Peter, artist, Dundee)*

In this sense participation in a very public community arts and exhibition space can involve a collective sense of rightful belonging forged through senses of neglect and marginalisation.

Beyond this displaying and reclaiming of a previously marginalised presence in the city, more prosaic concerns such as sustained funding levels and the physical placing of arts and mental health projects are meaningful in terms of both symbolic and literal senses of belonging. There are, of course, significant local differences in whether and how arts for mental health can secure a distinctive profile in premier cultural city spaces.

In the case of the Trongate Studios (http://www.trongate103.com) their well-funded location in the artist heartland of Glasgow, the Merchant City, aided a sense in which people with mental health problems have a role in the wider process of cultural place-making. Glasgow's self-conscious image as a 'city of culture', concerned for both the promotion of cultural industries and attaining social justice, combined with the City Council's inclusive arts objectives stating that 'arts organisations are a major resource for tackling some of Glasgow's most intractable problems in terms of health' (Glasgow City Council, 2001: 12). For the then artistic director of the Trongate Studios, this meant 'we have always been seen to be entitled to be part of the arts community in the city' (interview, March, 2005). Indeed, the redevelopment of the artistic quarter of the city included the Trongate Studios moving to a new building in a multi-million pound relocation package in King Street, where the project has been sited alongside 'mainstream' artists to promote further inclusive integration and to contribute to the marketing of the arts environment in central Glasgow.

For many artists and staff, though, inclusion in large-scale and visible cultural development is not the only way of sensing belonging in wider cultural geographies. Such belonging is also at least partly achieved through a more mundane embodied occupation of the city's artistic community spaces; feeling welcome and confident to sit in cafes and bars with other artists and workers, being invited to attend other gallery openings, and having access to mainstream exhibition space for the work of project participants:

> *I would call myself an artist now, aye ... You're in that community, an artist's community, you know, in that area. I still get that feeling of being, what's the word? like connected to the artist community. (Mick, artist, Glasgow)*

> *The feeling of coming to the Merchant City ... has given me the feeling of being part of the community I'm involved with. (Rene, artist, Glasgow)*

For some, this identification was based on new legitimised artistic identities arising as part of their art work. For others, this feeling of community was based more symbolically on notions of artists *also* being outsiders to more mainstream communities. Artistic communities are acknowledged as places where unusual working schedules, extreme emotional behaviours and experiences might be tolerated or even celebrated, perhaps as part of an alternative knowing of the city (Bain, 2003; Pinder 2005a, 2005b). Artists with serious and enduring mental health problems might be positively embraced in such communities of practice, although tensions with professional artists also surfaced over subsidised studio spaces and materials and regarding the allocation of 'undeserved' places in high profile cultural environments, buildings and projects, a concern raised by staff and artists from Trongate Studios when discussing the redevelopment plans highlighted above. Despite feelings of possible belongings, then, incursions into the cultural city can be difficult, involving senses of risk and stigma, and as a result some remain ambivalent about their identities as artists, despite extensive portfolios, experience of exhibitions and even advocacy for others:

> *I use art all the time, but I'm still not convinced I'm an artist. (Peter, artist, Dundee)*

> *I think we are probably treated with a lot of suspicion ... and there's a feeling in the studios when people talk about that, that they're the underdog ... we're damaged, and sometimes it feels quite excluded. (Tina, artist, Glasgow)*

One particular example elaborates what might be understood as an ambiguous positioning of artists with mental health problems in the city. The Glasgow Art Fair is an annual event that attracts artists from all over the UK and internationally. Project Ability and the Trongate Studios have had a stall there for some years, and this is seen as major recognition of the work of the project. Within the Trongate Studios, however, there were tensions about what and whose art work got selected for exhibition.[8] The artistic director of the Trongate Studios explained the dilemma:

> We cannot compete nor should we compete alongside galleries, you know, showing the work of professional artists. There are very few people who are working at that level, *so it's looking for different quality in the work, and that will sometimes have a quirkiness about it, an originality ... there's something surprising about it, that's what really grabs people and what we do that other people can't.* So the people who are doing okay-ish, you know, landscapes, would not get their work into the Art Fair because they shouldn't be shown alongside someone who has spent 30 years doing landscapes you know? ... *they are coming from a completely different place.* [my emphases].

Despite otherwise strongly denying the use of the category of outsider art, there is a hint here in the words of the artistic director, one also felt by project artists, that certain types of art are more or less suitable for representing an arts and mental health project in and to wider artistic (and viewing) communities. For the majority of studio artists whose work encompasses a variety of versions of fine art, a distinction is made between them and other professional artists. Their work is not deemed good enough to be completely inside the cultural project of the Art Fair. At the same time, the majority of studio artists do not produce versions of what might be identified as outsider art – as it is usually defined – as somehow sufficiently innate, naive, quirky, original. Some studio artists and their work are also therefore not 'outsider enough' to be inside the Art Fair. Their curious in-betweenness, as full-time artists located in the cultural quarter of the city, but who do not occupy fully insider positions through – ironically – not being categorised as sufficiently 'outsider', but nor being 'good enough', trained or time-served professional artists, means that their senses of artistic belongings are often ambivalent and tenuous. Whilst this problem could reflect an unwitting paternalism on the part of the Trongate Studios, it also

---

8. The Glasgow Art Fair was the only public exhibition that entailed a process of selection involving the Trongate Studios' artistic director at the time of research, a signal of the cultural and financial significance of the event for the organisation. The art works sold there raised significant funds for both individual artists and Trongate Studios (who take a small percentage from each sale). In general terms, art works produced within the two researched organisations did not generate consistent and significant income for artists, although this was a source of anxiety for some who did desire to generate sustainable income from their practice. There are not presently specific or supported pathways that assist artists to develop independent artistic livelihoods or occupation of independent studio spaces, and more state resources might be targeted at operationalising such inclusionary tactics.

points to a larger problematic of the cultural 'legibility' of people with mental health problems. Here there are risks that, as the boundaries between 'them' and the presumed mainstream ('us') fade from view due to participation in non-clinical (non-art therapy) arts-for-health projects that are also not orientated around productions of classic outsider art, then inclusionary possibilities are actually lessened. Put another way, the inclusion of 'others' can be seen as made available in only very tightly prescribed terms, with 'in-between' forms of artistic productions from in-between arts-for-health project spaces not being easily assimilated and valued in the artistic mainstream. The ambiguous positioning in the one cultural event discussed above might hence be read as symbolic of wider tensions concerning the project of inclusive cultural belongings, where positions of inside and outside are perhaps proving difficult, ultimately, to disrupt in practice.

Conclusion

An unproblematic and uncomplicated experience of belonging is not straightforwardly achieved through the linking of arts and mental health. Rather, I have suggested that important precursors for social and psychological stability – themselves crucial properties for the possibility of experiencing belonging for people with mental health problems specifically – might be cultivated through participation in creative spaces. Such stability, it is argued, enables artists more effectively to connect with themselves, with other artists experiencing mental health problems, with their immediate social networks, and with wider-interest communities in other social spaces beyond arts projects. In this way, the chapter empirically draws out particular meanings of 'belonging' for artists as related to feelings of connectivity, the possibility of being included in cultural and social life on equal and non-marginal terms, and through having potential access to new categorisations as 'normal' and 'participative' citizens.

Such a typology of possible belongings is nonetheless tempered by the knowledge that pairing creativity and belonging is an uncertain and unstable endeavour. The voices of artists have highlighted, for example, that the arts and art project spaces are both pleasurable and difficult social environments. Whilst embodied artistic practice can (but not always) have stabilising effects, and art project spaces can involve specific forms of social connectivity, engaging in artistic communities of interest in the wider city also holds differing and rather precarious opportunities for participants. Understanding participation in artistic geographies and the cultural city through spatialities of inside and outside has deliberately played on the 'limit cases' of outsider art and art therapy. The artist voices and projects represented above have been positioned as lying 'in between' these cases, and as neither fully inside nor fully outside 'the project' of the cultural city or the therapeutic project of recovery. As such these community artists occupy uncertain ground that renders a positive reading of the links between the arts and wider social belongings as always contingent.

This chapter hence shows that geographies of creativity are being imaginatively employed as pathways to particular versions of community insiderness, but these are also revealed as a highly contingent routes of (re)securing ill selves as 'participative cultural citizens', who still only precariously 'belong' in the mainstream social spaces of everyday life. The future of arts and mental health funding in an age of austerity further complicates the possibilities afforded to vulnerable people through creative engagement.

Acknowledgements

This chapter is an altered and edited reprint from Parr, H (2008) *Mental Health and Social Space: Geographies of inclusion?* London: Blackwell. Reproduced with permission.

References

Bain, A (2003) Constructing contemporary artistic identities in Toronto neighbourhoods. *The Canadian Geographer, 47,* 303–17.

Bondi, L with Fewell, J (2003) Unlocking the cage door: The spatiality of counselling. *Social and Cultural Geography 4,* 527–47.

Carter Park, D, Simpson-Housley, P & de Man, A (1994) To the 'infinite spaces of creation': The interior landscape of a schizophrenic artist. *Annals of the Association of American Geographers 84,* 192–209.

Crouch, D (2005) *Art and Belonging(s): How can the arts belong?* Paper presented at the Royal Geographical Society (IBG) conference, London.

Edwards, D (2004) *Art Therapy: Creative therapies in practice.* London: Sage Publications.

Glasgow City Council (2001) *Best Value Review: Museums, heritage and visual arts.* Glasgow: Glasgow City Council.

Haywood Gallery (1996) *Beyond Reason: Art and psychosis.* London: Haywood Gallery.

Hogan, S (2001) *Healing Arts: The history of art therapy.* London: Jessica Kingsley.

Jadi, I (1996) 'Points of view–perspectives–horizons'. In *Beyond Reason: Art and psychosis* (pp. 12–26). London: Haywood Gallery.

Laing, J (2000) *Angus McPhee: Weaver of grass.* Harris: Taigh Chearsabhagh Art Centre and Museum.

Lombroso, C with Lombroso-Ferrero, G (1972) *Criminal Man, According to the Classification of Cesare Lombroso*. New Jersey: Putnam and Patterson Smith. (Original work published 1911)

Maddern, C & Bloom, T (2004) Creativity, health and arts advocacy. *International Journal of Cultural Policy, 10*, 133–56.

Malchiodi, C (1999) *Medical Art Therapy with Adults*. London: Jessica Kingsley.

Parr, H (1999) Delusional geographies: Experiential worlds of people with madness/illness. *Environment and Planning D: Society and Space, 17*, 673–90.

Parr, H (2000) Interpreting the 'hidden social geographies' of mental health: Inclusion and exclusion in semi-institutional places. *Health and Place 6*, 225–37.

Parr, H (2007) Collaborative filmmaking as process, method and text in mental health research. *Cultural Geographies 14*, 114–38.

Philo, C (2006) Madness, memory, time, and space: The eminent psychological physician and the unnamed artist-patient. *Environment and Planning D: Society and Space, 24*, 891–917.

Philo, C, Parr, H & Burns, N (2005) An oasis for us: 'In-between' spaces of training for people with mental health problems in the Scottish Highlands. *Geoforum, 36*, 778–91.

Pinder, D (2005a) Arts of exploration. *Cultural Geographies, 12*, 1–29.

Pinder, D (2005b) *Visions of the City*. Edinburgh: Edinburgh University Press.

Rexer, L (2005) *How to Look at Outsider Art*. New York: Harry N Abrams.

Rhodes, C (2000) *Outsider Art: Spontaneous alternatives*. London: Thames and Hudson.

Rose, G (1997) Spatialities of 'community', power and change: The imagined geographies of community arts projects. *Cultural Studies, 11*, 1–16.

White, M (2003) *Mental Health and the Arts: A discussion paper*. London: Institute of Public Policy Research Seminar.

Willis, J (2002) *The Art of Good Health: A practical handbook*. London: National Health Service Estates.

CHAPTER TWO

Is Art Therapy?

Langley Brown

My eye

There is a sweep of time.

My motive for undertaking a doctorate was autobiographical. There were times to make sense of.

I was born the week Nye Bevan presented the National Health Service Bill to Parliament.

Three years earlier my father had been transported as an RAF prisoner of war into Nazi Germany, where in a draft for his intended book he pencilled my intended name *Ronald Langley Brown*, as a chapter heading.

Pre-conceptions

At 11 I was permitted to stay up for a television documentary *Watch on the Ruhr* (ITV, 1957). This contained footage of the liberation of Bergen-Belsen concentration camp. This was the first I had known of what is now called the Holocaust.

I've had a few good nights' sleep since.

Before entering Stalag IVB at Mühlberg my father's group spent a week in a nearby camp at Jacobsthal, where he witnessed the suffering of Jews and Russians.

People often behave how they are treated.

Expectations

'In 1937 I knew what Hitler wanted,' my father told me after that programme. 'That's why I joined up as soon as we declared war.' My noble dad, standing in the teeth of horror.

Ten years after he'd pencilled my name in Germany, I began a decade of boarding school.

This was a surprise too. I had been enjoying a happy childhood.

I went 'away to school' despite the protests of my mother and her parents.

'Your father thought blokes who survived POW camp best were the ones who'd been away to school,' she told me.

Years later she told me this too: 'You know, he had a bit of a crush on another prisoner.'

When he died in 1998 I found amongst his long-hidden (but not thrown away) wartime papers a foolscap sheaf of faded pencil describing his feelings towards this army sergeant and towards the wife he'd married just before his final mission.

Rationalisations

Two years before his death I was recalling my lifelong admiration of his reasons for joining up. 'Oh no, no, no,' he said, 'no; I did it to save the Empire.'

Illusions

When I left school I applied for law school. I didn't get in.

In 1966 I entered art college. Free-fall through the greys of bourgeois restraint.

Exhilaration!

I painted and made collages. I saw myself as a surrealist.

At about 30 I was interviewed for a job as caretaker at our village school. I didn't get it, but one of the governors invited me for a drink afterwards. He introduced himself as Peter Senior, and told me about a scheme of his for artists to work in hospitals.

This did not sound like an appealing notion.

My wife persuaded me to go for another interview – for a job I didn't want.

Another surprise. I was offered the job.

'But what on earth did they think of my work?' I asked Brian Chapman, the new arts team's leader.

'They said it was self-indulgent.'

Half a century after our twin birth I became the NHS's first artist (non-therapist mode) to take early retirement, following half a century in what is generally known as 'Arts and Health'.

A decade later I was awarded the doctorate that is the subject of this chapter.

Reconciliations

Doctor, doctor, I don't think I'm a therapist

I suspected an autobiographical motive would not be enough to begin a research degree. I might need something less self-indulgent.

Two issues during my career had particularly concerned me: the wellbeing of the artist, and the problem of therapy.

As I worked from the early 1980s in mental health services, I came to suspect that the preconceptions applying to people as cases for treatment – as *patients* – exerted an inhibiting effect on their autonomy and were to some extent counterproductive. 'They want me to do psychodrama', 'I don't talk to my doctor about my *painting*'. This led to the notion that the application of art as medicine – as *therapy* – formalised and diminished art just as much as the codices of 'mental illness' added seemingly impermeable layers of labelling and disempowerment upon those who found themselves in the psychiatric hospital, their skills and potential abandoned in the world outside an institution which persistently failed to recognise the potency of these attributes as engines of restoration. There was, as I perceived it, an *illness* dance going on, a collusionary arabesque between patients and staff.

Whenever art therapists questioned the role and appropriateness of non-therapy-trained artists in the mental health arena, my response had been to assert the irrelevance of clinical case history, psychiatric theory, and therapeutic intent to the mission (as I saw it) of our cohort of artists to collaborate with patients (as they were then known) in sidestepping the illness dance and engaging artistic resources to address issues in the world beyond the psychiatric hospital.

So would my thesis be a self-indulgent blend of autobiography and polemic? I had to lay my cards on the table. The way to get away with what I wanted was to clearly frame myself and my gripes within the picture, to delineate the cultures – interior and exterior – within which I would place the author's autoethnography and my own predisposition to diatribe. Then would I gather and scrutinise my data.

Well stop talking and start painting

I had observed, in myself, in my children, in my artist wife, and in those with whom I worked in the psychiatric institution, the 'flow' (Csíkszentmihályi, 1996) that is experienced when people engage in art – or in any absorbing activity; that altered state, where time and surroundings become dreamworld and the interaction between media, limb and brain becomes transcendent reality. I had observed this state eliciting tangible results (painting, mosaic, text, music, movement) and the participants' enhanced self-positioning within the world she or he finds on emerging from that altered state. 'Blimey – did *I* do that? It's quite good, isn't it?' 'Yes, Bill. It is.' Dead simple. Obvious. Evidence-based medicine? Get away! Talk about the emperor's new clothes.

Actually, I think I'll do a Ph.D.

> *Someone: So ...* what *do you do then?*
> *Me: I'm an artist.* (a beat) *I work in the health service ...*
> *Someone: Oh. An art therapist ...*
> *Me: ... er. No, ...*
> *Someone: ... what?*
> *Me: An artist ...* (pause ...)
> *... and a researcher.*

Shortly before my 60th birthday I completed a decade doing a doctoral thesis that drew upon and extended my own continuing experience in the arts and mental health field.

Although I'd finally set out to nail an issue that hadn't adequately been explored – the relationship between art therapy and non-therapy art – my three initial interests had been: to make a narrative out of what I'd been doing for the past 25 years; to ascertain the benefits to emotional wellbeing of engaging in the arts; and to peek at the corollary: what is the effect of *not* engaging in the activities we call the arts?

The study (Brown, 2006)

Introduction

So by now I was concerned with two approaches to visual creativity in mental healthcare: art therapy, where the emphasis is placed on healing, with the client as patient-to-be-cured; and non-clinical arts activity, where the emphasis

> **• BIZARRE •**
>
> BIZARRE • TO HAVE SPENT TEN YEARS RESEARCHING AN APPARENTLY IMAGINARY PROBLEM ANY SOLUTION TO WHICH SEEMS OBVIOUS TO ANYONE INVOLVED IN THE ARTS AND HEALTH MOVEMENT IF NOT TO ANYONE INVOLVED IN THE ARTS FULL STOP • IN THE FACE OF THE OBVIOUSNESS OF THE SOLUTION - IN THE TEETH OF THE READINESS OF A REPUTEDLY LOGICAL ESTABLISHMENT TO DOWNGRADE THE ARTS TO A DEGREE THAT APPEARS PERSECUTORY AND TO DO THIS ALL THE MORE READILY AT THOSE VERY TIMES OF CRISIS WHEN THE ARTS BECOME MORE SOUGHT AFTER AND ESSENTIAL THAN EVER - MY RESPONSE HAS OFTEN BEEN TO RESORT TO POLEMIC, SOMETHING AN ASPIRING ACADEMIC SHOULD AVOID OF COURSE & THE FACT I DID NOT ALWAYS DO SO DID NOT MAKE ME A BETTER RESEARCHER BUT I HOPE IT DID ACCURATELY REFLECT OUR FRUSTRATION AT THE ESTABLISHMENT'S REQUIREMENT THAT THE ARTS SURRENDER THE KIND OF EVIDENCE REQUIRED OF OTHER ACTIVITIES AND INTERVENTIONS REGARDLESS OF HOW MEANINGFUL OR NOT SOME OF THE ALLEGED EVIDENCE (NOT ALWAYS DEMANDED!) FOR OTHER INTERVENTIONS MAY BE • IT IS ACCEPTED THAT MANY TREATMENTS WORK THAT ARE BACKED BY LITTLE OR NONE OF THE EVIDENCE REQUIRED OF THE ARTS, AN AREA OF HUMAN ACTIVITY FOR THOUSANDS OF YEARS BEFORE SOME OF THE QUASI-MEDICAL PRACTICES THAT HAVE BEEN SUPPORTED BY THE NHS • HOMOEOPATHY FOR EXAMPLE WHETHER IT 'WORKS' OR WHETHER IT IS A PLACEBO OR WHETHER THAT'S A POINTLESS 'WHETHER' THERE IS STILL NO *MEDICAL* EVIDENCE FOR ITS EFFECTIVENESS • THE FACT THAT IT MAY BE *BELIEF* IN SUCH INTERVENTIONS THAT STIMULATES HEALING ENDORPHINS IS ONLY NOW BEING RESEARCHED PLACES MEDICAL RESEARCH AND PRACTICE IN A QUANDARY • BUT HOW EFFECTIVE, BECAUSE SO INTRINSICALLY ESSENTIAL TO THE HUMAN EXPERIENCE, IS THE SUITE OF ACTIVITIIES LOOSELY BANDED UNDER THE FLAG OF CONVENIENCE 'ART' ! IT IS TRAGIC - NOT TO USE THE WORD CARELESSLY - THAT THE STUBBORN REFUSAL OF THE ARTS TO YIELD QUANTITATIVE EVIDENCE CONSTANTLY GIVES THE ESTABLISHMENT THE COP-OUT TO PERSISTENTLY REDISESTABLISH ONE OF THE ESSENTIALS OF
> ***WHAT IT IS TO BE HUMAN.***

polemigram 1

is on art, with the participant as artist-in-the-making. I described the history and modes of practice of each approach, identified areas of contention, and laid some foundations for collaborative working between the modes of practice in pursuit of a continuum of creative opportunities for people experiencing mental health problems.

I hoped that the contribution made by my study would lie, firstly, in its heuristic documentation and analysis of the experience of myself as a player who may have had occasional influence in the field; secondly, in its laying of foundations for a synthesis based upon mutual understanding and collaborative practice between the approaches found; and, thirdly, in its furnishing future investigators with a wealth of data and new starting points.

Background

The period from the mid 1970s into the first decade of the second millennium encompassed my work in and for the UK's National Health Service (NHS) as artist, director, and arts-in-health consultant. This period saw an increasing application of the arts as a component of health and social care and community development, in the UK and elsewhere. In particular, there was a growing engagement in the mental health field by artists who saw themselves as artists, not therapists; the former I defined (however cumbersomely) as *non-therapy-oriented artists*. These may also be availers of mental health services, of course (as may be therapists; as indeed have I been). And yet a frequent assumption made with regard to any artist working in the health field has been that she or he must, by definition, be an art therapist. I didn't invent the dialogue above; I've been party to it many times.

My peers and I may be artists, but we are definitively not therapists. And many of us would not claim that our work is therapeutic; that claim might be made by others, but, as artists, we couldn't possibly say; nor would we be wise to do so. And therein may lie the strength and the weakness of the mental health-oriented work of these artists; as my study in part argued, one reason why their work is effective may simply be because it bypasses a cocoon of caring, of 'treatment', in favour of a focus on the world beyond the therapist's room.

And yet the potential of these artists' work – not just as art but as a catalyst for social engagement and action and arguably wellbeing – has consistently been at risk of being undermined by pressures from various forces: from threats arising from the legal professionalisation of the clinical practice of art therapy; from the clinician's view (arguably correct and apposite) of artist as maverick; from movement towards such standardisation of codes of practice in Arts in Health as may dilute that maverick impulse; and from socio-political and corporate agendas manifested in the *Scylla and Charybdis* of social inclusion and the expectations of sponsors out of synchronisation with the ethos of artists. For artists to navigate these perils without losing autonomy and integrity, whilst offering their skills and sensibilities in the service of individuals and communities, is an increasingly difficult course to plot.

One of the many contemporary dilemmas facing the artist is to reconcile social purpose with personal vision, whilst retaining artistic, moral and human integrity. This dilemma has been a concern of mine throughout my career in the health domain. It gave rise in the 1980s to my part in instituting a short-lived 'monthly sabbatical' for artists working full time in a hospital: time out from the clinical domain to reinvigorate the artistic batteries; to my initiation in the 1990s of an (again short-lived) 'rusty artists' group, bringing together practitioners across several Arts and Health projects; and, in the 2000s, to my involvement in Bridgehead Arts, a cross-artform company one of whose aims was, not merely to restore creative energy to artists working to social agendas, but to build upon their experience to impart a better understanding and application of their skills to our cultures during a time of crisis and transition.

Methods used

As indicated, the prime impetus for my study had been shamelessly autobiographical; I wanted to make sense out of what I'd been up to, to place it in the context of my life, of a wider culture, and of the times in which I have lived. At the same time I wanted to address one of the more intransigent problems that arose in my career as an artist in the NHS: the sensitive relationship between art therapy and what has become awkwardly known as Arts and Health.

Weighing up methods that might suit the purposes of my research I decided on heuristic and autoethnographical approaches, alongside narrative case studies and cross-case and within-case analysis.

Ellis (2004) described autoethnography as:

> ... research, writing, story, and method that connect the autobiographical and personal to the cultural, social, and political. (p. xix)

Krizek (2003) warned of some of the pitfalls of this approach, concluding that, if it is to avoid narcissism, autoethnography should always connect to some larger element of life. The cultural domains to which my autoethnography connected most intimately were those of 'mental health/illness' and 'the arts', as well as, of course, to my concept of the 'me' as one among the millions living through the second half of one of the more dramatic centuries in human existence – and one in which horrors ran so spectacularly amok.

In view of the inadequacies, discussed by Angus (1998/2002) and others, of quantitative methods in assessing the relative merits to our mental wellbeing of engaging in any suite of activities as intangible as the arts, research of a personal nature was more likely than any attempt at objectivism to impart richer insights into problems often overlooked in the culture at large and in the medical domain in particular. As Andrea Gilroy observed:

> We need the facts, we need the figures, but we need the stories and the pictures, too. (Gilroy, 2006: 150)

The former Chief Medical Officer of England, Sir Kenneth Calman, applied more pith:

> I'm not interested in the figures, just give me the story! (1999; paraphrased from my memory)

I would be reflective and reflexive; explicit from the outset about my 'I'.

I studied research methods in the respective fields of the arts, health and art therapy, reviewing several authors' search for a methodology that respected and to some extent met the conflicting needs of artist, academic, and healthcare manager. I gave examples of research in the field, and explained my reasons for choosing a qualitative approach using case study, reflective practice and personal ethnography.

The methods I used included a questionnaire survey, and a directory that is a historical snapshot of activity in the mental health field in the UK at the turn of the century. Multiple case studies – using action research, interviews, participant observation, documentation, archives and visual material – described stakeholders' experiences of participatory visual arts practice in the mental health field. The case studies represented a range of practice and approaches.

The data was scrutinised using within-case and cross-case analysis, employing indicators devised partly through the research aims, propositions and questions, but also in partnership with project stakeholders; these indicators arose in the course of the research and were embraced in order to clarify the benefits that stakeholders themselves identified as arising from their engagement in the visual arts. This might then help distinguish benefits arising from non-therapy visual arts from those provided by art therapy.

My study exhibited a marked and deliberate contrast in style between *Background* and *Methods* on the one hand, and *Case Studies* on the other. This contrast had been carefully considered; I embraced it in order to present as much of an 'objective' overview as is possible within which to place the subjective view of the author, whilst, conversely, enabling the reader to place and assess the 'objective' data within the personal context of an author who had been emotionally, professionally and pivotally involved in the field of practice that was the subject of the study. I had hoped, then, that by adopting this triangulatory approach, an approximation to more revealing and useful 'truths' might be caught in the cross-beams projected by these two sources of illumination. Writing now, I confess to engaging in some tongue-in-cheek playfulness when toying in the language of academia.

My 'I' as observer and actor, then; my starting point essentially my own experience, as reflective practitioner (Schön, 1995); experience recorded in diaries, notebooks, correspondence, minutes, papers, speeches, visual material and personal memory, and corroborated wherever necessity demanded and possibility allowed.

Two studies described action research projects that had informed or were integral to my research. These, firstly, added to my own knowledge as researcher, and, secondly, aimed to improve participants' quality of life through engagement in art. Here again I was both practitioner and researcher.

Who did what? Thoughts on confidentiality

The question of confidentiality required complex decisions.

Non-therapy artists working in the mental health circus are more likely to view *participants* as just that, or as artists, or, as at START in Manchester in the early years, as members, and, as at START more recently, as students or trainees. Impatient with the titles 'patient' and 'client', and sceptical of the titles 'user' and 'survivor', I had always encouraged participants to see themselves as artists, with the confidence to permit their artist persona to override the stigma of mental illness with its blanketing anonymity. However, as it was not possible to contact all informants, I decided to change the names of contributors wherever there could be the slightest uncertainty regarding to their wish to be named or otherwise.

And yet a difficulty arose, insofar as one of the contributory aims of the study was to present a historical overview of the arts in mental health and compile a directory of practice and practitioners at the turn of the millennium. It is not known – because the question was not asked, for it was seen as inappropriate – whether contributors to the directory defined themselves as artists or as service users. The way in which informants did actually define themselves and their groups was open, prompted by the first heading printed on each respondent's copy of the directory questionnaire: 'i [*sic*] am …', 'we are …'.

Among the professional artists in the study were several who experienced states of mind that included schizophrenia, depression and anxiety. As a group they represent to the clinician, no doubt, a panoply of commonplace pathologies. For a significant few of these artists a psychic journey, with heights and depths, had informed, or in at least one case impelled, their artistic practice. Wherever I was unequivocally certain of the wishes of such informants, real names were used.

Similarly, those professionals in the arts, health, social, academic and other domains who were well known in their field appeared under their own names, with exceptions made where there was even the slightest concern that the revealing of an informant's identity would be problematic, either for that person or for those with whom they worked.

Definitions and contexts
'Art'

> Art, *n*. This word has no definition. (*Ambrose Bierce: The Enlarged Devil's Dictionary,* first published 1906, Hopkins, 1967)

I began by recognising the need to find a way of defining art, and of understanding its origins and function, that would embrace such diverse and often seemingly contradictory aspects as, for example, the Western 'art world', tribal art, community arts, amateur arts, romantic and classical art, and modernism and postmodernism. Viewing it as an evolved biological *behaviour*, Ellen Dissanayake (1988) defined art as the *making special* of our experiences. However clumsy in itself, I felt her term encompasses the different and often contradictory approaches to be found in any discussion on the arts in general, and in the mental health arena in particular. The more recent term, *participatory arts*, nicely embraces community arts and reflects Dissanayake's helpful view.

Also helpful – in that it not only describes those processes of artistic creation that may be indicators of mental wellbeing, but also hints at the creative aspects of those states of consciousness pathologised as *schizophrenia* – was Steven Mithen's (1996) concept of *cognitive fluidity*, which explains the evolution of the ability to link domains of consciousness previously confined in separate, specialised mental compartments.

Mental health and illness

Mental health and mental illness were as difficult to define as art.

After discussing several attempts at definition I adopted the World Health Organization's (2010) definition of mental health as:

> a state of well-being in which the individual realises his or her own abilities, can cope with the normal stresses of life, can work productively and fruitfully, and is able to make a contribution to his or her community.

This definition, which acknowledged the complexity of a phenomenon that can be determined only by a combination of social, environmental and biological factors, supported the view that engagement in community is central to the fostering and maintenance of mental health and in combating isolation and emotional distress.

I discussed the idea of 'mental illness' as spiritual crisis, a gateway to personal growth, citing an example from a traditional society of positive cultural response to behaviours that in the West would probably be treated as pathological (Obeyesekere, 1981).

Responses

I considered the 'delivery' of mental health services in the light of changes brought about by advances in pharmacology. The gradual reduction in the side effects of 'antipsychotic' drugs was noted, as was the accompanying virtual disappearance of what had infelicitously been called 'psychotic' art. The relationship between 'outsider' and 'insider' artist is discussed elsewhere by Hester Parr (2006 and this volume, Chapter One).

I touched upon the problems and their legacy surrounding the discharge in the 1990s of people from the asylums into an under-resourced 'community care', noting how artists had been increasingly involved in this process, and that this had given rise to a growing recognition of the role of the arts in challenging some of what my mental health services manager saw as 'the impasses of community care'.[1]

Art in healthcare

I reviewed the history of the arts in healthcare and described philosophies and practices ranging from participatory to prestige art, noting that all these approaches were accommodated within Dissanayake's term 'making special', the adoption of which could go some way towards obviating an observed tendency among practitioners towards suspicion, polarisation and protectionism. I introduced some of these tensions, particularly a division between the advocates of participatory arts and those who champion the commissioning of prestigious art works and who may decry popular and participatory arts.

I wound up my discussion of definitions and contexts by considering the different meanings of *therapy* and *therapeutic* in terms, respectively, of treatment and healing. I listed a range of therapies (some bizarre) and ended with a short review of Smail (1998), Masson (1989) and others who criticise the very concept of therapy.

---

1. Tom Butler, in conversation with author, 1995.

The art of mental health
Artists seeking a role

To place Arts and Health in a wider cultural perspective I discussed views on the changing role of the artist in society, and the impact of such change on the mental healthcare domain.

In the 1990s Suzie Gablik (1991) called for artists to re-engage with the social, spiritual and ecological issues in need of attention at this time. She linked our general feeling of estrangement to the fragmentation of society and to the decline of a spiritual basis to life, citing Erich Fromm's equation of a sick society and sick people, and his assertion of the human need for relatedness, identity and transcendence (Fromm, 1979).

Gablik's (1985, 1991) call for a 'pragmatic idealism', for a spirituality based on ecological principles, a 'lifelike' art (citing Kaprow, n.d.) in the neo-shamanic tradition of Josef Beuys, may not, in the opinion of Bocock (1993) for instance, be enough to re-engage populations outside the sphere of influence of the arts. Bocock's (1993) controversial suggestion was that it may only be by positively engaging *with* – at the same time as challenging some of the assumptions *of* – the world's religions that a new ecological, non-consumption-oriented paradigm may take hold among the wider population.

Gablik and others helped illuminate the background to the growing social commitment of artists, on the one hand, with, on the other, the need expressed by the health (also known as *illness*) sector to foster 'mental health-promoting communities'.

polemigram 2

Artists and mental health

A number of strands had been drawn together: the problems of the alienated individual in a consumer society; the call for artists to re-engage in social issues; and the needs of mental health service planners to foster 'mental health-promoting communities'.

I then described the origins and evolution of art therapy from the 1940s to its recognition 50 years later as a Profession Allied to Medicine (PAM), covering initial attempts to integrate the profession within the education sector before aligning it with medicine. I suggested that the considerable length of art therapy's journey to (a nonetheless insecure) institutional integration may not have been unconnected from a subversive strand that was evident in the profession's pioneers and which had persevered among some of its practitioners. Indeed, the subversiveness of the pioneers of art therapy was a quality they shared with some of the post-1970s influx into the health field of non-therapy-oriented artists.

I clarified by identifying two strands in art therapy: on the one hand, the view of the pioneers and their followers (shared to some extent by the non-therapy, participatory artists) that it is in the actual making of art that healing occurs; and, on the other hand, the view of the psychodynamic schools who believe that image making is merely a part (albeit a central one) in the therapeutic transaction between client and therapist. I commented on the virtual absence (at the time of writing) in the art therapy literature of informed debate on non-therapy arts practice in the health field. The British Association of Art Therapists has since published a *Statement of Principles* representing discussions between the two modes of practice: *www.baat.org/Arts_in_Health_Arts_Therapies_11_Jul_10.pdf*

The art therapist Kaplan (2000) also cited Dissanayake's 'making special' to underpin her profession. However, the suggestion that 'making special' underpins all arts practice may be seen either as undermining the claim for any exclusivity for art therapy, or as a timely bridge towards more collaborative practice. Or both. Nevertheless, I cited examples of how the professional demarcations between art therapy and non-therapy-oriented art had continued to give rise to problems that helped neither; nor, crucially, had such tangles helped availers of mental health services in which these practitioners operated.

I then turned to the non-therapy-oriented artists in the mental health system. Whilst their contribution may be seen as that of the individual artist, such artists more often see their role as grounded in engagement within a community, often in an activist role. Their work is frequently seen to be, and may even be claimed to be by some artists, therapeutic, but its intention is primarily artistic and/or social; some artists may well see their role in terms of healing, perhaps by definition, but not as treatment or therapy. Indeed, they may even see their activity as an antidote to what they perceive as the patronising and disempowering effects of therapy.

Impacts of participation in the arts

I then reviewed the literature concerning the healing (also known as *therapeutic*) potential of the arts in relation to the mental health of the individual and the community. Citing Matarasso (1997) and others, I considered the impact of participation in arts programmes as a means of addressing a range of social objectives, discussing health and social aims, methods, problems and impacts of art in the community, and the benefits of engagement in the arts to the individual. I considered the processes involved, giving texts exemplifying such benefits and processes.

I gave two examples epitomising synergy between distress and social action. Firstly, an account of social practice in which an arts group had worked with a Traveller community to visualise what they needed to live in dignity and to persuade a local council to see their vision through (Gould, 2000); and secondly, an aspect of Joseph Beuys' teaching where, after his quizzing of a student regarding her lack of work and her replying that *he* should try living on a deprived council estate, he suggested that her neighbourhood was her 'terrifying material', which resulted in her becoming an activist working to improve conditions on her estate (Sacks, 1995).

I now discussed Arts and Health-related research up to the time of writing (mid 2000s), listing several relevant studies before examining François Matarasso's (1997) seminal *Use or Ornament? The social impact of participtation in arts programmes*, which found that the arts are an essential ingredient of society with positive impacts on community and individual wellbeing. Matarasso found that the mental health benefits felt by his respondents related particularly to enhanced confidence and sense of belonging. Negative findings arose as a result of a project's inadequate resources, as well as of the tensions that generally accompany change of any kind.

Mental health benefits for the individual of engaging in the arts were examined more closely, beginning with the finding of Colgan et al. (1991) that attendance at an arts studio significantly reduced users' needs to attend other psychiatric services.

Making art had been said (Kaplan, 2000) to include benefits relating to the social field, mind–brain development, problem solving, communication, the accessing of inner experience, and 'optimal experience' – the term used by Csíkszentmihályi (1996) to describe what he also calls 'flow'; that is, a complete and absorbing engagement in a task. Flow, said Csíkszentmihályi, gives life both joy and meaning. These are, perhaps, two central pillars of mental health that are so obvious – and so removed from the clinical and the pathological – that they do not get a mention by the authors I had discussed in my review of definitions of mental health. Nor had I found much evidence of their consideration during my career in the mental health field; not even at times when such consideration would (in my view as borne out by my experience on several occasions) have been of benefit to people in emotional distress by addressing profound needs via cultural and creative approaches.

Research by the Health Development Agency (2001) had again confirmed what artists know: that the richest benefits arose for participants when arts projects were not 'easy' but constituted a challenge; although it was clear from the views expressed by participants that their initial introduction to group arts work should be within a relaxed, pressure-free atmosphere.

After a brief discussion on the relationship between catharsis and therapy, I pointed out that the evidence from the literature unequivocally suggests an obligation by policymakers, commissioners, providers and availers to ensure that the arts become an integral part of mental healthcare.

polemigram 3

Case studies

As described earlier, the case studies explored a range of approaches and practice, employing different methods to describe stakeholders' (including my own) experiences of participatory visual arts practice in the mental health field.

Autobiography

The first of four case studies was an autobiographical narrative that positioned the 'I' as author within the research, narrating life and career events relating to my part in the development of the arts in mental health from the mid 1970s, through my early retirement in 1996 due to burnout, and a subsequent career as consultant, researcher and artist. The role of humour in these processes was made explicit.

Trafford

The second case study described and analysed the ad hoc arts in mental health provision in 1998/99 in Trafford, where I was commissioned by the borough to conduct an audit and propose foundations for the planning of more coordinated activity. This study identified little understanding in the locality of the difference between art therapy and non-therapy-based art, and found that staff offering 'therapies' using very basic arts-related techniques predominating over projects involving professional artists. This audit was influential in the formation and development of BluSci (http://www.bluesci.org.uk).

Pathways

The third case study described the planning, delivering and evaluation of a pilot *Neighbourhood Renewal* scheme to merge artistic, therapeutic and research practice in Wythenshawe, a Manchester City district with the highest level of social deprivation in the UK. I worked as action researcher, with Lime (http://www.limeart.org/index.php), to help set up and evaluate (with Dr Rae Story) the Pathways Pilot project. Contrasts and synergy between artistic and therapeutic concepts and practice were examined, as too was the question of support for artists working in stressful situations.

Art therapy

The final case study began with an account and analyses of episodes from my own experience of skirmish between 'art' and 'therapy', before presenting three short case studies: a conversation with an art therapist who described division within the profession between the 'psychotherapeutic' and the 'artist/studio' wings; a discussion with the Pathways lead artists, whose practices blurred the boundaries between therapy and art; and an open letter from the British Association of Art Therapists (BAAT) offering 'supervision' to non-therapy-trained artists.[2]

---

2. On being shown this letter, one non-therapy artist (who understandably remains anonymous) said 'Well, they can fuck off!'

Cumulatively, the case studies, together with the *Directory*, form a comprehensive picture of arts and mental health practice either side of the millennium.

Findings, discussion, conclusions

In the early stages of my research I had articulated three central issues that formed a triangular core running through the study:

- the problem of the alienated individual in a consumer society
- the call for artists to re-engage in social issues
- the need expressed by mental health service providers to foster 'mental health-promoting communities'.

A growing number of artists are adopting a societal and ecological practice that is likely to impact upon the mental health domain – or, to put it in another (less clinical and thus more obvious) way, upon culture at large. Fromm's (1979) equation, summed up as 'sick society = sick people', and his assertion of the human need for relatedness, identity and transcendence, find a response in Kaprow's call for a 'lifelike' art , in the neo-shamanic tradition of Beuys. But for such a non-consumption-oriented paradigm to take hold among populations it may require (argued Bocock, 1993) positive and challenging engagement with the erstwhile and dogma-ridden guardians of the spiritual theatre, namely, the religions.

A comparison of art therapy and non-therapy arts practice suggested that one area of common ground may be found in a subversive furrow that is prevalent among the latter practice and which has persevered in some (but by no means all) sectors of the former. Once the principle threads had been drawn together regarding the relative merits of various modes of participation in the arts for people with mental health difficulties, the overriding conclusion was the need to recognise and realise a continuum of practice responsive to the needs and aspirations of participants and artists.

The conclusions had been drawn from those narratives and discussions that led to an understanding of respondents' perceptions of 'art', 'therapy' and 'the therapeutic' that arose during the course of the case studies. Having examined the differences and similarities – in approaches, attitudes, philosophy and potential outcomes of the different practices of art-as-therapy and art-as-art – the study concluded that a series of continua and virtuous circles emerged from the findings.

In the final discussion I also reviewed findings already delineated within the study concerning the support, mentoring or supervision of artists working in potentially stressful situations. I suggested that without support for artists such work may not be sustainable; and that a key aspect of this support must be to enable the artists to pursue their artistic vocation.

For myself, this research had been a lengthy adventure that challenged my own preconceptions and threw up unexpected discoveries. It was like advancing along the corridor in the Beatles' *Yellow Submarine*, doors opening and closing on unseen rooms off an endless corridor. Additional avenues of investigation were glimpsed, with several discussed in detail and suggested as topics for further research.

polemigram 4

Afterthoughts before a long goodbye

There is the sweep of time. Maybe noticing such things is just one of the things that helps you become more aware of your place in the world.

The word 'aesthetic' relates to 'noticing'; it is derived from the Greek αισθητικοζ (*aisthetikos*): aesthetic, sensitive; which itself was derived from αισθάνομαι (*aisthanomai*): I perceive, feel, sense:

I began my decade-long research interlude to try and make sense of myself, what I'd done, and the times I'd lived in. Halfway through this journey an academic reviewer criticised my emerging thesis as:

A manifesto for a profession in the making.

If that's the case I'm glad I got away with it.

I took early retirement as an artist in the NHS in 1996. I declared I was doing no more Arts and Health work in 1999, after the World Symposium on Culture, Health and the Arts. In 2003 I said I would do no more Arts and Health work so I could focus on Bridgehead. In 2005 I decided not to complete my thesis. In 2006 I did. In 2007 my friend Aidan Shingler and I announced simultaneously that we were giving up campaigning against abuses in the psychiatric system and arts in health respectively. In 2008 I gave up Arts and Health work to return to practising as a painter.

In 2010 I was invited to contribute to this book, and began working to establish an Arts for Health archive at the Manchester Metropolitan University as part of a virtual warren of archives that will enable future researchers to build as accurate as possible a history of the Arts and Health movement.

Resolution:

… now I'll get back to painting …

polemigram 5

References

Angus, J (2002) *An Enquiry Concerning Possible Methods for Evaluating Arts in Health Projects* Durham: CAHHM, University of Durham. (Original work published 1998)

Bocock, R (1993) *Consumption*. London: Routledge.

Brown, L (2006) *Is Art Therapy? Art for mental health at the millennium*. PhD thesis, Manchester: Manchester Metropolitan University

Calman, K (1999) Speech at the *World Symposium on Culture, Health and the Arts* (CHARTS99). Arts for Health. Manchester: Manchester Metropolitan University.

Colgan, S, Bridges, K, Brown, L & Faragher, B (1991) A tentative start: Evaluation of alternative forms of care for chronic users of psychiatric services. *Psychiatric Bulletin, 15,* 596–8.

Csíkszentmihályi, M (1996) *Creativity: Flow and the psychology of discovery and invention.* New York: Harper Perennial.

Dissanayake, E (1988) *What Is Art For?* Seattle, WA: University of Washington Press.

Ellis, C (2004) *The Ethnographic I: A methodological movel about autoethnography.* Walnut Creek, CA: AltaMira Press.

Fromm, E (1979) *To Have or To Be?* London: Abacus.

Gablik, S (1985) *Has Modernism Failed?* London: Thames and Hudson.

Gablik, S (1991) *The Reenchantment of Art.* London: Thames and Hudson.

Gilroy, A (2006) *Art Therapy, Research and Evidence-based Practice.* London: Sage.

Gould, H (2000) Creative exchange: Creative approaches to health, rights and development. In F Turner & P Senior (Eds), *A Powerful Force for Good: Culture, health and the Arts World Symposium: An anthology* (pp. 48–9). Manchester: Manchester Metropolitan University.

Health Development Agency (2001) *Art for Health: A review of good practice in community based arts projects and initiatives which impact on health and wellbeing.* London: Health Development Agency.

Hopkins, EJ (Ed) (1967) *Ambrose Bierce: The Enlarged Devil's Dictionary.* Garden City, NY: Doubleday. (Original work published 1906)

Kaplan, F (2000) *Art, Science and Art Therapy: Repainting the picture.* London: Jessica Kingsley.

Kaprow, A (n.d.) Interview by Robert C. Morgan, *Journal of Contemporary Art*: http://www.jca-online.com/kaprow.html

Krizek, RL (2003) Ethnography as the excavation of personal narrative. In RP Clair (Ed) *Expressions of Ethnography: Novel approaches to qualitative methods* (pp. 141–51). Albany, NY: State University of New York Press.

Masson, J (1989) *Against Therapy.* London: Collins.

Matarasso, F (1997) *Use or Ornament? The social impact of participation in the arts.* Stroud: Comedia.

Mithen, S (1996) *The Prehistory of the Mind: A search for the origins of art, religion and science.* London: Thames and Hudson.

Obeyesekere, G (1981) *Medusa's Hair.* Chicago: The University of Chicago Press.

Parr, H (2006) Mental health, the arts and belongings. *Transactions of the Institute of British Geographers, 31*(2), 150–66.

Sacks, S (1995) Joseph Beuys' pedagogy and the work of James Hillman: The healing art and the art of healing. *Issues in Architecture, Art and Design, 4,* 1.

Schön, D (1995) *The Reflective Practitioner: How professionals think in action,* Aldershot: Arena.

Smail, D (1998) *How to Survive without Psychotherapy.* London: Constable.

World Health Organization (2010) Mental Health: Strengthening our response *Fact Sheet N° 220:* http://www.who.int/mediacentre/factsheets/fs220/en/index.html

CHAPTER THREE

Innovation, Arts and Mental Health: An evaluation of four innovative arts-based mental health projects

Helen Brooks & David Pilgrim

Introduction

The Challenge Programme was set up by the National Endowment for Science Technology and the Arts (NESTA) in 2006 with the aim of exploring innovations in response to major social problems. In November of that year, mental health emerged as one of the major topics that the programme should target. NESTA recruited a number of expert partners from the mental health field to be involved in the selection and management of the funded projects. The call for funding was released and projects were asked for that could demonstrate:

- multi- and interdisciplinary working
- use of arts in the mental health field
- innovation had to be central to the concept of the project
- service user engaged or led.

As a result of the call for funding over 500 applications were received, which varied greatly in their content and scope. From this pool of applications, 11 were finally selected to receive funding. Of these 11 projects, four had a particular focus on arts-based activities and the evaluation of these will form the basis of this chapter. These projects are outlined briefly in a later section.

The Department of Social Work based at the University of Central Lancashire undertook the evaluation of these projects and used a realistic approach to evaluation. This involved acquiring a deep understanding of the projects under consideration to fully comprehend the extent of success for each project and to also allow the evaluators to draw conclusions about these successes from both within and between projects. A fuller explanation of the methodology used can be found in the methodology section below.

Context

Generally, there are two types of change that occur within mental health services: transactional change (adhering to pre-set targets and agendas by changing roles, responsibilities and tasks), and transformational change (which is a deeper change and aims to do something entirely new). The focus of the projects described in this chapter, and the premise on which the projects were selected, was innovation which is aligned with transformational change. However, this type of change is often hampered within health services by transactional priorities or targets, which can be a constant threat to developing something entirely new or innovative.

There have been constant policy pressures on the NHS, including mental health services, to 'modernise' and increase efficiency within services. However, this has been difficult to achieve. Reasons for this were described by Sheaff and Pilgrim in 2006 and include:

- constant change within the wider system (e.g., the introduction of new policies and procedures regularly and rapid staff turnover)
- a focus on routinisation especially in terms of clinical practices
- a lack of ring-fenced learning time for staff working within health services
- resource constraints.

In particular within mental health services, modernisation has been driven by notions of citizenship and recovery (Pilgrim & Ramon, 2009). The projects described in this chapter reflect this notion of recovery and, in particular, the notion of social inclusion and the need to offer choice to service users who often have diverse needs (Care Services Improvement Partnership, 2006). However, this modernisation drive has been hampered by the risk-averse culture that operates within mental health services and the underfunding of mental health when compared with other services. It is worth noting then that any project operating within statutory services works within this environment where there is tension between a recovery ethos (which by its nature requires some risk by encouraging people to live on their own in their own way) and the risk-averse nature (e.g., focus on patient safety) of services (Repper & Perkins, 2003).

Despite a call for increased funding within mental health services following the National Service Framework (NSF) for Mental Health (Department of Health, 1999) and a report from the Sainsbury Centre for Mental Health (Sainsbury Centre for Mental Health, 2003), these services still remain underfunded (Pilgrim, 2009). However, the NSF did encourage service development around recovery and user involvement. As previously discussed however, these are likely to encounter tension within services when they challenge the risk-averse status quo.

Resource constraints are a constant pressure within services and this is likely to become exacerbated by the new pressure on funding through the budget cuts introduced, and to be introduced, by the new coalition government. It may be that innovation and/or transformational change become victims of this streamlining of services to enable the organisation to focus on transactional forms of changes. It is perhaps difficult to foresee that innovation per se will find it easy to generate support within statutory services in the difficult times ahead. It is worth then considering the provision of these types of projects/services from a different sector or different type of provider.

This section has highlighted the drivers of change in terms of policy documentation within mental health services as well as some of the challenges that may arise during their implementation. The four projects under evaluation here have a strong user-involvement focus and are described in more detail in the next section. Three of these arts-based projects were undertaken externally to the NHS from the outset whilst the remaining project started within statutory services and moved outside during the process of developing the project.

Description of projects

The projects funded by NESTA varied in a number of ways. Some were new and developed entirely in response to the call for funding, whereas others were extensions of existing projects. The ethos of Project B and Project C was around normalisation and citizenship, focusing on providing access to artistic activity for a group of individuals who were normally denied it. Projects A, B and C used artistic activity as a vehicle for the innovation behind the project whereas Project D was clinical in its orientation whilst utilising innovative methods.

The projects under consideration for the purpose of this chapter are outlined below:

- *Project A*: The provision of a tailored programme of user-defined arts-based activities for a group experiencing the double disadvantage of mental ill health (no diagnosis specified) and homelessness. This was undertaken in partnership with a major arts and social inclusion agency. The project was perceived to be innovative within its context due to the collaboration between mental health services, a local homeless drop-in centre and the arts sector, and through using creative activities to explore the individual challenges that these service users faced.
- *Project B*: The production of an informative DVD documenting and acting out situations in which subtle abuse (e.g., false befriending, postal scams) of vulnerable adults can occur. The idea for the project came from service users who had themselves suffered this type of abuse. They worked with a filmmaker to write, perform and film the scenarios suggested by the group. The project innovation arose through its focus on self-determination and personal empowerment, using these values to produce a concrete outcome.
- *Project C*: The provision of a programme of arts activities within a medium-secure psychiatric unit. The delivery was split between workshops that service users engaged in and performances where service users were the audience (e.g., cabaret evenings, poetry readings etc.). The innovatory nature of this project was specific to the context and centred on the introduction of arts activity (as opposed to arts therapy) within secure mental health services.
- *Project D*: A project which explored the therapeutic potential of animation for vulnerable children and families. Initially based within statutory services, the funding enabled the project to move outside of traditional services into a third-sector (voluntary) context. The use of animation within therapy was new in this context and with this particular client group.

While the specifics of the problems each project sought to address were different, they did appear to converge under the broad umbrella of addressing a perceived lack *of meaningful activity for mental health service users to engage with.*

There were also some similarities between the factors perceived by those involved in the project to be sustaining the problem, and these are outlined in Figure 3.1.

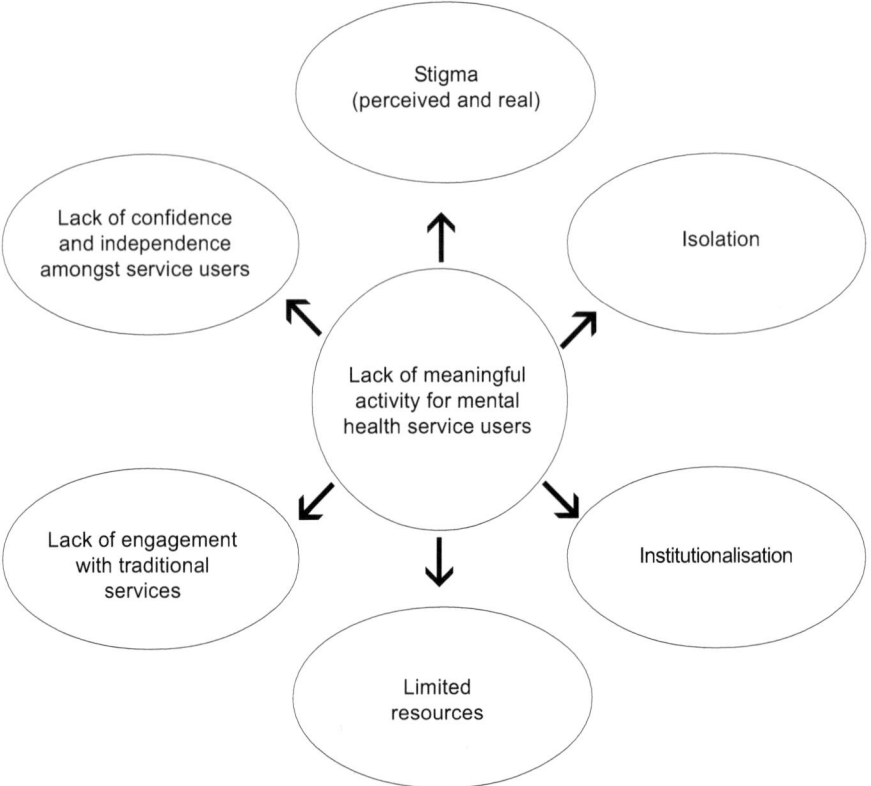

Figure 3.1: Factors perceived by stakeholders to be sustaining the problem of lack of meaningful activity for mental health service users

Table 3.1 provides further information on the projects, including outlining the position of the different projects in relation to statutory services, detailing any changes to the hosting of the organisation, in addition to briefly summarising the impact and the success of each project.

Methodology

The methodology for this evaluation followed a realistic evaluation approach based on the work of Pawson and Tilly (1997) with an emphasis on the links between processes and outcomes within and between different projects. This method advocates obtaining a deep understanding of individual projects

	Project A	Project B	Project C	Project D
Relation to statutory services	External	External	External	External
Changes to the hosting of the project	No	No	No	Yes – moved outside statutory services
Level of development prior to the NESTA grant	New	New	Expansion	New
Output: product vs. activity	Activity and product(s)	Activity and product(s)	Activity	Activity and product(s)
Ethos of the project				
Therapy low/high	Low	Low	Low	High
User Inclusion low/high	High	High	High	High
Impact/Success	Both this evaluation and the local evaluation demonstrated a clear impact on those that accessed the project. This related to improved self-esteem and confidence and a substantial development of their creative skills. This was achieved through the showcasing of products at local accessible community venues.	This evaluation demonstrated that this project worked best for those people who had previously been involved in an artistic area and were considered stable in terms of their current mental health. For these individuals, confidence was increased and they often went on to develop their artistic skill through further education. The project was set up so that other people not considered in this category could also take part in other ways e.g., set production.	The local evaluation was not ready at the time of going to print. However, findings from the interviews and analysis of project documentation indicate that sessions were well attended and those who attended benefited in a number of ways. The impact related to enhanced creative skills, improved relationships with other users and staff, as well as enhanced integration with the local community.	The project was not complete at the time the evaluation went to print. However, interviews with stakeholders revealed that the response from therapists and service users has been very positive to date.

Table 3.1: *Further information on the four projects under evaluation*

with a particular focus on understanding the mechanisms operating in particular contexts to produce outcomes. In addition, the researchers then aim to formulate an awareness of *what* is working and for *whom* in *which* circumstances. In this evaluation this was achieved through semi-structured interviews with the stakeholders involved in each project. In this study, this methodology was applied to each of the individual projects which allowed the researchers to formulate conclusions about each project whilst also enabling comparisons to be made across the different projects.

This chapter reports on the findings of 27 interviews with key stakeholders involved in the different projects (11 from Project A, 5 from Project B, 6 from Project C and 5 from Project D) in conjunction with site visits and a thorough examination of any relevant project documentation (including manuals, individual evaluation reports, minutes from meetings etc.). Contacts for initial stakeholders were provided to the research team from the funding body and then a snowballing approach was utilised to ensure full representation for each project. Stakeholders included those running the projects (defined as project champions), other staff working on the project, service users, and key people who were instrumental to the project setup.

The interviews were analysed along the following domains and are reported on this basis in the subsequent sections.

- *Conducive conditions*. What evidence was there about the extent of conducive conditions for the success in each of the projects? In this sense the study aimed to identify the factors that gave rise to the projects' success or lack of it.
- *Ontological depth*. One of the key tasks associated with this study was to gain, through interviews with key stakeholders, a deep understanding of each project from the point of view of those involved.
- *Mechanisms*. The interviews aimed to generate information relating to two types of mechanisms. The first related to stakeholders' perceptions about the causal factors that led up to the issues or problems that the projects sought to address. The second type of mechanism and the type this chapter will focus on was the mechanisms central to the remedial effects noted by individual projects.
- *Context–mechanism–outcome configurations*. Once the interviews were completed, the next task was to look for patterns between the context in which the innovation operated, the mechanism involved and the observable or identifiable outcomes. At this point, any similarities and differences within and between different projects were identified.

- *Open systems.*[1] In line with the aforementioned methodology utilised, the researchers assumed that the evaluation was being carried out in an open, rather than closed, system. Any findings or noteworthy data relating to the impact of open systems were noted.

The evaluation commenced in 2008 and all relevant ethical and research governance clearance was obtained in the Spring of that year. The evaluation was completed by September 2009.

Findings

All four of the arts-based mental health projects reported in this chapter appeared to be highly successful (see Table 3.1 for details on individual successes). All the projects achieved the aims established originally at the outset of the funding and all appeared to have high levels of engagement from service users. In addition, the projects produced high-quality artistic outputs that were disseminated both locally at accessible venues, nationally and, in one case, internationally. The potential conducive and impeding factors related to these successes are outlined below.

1. Context
Conducive conditions
Structure and position of the host organisation. Three out of the four projects were run by independent organisations outside of statutory services. The remaining project started off within statutory services but during the course of the project moved outside of the NHS due to changes within the local trust which meant the project was no longer feasible within the NHS. All four projects felt that the position of their host organisation outside of statutory services was conducive to success for a number of reasons:

- These organisations were often smaller with a relaxed, flat team structure or hierarchy. Those interviewed felt that smaller organisations were less confined than larger ones and this appeared to be related to levels of bureaucracy. This seemed to be supported by the findings from other projects undertaken within statutory services.

---

1. An open system is one that regularly exchanges information and obtains feedback from its environment and has the potential to change/learn as a result of this feedback. In comparison a closed system has firm boundaries which do not allow for information exchange.

> The project champion within Project B had responsibility within the organisation for running the project, which allowed flexibility in the design and delivery of the project. This encouraged a sense of ownership for all those involved in the project. The sense of ownership was also encouraged by the non-specific brief and the ability to be able to experiment with the process of developing the DVD (scripts and characters had been drafted before the workshops started but it quickly became apparent that these would not be appropriate and scripts and characters were then developed by service users).

- The project was more likely to be aligned with the core business of the host organisation and therefore more easily incorporated into daily routines.
- There were perceived to be fewer competing targets or agendas when stakeholders compared their organisation to statutory services.
- Stakeholders felt that the smaller size of the organisation increased the ability for more flexible delivery of the project.

There was a perception amongst those interviewed that the voluntary sector was the innovator in the mental health field and that the voluntary sector's flexibility meant they could adapt services and mainstream what worked. Staff within each of the organisations had significant experience of working with the service users the project targeted.

There was also a perception that the environment within the host organisations of the projects described here provided a 'safe and comfortable' setting with less stigma attached for those involved in the projects. Care was taken to ensure that it was clear that the focus of each project was collaborative activity rather than any form of traditional therapy. This allowed the focus of the projects to be on social interaction and engagement with meaningful activity which encouraged long-term engagement from those involved. The use of non-traditional roles (discussed later) further facilitated this.

Impeding conditions

Structural instability. Structural instability in these arts-based projects related specifically to changes within the host organisation. These changes varied between projects and included changes to key personnel (including in one case the project champion) and the introduction of new systems and procedures which had the potential to derail individual projects.

Resistance. Initial resistance occurred in all the projects under evaluation, but to varying degrees. However, it should be noted that this resistance was minimal when compared with projects run within statutory services. This resistance could come from a number of different areas. Perhaps the most pervasive was *initial* low expectations amongst some front-line staff within the host organisations. These related to perceptions that service users would not fully engage with the project and would consequently drop out. However, individual projects were able to challenge these expectations by the staff seeing first hand the high levels of service user engagement with the project and subsequent impact it had on them. This eliminated the resistance and the subsequent positive involvement of staff contributed positively to the process of delivering the project.

Media response. In one of the projects, stakeholders reported that the negative media response to the project and its activities locally could threaten development. This negative coverage threatened confidence in the project through its reinforcement of the stigma associated with mental health problems.

2. Process and Outcome
Conducive conditions

Project champions. Perhaps the strongest lesson to be learnt about the success of arts-based mental health projects was the importance of having a 'project champion' responsible for driving the project forward. The utility of the project champion was further enhanced if they had an in-depth knowledge of statutory services often as a result of having worked within them previously. This became particularly useful if the project worked directly into statutory services (Projects C and D). In order to maximise the impact the project champion could have, projects needed to ensure that the responsibility for running the project was fully devolved to them. This increased the flexibility of delivering the project. This devolved responsibility also engendered a sense of ownership amongst those involved in the project.

Whilst project champions were necessary for projects to succeed, it did not appear that they were solely sufficient for the success of individual projects. Stakeholders involved felt that building up a constellation of supporters of the project was critical to succeeding, in addition to having a project champion. 'Supporters' could include those within the host organisation, within statutory services, or from arts organisations in the locality. This network became particularly useful if the project champion could identify supporters in areas unfamiliar to them.

> The project champion within Project D solicited a constellation of supportive individuals to help her with the delivery of the project. This was important as there were often elements of the project that the project champion needed support with (e.g., legal and financial issues) and needed to feel comfortable to ask these individuals for help. This network of supporters also helped drive the project forward when it encountered any resistance.

Positive input from staff and service users. The success of each project was facilitated by the positive role of staff working on the project and of the service users involved in the project. The fact that all those involved in the project were working towards a common goal encouraged involvement with the project. Service users were keen to be involved in each of the projects described here and their motivation appeared to result from a desire to improve services for future generations of service users. The fact that stakeholders could see first hand the impact of the project further enhanced this engagement and contributed to the integrity of any outputs produced.

Artistic integrity. The artistic integrity of the arts activity involved and/or any outputs produced appeared important to the success of the individual projects. The use of professionals such as artists was perceived by those interviewed to increase engagement from those involved due to the enhanced authenticity of the outputs and activity. These became particularly useful if sufficient responsibility was devolved to these roles within the project to allow artistic freedom and flexibility of delivery.

The outputs produced by the projects in the form of films, photographs and theatre performances were exhibited locally, nationally and, in one case, internationally, which served as external validation of the projects. This was positively acknowledged by those involved, especially for those that were exhibited locally at accessible venues. There was a perception amongst those interviewed that this enabled service users to feel more 'visible' in their communities through the displaying of artistic outputs at these community venues. Those interviewed also reported that this served to empower the service users involved in the project. Service users often went on to pursue further artistic activity after the project finished, including further education. This was particularly marked for those who had undertaken some form of arts activity previously.

> In Project A, the high quality of the art outputs (photographs) generated shared pride amongst those taking part in the project. This was further enhanced through the final exhibition at an accessible local venue which served as external validation of the project through its display and acceptance within the community. There was a perception amongst those interviewed that this had the potential to be empowering for all those involved. This also enabled users to feel 'visible' in the community through the displaying of photographs at community venues. Photographs were also entered and won national photography competitions.

Working towards a common goal in the form of a final product, particularly one perceived to be of a high quality for the aforementioned reasons, fostered a sense of pride amongst those working on the project and was in itself helpful to the projects under consideration. Those involved had clear goals to work towards whilst also being able to see quickly and clearly the benefit of taking part. In addition, not having an explicit focus on individual diagnoses further facilitated this engagement and contributed to the focus on social interaction rather than traditional therapy.

External drivers. Having a dedicated funding source was imperative to the success of the individual projects. NESTA also provided opportunities for the projects to network with each other and provided projects with mentors to further support them. Both this and the financial support were reported in each project to be crucial to the successful development of the projects. The stability of funding (in some cases three years) further facilitated the individual projects.

Impeding conditions

Resistance from statutory services. For those projects working directly into statutory services (Project C and Project D), some resistance was encountered from within the NHS. Often for staff within statutory services, this was the first time they had seen projects of this nature and they often had concerns about issues such as health and safety and whether users would engage with the project. Again in line with the resistance encountered from staff within the host organisation, these concerns were allayed by seeing first hand the engagement with, and impact of, the project.

> There was some internal resistance from staff within statutory services during the implementation of Project C and this impacted on the engagement with the project. Staff within statutory services were concerned about the use of drama and the arts and described being worried about service users becoming 'over excited' during the activities. Artists had to overcome this resistance during the course of the project through the staff seeing first hand the positive engagement from service users.

Tension between artistic integrity and user-led services. Those interviewed reported on occasion finding it difficult to make collaborative decisions in relation to the dissemination of outputs or the content of arts activities. Artists working on the project often had different ideas about this than the service users involved, which could cause difficulties. This seemed to be symbolic of a tension between artistic integrity and the development of user-led services.

3. Potential context–mechanism–outcome configurations

Table 3.2 provides a summary of the potential relationships and configurations of context, mechanisms and outcomes that were derived from the interviews with stakeholders. This diagram aims to give readers a summary of the factors related to successes that spanned across projects and which have already been discussed. These factors were selected due to their relative importance as attributed by those interviewed during the data collection period. The table should also aid the visualisation and understanding of how mechanisms interact in a given context to produce outcomes across different projects as reported by those involved in each one.

Discussion

The four projects described and discussed in this chapter varied in terms of their delivery and content. However, all four were arts based, (eventually) external to statutory services, and had a focus on social interaction and patient centeredness. All four projects appeared successful in terms of their outcomes and encouraging engagement from service users (see Table 3.1). The evaluation highlighted the utility of arts-based activity when working with people who are highly marginalised in society and who statutory services may find difficulty in engaging for help. This was achieved through a focus on social interaction and engagement with meaningful activity rather than a focus on traditional therapy. This was facilitated by the project's position

Context +	Mechanism =	Outcome
Organisations that ...		
• have a project champion to take responsibility for the project who has knowledge of statutory services • are independent of statutory services • are small with a flat, relaxed team hierarchy • can align the project to the core business of the organisation • offer a safe and secure environment	• identify a constellation of supporters • use non-traditional roles to delivery the arts activity • collaborative working between artists and service users based on the production of high quality artistic outputs • responsibility devolved to front-line staff to allow flexibility of delivery • project focuses on social interaction and engagement	• increased likelihood of challenging any problems that arise through combined skills and experience • increased acceptability of the project amongst service users • external validation and increased perceived visibility in the local community which reduces stigma • increased appropriateness of project through flexibility of delivery and less systemic resistance to the project • enhanced engagement with the project which impacts on self-esteem and confidence

Table 3.2: *Potential context–mechanism–outcome (CMO) configurations*

outside of traditional services. The projects responded successfully to the policy emphases of user involvement and diverse expressed needs described previously (Pilgrim & Ramon, 2009; Care Services Improvement Partnership, 2006). In addition, the findings appeared to show that there is a potential creative role for the third sector in engaging with specific groups of service users who often fall outside of traditional statutory provision. For example, Project A targeted homeless individuals who also had mental health problems and engaged them in a way that was acceptable and appeared to be beneficial to them. However, more substantive analysis and examination of outcomes would be required to fully demonstrate any beneficial effects.

It is worth highlighting at this point that whilst approximately 90% of mental health problems are treated within primary care, the four projects discussed in this chapter were aimed at those with mental health problems who were, or might typically have been, receiving specialist mental health services. There were no 'primary care only' projects included in the projects funded. However, it could be argued that these projects would have been applicable in other fields, not solely the ones in which they were based. For example, Project C could be taken into any setting, community or otherwise, where individuals with mental health problems come together.

As outlined in the context section above, there is a tension between the risk-averse nature of mental health services and new innovatory projects which take risks in their attempt to become patient centred and responsive to individual service user needs. The projects described here encountered this tension to some extent and this was manifested in Project C more than the others. This is likely to be due to the fact it was the only project of its type working into a service that by its nature focuses on the loss of individual freedom.

To conclude, the methodology utilised in this study, based on the work of Pawson and Tilly (1997), allowed the growth of a rich understanding of the individual projects before drawing lessons in relation to factors that might contribute to or inhibit successful development (specifically conducing and impeding factors relating to context, process and outcome) of these types of projects. All projects described in this chapter benefited from their external position in relation to statutory services. Reasons for this were related to their smaller size, flatter team structure and increased ability to align the project with the core business of the organisation. There are various other lessons, however, that can be taken from the findings that may be relevant to any future arts-based activities attempting to operate outside of statutory services:

- Having a *project champion is critical* to the successful development of any project to be undertaken. Project champions with an in-depth knowledge of statutory services can be particularly beneficial to anticipating or combating any problems that may arise.
- Project champions should seek to obtain a *constellation of supportive individuals* for the project, particularly in areas with which they are unfamiliar. This will help when/if the project encounters resistance.
- *Devolving responsibility* for running the project to the project champion or other front-line staff working on the project (e.g., artists), where possible, as this encourages the flexible delivery of the project.
- Projects should *focus on social interaction* with a move away from the label associated with a diagnosis of mental health problems. This encourages ownership and engagement with the project.
- *Stability of funding* is important to successful delivery.
- Working towards a common goal and in particular producing *high quality artistic outputs* engendered a sense of pride amongst service users and

facilitated engagement. This was facilitated by the use of non-traditional roles in the delivery of the project (e.g., artists, animators, actors). However, projects should be aware of the potential tension between artistic integrity and user-led services and consider this in any design.

- Engagement in arts-based projects can be used as a *stepping stone to further activities* for those involved. This should be encouraged where relevant and can be beneficial for those involved.

References

Care Services Improvement Partnership (2006) *Our Choices in Mental Health: A framework for improving choice for people who use mental health services and their carers.* London: National Institute of Mental Health in England.

Department of Health (1999) *National Service Framework for Mental Health: Modern standards and service models.* London: Department of Health.

Pawson, R & Tilly, N (1997) *Realistic Evaluation.* London: Sage.

Pilgrim, D (2009) 'Recovery' and current mental health policy. *Chronic Illness, 4,* 295–304.

Pilgrim, D & Ramon, S (2009) English mental health policy under New Labour. *Policy and Politics, 37*(2), 273–88.

Repper, J & Perkins, R (2003) *Social Inclusion and Recovery.* London: Balliere Tindall.

Sainsbury Centre for Mental Health (2003) *Money for Mental Health: A review of public spending on mental healthcare.* London: Sainsbury Centre for Mental Health.

Sheaff, R & Pilgrim, D (2006) Can learning organisations survive in the newer NHS? *Implementation Science, 1,* 27.

CHAPTER FOUR

Creating Something Beautiful: Art in Mind

Theo Stickley

> Another thing we should do ... is to switch the aim of research in the arts to finding out not what critics think about this or that artwork ... but how art has affected and changed other people's lives. (Carey, 2005: 167)

A little history

Prior to my mental health nurse training in the early 1990s, I had a period of some six months working voluntarily in the old Mapperley Hospital, before its closure as a mental asylum. The environment was bleak and treatments appeared to me to be very limited. Wishing to bring an element of creativity into the area where I was volunteering, I was given permission to run a drama group on a Friday evening. This group ran for some months and was very popular amongst the patients. My perception at the time was that the group provided an opportunity for people to be expressive about their confinement in hospital and experiences of mental distress.

Once qualified as a nurse, I endeavoured to incorporate creative approaches in my nurse practice. I had degrees of success; however I felt frustrated at the lack of opportunity for people to express themselves creatively. A small group of nurses commenced a monthly meeting within the Trust to discuss ways in which creative approaches could be encouraged. It was in the late 1990s that I began to imagine an arts programme for people with mental health problems. Over time, I became acquainted with people working in community arts and realised that there existed projects that engaged with people using mental health services. In February 2002, I arranged a meeting of potentially interested people. This meeting included two statutory workers, six professional community artists and four service users/local residents. This group continued to meet monthly for nearly three years working on a proposal to the government's New Deal for Communities. The proposal was successful and funding (£260,000 over two and a half years) commenced in September 2004.

I've called this chapter 'Creating Something Beautiful' because when I now pause and look back at the work that has been done over the last seven years, I realise that it has touched many lives. Something beautiful has been created. Literally hundreds of people have, one way or another, come into contact with the programme of work. I have published elsewhere about the work (Stickley & Duncan, 2007; Stickley et al., 2007; Stickley, 2010a, 2010b, 2011), but this is the first time that I have written about the research I conducted with those who set up Art in Mind in Nottingham. This chapter catches what I saw developing at the time; genuinely caring and creative people with a shared vision for community-based arts, working together, unselfishly, to make it happen.

Researching people who developed a community arts project

Quite early on, I decided to conduct some research focused upon the Steering Group itself. Whilst there were many research studies looking at how participants benefited from engaging with participatory arts, I knew of no study that explored the motivations of people developing and managing programmes of work. I originally set out to ask questions of participants about their experiences of being involved; however, because of the personal nature of the answers I was getting, the focus of the research shifted to eliciting people's stories. This was mainly because although I was asking questions from an interview schedule, people digressed from my questions, and simply wanted to tell their stories. This was an important learning experience for me about research itself. The researcher should be open to new methods and new information that comes back from conducting the research itself. We shouldn't be rigid in our methods; sometimes we should listen to what the research is telling us and go with the flow.

I therefore realised that the focus of the inquiry needed to be one that centred upon narrative. More than this though, I wanted to get a sense of what collective narrative was being constructed. Thus, I decided upon contextualising the entire work in a narrative framework.

Some narrative theory

The social science research world is replete with narrative-based literature and methods. This *narrative turn*, as it has been called, may be first attributed to the work of Roland Barthes (1977) who first proposed that the social sciences should employ narrative methods. Although originating in the arts, narrative inquiry has more recently emerged in medicine and nursing under the umbrella term of 'illness narrative'. Furthermore, there are those who have combined discourse approaches with narrative inquiry in various disciplines. Naturally, there are those who are 'discourse analysts' and others who are 'narrative analysts', ultimately however, there is no conflict in bringing the two together as narrative constructs discourse and (some would argue) a discourse is a narrative. This multiple lens, multiple voice approach (Chase, 2005), has been said to begin to generate '… a new form of consciousness' in research approaches (Gergen & Gergen, 2003: 603).

I am not, neither have I been, a passive observer. This study is based upon the part that I have played in the project. Reflexivity therefore has been central to my research. Over the years, and throughout the research process, I have maintained a reflective research diary. In this, I include my own story. Where appropriate I have drawn from this work to create the narrative in my chapters in this book. It was Riessman (1993: 1) who reminded us that, 'Narrative analysis takes as its object of investigation the story itself'. It is not just the research transcripts that are central to this study, but the researcher's journey through this research, and my narrative is interwoven throughout the text. I am co-constructing a narrative (Gubrium & Holstein, 2000; Gergen & Gergen, 2003) with others who I have worked with and interviewed. Conducting this research over several years has enabled me to see not only change over time, but change in co-constructed concepts over time too.

The following extract from my research diary illustrates the development of my ideological motivation to work outside of the psychiatric system and illustrates the use of my own narrative within the text:

I went to work in psychiatric nursing not knowing what I would find or where that career path would take me ... When I became a nurse, I found out that the system did not provide what was needed for people with mental health problems. It was obvious to me that people needed compassionate care that involved listening and creativity. In psychiatric wards, I discovered nothing much more than basic physical provision, controlling people's behaviour and much medication. I sat in on ward reviews that humiliated the person and observed paternalism that disabled people and stripped them of their independence and dignity. What began to grow was a determination that I could do better. People needed relationships, friendship, someone to listen. Furthermore, people needed the opportunity to be their creative selves. (Extract from my research diary, 29th January, 2004)

Narrative defined

While the theoretical underpinning of both narrative inquiry and discourse analysis is presented, throughout this work I use the words 'narrative' and 'discourse' interchangeably. Although the two expressions may have developed an independent canon of academic literature, the two are also merged at times, notably in the field of 'discursive psychology' (Edwards & Potter, 1992; Harré & Gillet, 1994; Edwards, 1997; Brockmeier, 2001). Both narrative and discourse have a sense of the way people construct their worlds and tell their stories. The Cambridge English Dictionary (2007) defines *narrate* as: 'verb; to tell a story, often by reading aloud from a text, or to describe events as they happen', and *discourse* as: 'noun; communication in speech or writing'.

Therefore, the word 'narrate' may be considered the doing (transitive verb) of the noun, narrative. People may construct their narrative (in the same way that people may construct a discourse). Similarly, the terms throughout the research literature are used for both personal and collective constructs and descriptions. Riessman (1993: 3) defined *narrative* as: '... talk organized around consequential events'. This chapter is text organised around consequential events.

As I write the words for these chapters, I imagine a reader as my audience. My reader is seriously interested in research; otherwise they would not have bought this book or got this far in the text. As I imagine, I am performing in my writing. In reality, the audience is limited (textbooks are never bestsellers!), and the script (my performance narrative) is my account of my research journey. Furthermore, in reality, the notion of performance does not imply falsehood on my part, rather an acknowledgement that in conducting this research and writing it up I am doing so in a social role. I am a social performer in the role of mental health and the arts researcher. I have attempted to present the qualitative interviews that make up my data set not as products of a potentially cold and sterile activity of a 'scientific' researcher but as living human interactions. For research interviews should be:

> ... not as a method of gathering information, but as a vehicle for producing performance texts and performance ethnographies about self and society. (Denzin, 2001: 24)

Interview method

In qualitative research the interview, contents, structure and relationship are critical to the sense and purpose of the research study (Mishler, 1986). For Ricoeur (1981, 1984, 1991) the interview is a place where the narrator recounts the story and produces the plots. The telling is not mere repetition but it is a dynamic process with a new reformulation, thus new meanings may emerge; the narrator and the listener are reborn. It is generally accepted therefore that the more open the interview schedule, the better (Labov & Waletsky, 1967; Riessman, 2004). It is with some regret that I asked as many interview questions as I did in the early interviews, although later interviews were less directive.

In narrative research, it is largely held that people already possess constructed and rehearsed discourses of their life experiences and the role of the researcher is to elicit the narrative (Mishler, 1986). However, this should not diminish the role and effect of the interviewer in terms of human interaction (Silverman, 2006). Furthermore, research interviews do not always evoke narratives; some may consider the interview process as a kind of scientific environment where it is inappropriate to tell stories (Czarniawska, 2004). This could be remedied by the interviewer inviting the story rather than adhering to an interview guide (Gubrium & Holstein, 2000). It is possible however, given the experiences of narrative researchers cited in this chapter, that narrative will emerge irrespective of the interview guide. For this research, I interviewed seven members of the Steering Group. Five were arts voluntary sector workers and two were local residents. Ethical approval was granted before the research commenced. Pseudonyms are used throughout.

The people interviewed (Winter 2004–5)

Name	Designation
Rupert	Local resident
Wendy	Local resident
Clare	Arts voluntary sector worker
Roger	Arts voluntary sector worker
Veronica	Arts voluntary sector worker
Simon	Arts voluntary sector worker
Belinda	Arts voluntary sector worker

These are the questions I set out to ask each of the participants:

Vision
What was the vision that the original group shared?

What has kept the group going?
1. Motivation for being in this group?
2. With no money, how has the group been sustained?
3. Given the potential different and competing agendas of people within the group, how has this group been successful?

How has the group worked together?
1. What have been the difficulties?
2. What conflicts have arisen in the development of the proposal?
3. How have these been resolved?
4. How has being a part of this group helped individuals?
5. What have people learned by being in this group? (About developing a proposal and about themselves)
6. What advice would people give to others seeking to develop this kind of initiative in the future?

Themes from the research

The themes from the research interviews are presented, firstly, thematically and secondly, collectively. The questions elicited answers relating to the nature of the group and its processes. Asking open questions and encouraging participants to talk freely, and not to be overconcerned about being restricted by the questions asked, encouraged narrative responses.

NVivo software was utilised to aid the thematic analysis. Each of the transcripts was read several times before attempting the analysis. It became obvious at an early stage that some participants used narrative accounts to answer questions. Each participant incorporated personal elements in their responses by either illustrating how their own life stories impact upon their work or the significance of creativity for their own wellbeing. The seven interviews elicited a large quantity of data. The quotations that are used in this section are selected representative examples from the data.

Originally, six themes were identified:

a) Belief in the work
b) Human connection
c) Art, therapeutic value and healing
d) Personal experience
e) Concepts and philosophy
f) Working together

After further re-reading of the identified selected passages that best illustrated each of the themes, the themes were collapsed into three broad categories:

Theme	Sub-theme
The benefits of creativity	b) Human connection
	c) Art, therapeutic value and healing
	e) Concepts and philosophy
Experiences and beliefs	a) Personal experience
	d) Belief in the work
Effective collaboration	f) Working together

Table 4.1: *Themes*

First Theme: The benefits of creativity
Sub-theme 1: Human connection

Four participants talked about the place of human connectedness, both socially and on a personal, deeper level. Creativity and values are considered common bonds that united the group:

> *... it felt like the passion that connected people together was a direct passion of their own experiences, rather than ironically just a belief or a thought or an idea or what they had been told. It felt like we were all there because this is, somehow connected to our lives and our life choices and what we want to do, whether that is professionally or um ... for other reasons. (Veronica, 39–44)*

> *I just am a firm believer that there's not a lot out there for people um ... to do, to connect with um ... and I feel it's just so important that there are other avenues into um ... being able to develop the healing process. (Clare, 36–9)*

> *Uh ... I mean just talking with um ... the three Art in Mind people the other day ... that sense of how we're connecting with others and the network effect of it and the creative possibilities of that. (Simon, 169–72)*

> *If it's fun and can be engaged with at some level then in one sense it's all worth while because you've made a connection, people connect with you. (Simon, 310–12)*

Sub-theme 2: Art, therapeutic value and healing

Three participants talked about the therapeutic potential of creative expression and the potential for personal growth:

> *But um ... uh ... so and I think, I think the concept was about the care within the community and what was actually lacking for people and I think it was also about the fact that we all know that the arts are a humongous healing process and you can work so much through, uh, in your own head through art in so many different ways. (Clare, 66–70)*

> *That I think essentially ... I'm very scary around the words ... but creativity is healing. Creativity improves mental health just very basically and is what people are craving for and I think what people want in their lives. (Veronica, 55–7)*

> *I think tied up in the whole function and value of art at its very core is um ... is ... good mental health practice in the sense that art does have a good therapeutic value. (Simon, 219–21)*

> *Because it is about all of us and ... you know, it's about developing, it's about healing, it's about growth ... (Clare, 650–1)*

> *Healing potential, just a health potential actually more than just the healing. Just the potential for health to be living our full potential on, in this world, in this community, in our lives. That even if we consider ourselves to be healthy there's always more. (Veronica, 72–5)*

Sub-theme 3: Concepts and philosophy

Participants articulated their personal philosophy of community arts in one way or another. This philosophy underpins their vision for the project:

The thing that I think is crucial is about access and it kind of builds on some of the ownership things that we've been saying. When I thought about Art in Mind, I always ... I thought ... that it would be a really safe space that people knew was there ... (Belinda, 253–7)

Um ... giving them somewhere where there is a bit more light, just helps to lift. (Clare, 104–5)

But you know ... that it is about just seeing people as people ... that it's for a broad group of people. (Belinda, 632–4)

... yes it would be good to see individuals from that community of their own volition wanting to take charge of some of the initiatives that arise from the project. Uh ... so that it can become in a sense self-governing. (Simon, 750–3)

...within the Art in Mind we wanted to be something, we wanted to fulfil our own dreams as well. (Wendy, 248–50)

You know, that it's actually really working with the social capital model and giving people the chance to meet people outside of their ordinary social circle ... It's that broad approach as well as wellbeing and people feeling good about themselves. (Belinda 636–9)

But also, giving them, giving people the comfort zone as well because I think we all need that. Um ... and just having a place that you can go and a place that you can be happy in and be comfortable in. (Clare, 99–102)

I, think that, probably, people felt that there was no other outlet and that they were sort of like, 'ooh, well, let's try this and just see how, where it will go', like, you know, because people feeling, like, lack of opportunity. (Rupert, 13–16)

I think, also, providing various opportunities for, for people, yeah, I'm trying to think, yeah, to provide opportunities for creative outlets, for people who maybe ... perceive themselves to be, you know, a mental health service user, so, I think those were the, the two sort of core values, sort of an educational thing for people who, who don't perceive themselves to be in any way involved with mental health issues, and for those people who, who understand that to be true of themselves, but to, to provide places, situations, but through, through creative ways where they can come and relate, respond to one another, you know, those probably were the two areas that I felt that we were trying to, to go towards. (Roger, 266–76)

> *There's one area which is very positive because it's safe and it's comfortable and but there's then another side of it which means that um ... we ... we have got to give other opportunities and ... and make sure that we can broaden people's horizons and show them new places to go and show them new things and, and show them that um ... there, there is more out there for them. (Clare, 188–94)*

> *When you do it through an art form ... you, you will have, in some ways, created a something, you know, whatever that something may be, a poem, a song, a dance, or sculpture, a painting, or whatever, which can be a thing of beauty, will be a thing of beauty. Which is inherently that person, really. (Roger, 365–71)*

> *It's because what I feel that's happened is that people are transforming to higher levels of themselves or to greater levels of themselves. (Veronica, 527–30)*

> *... we can feel good about ourselves ... we can! Um ... we can feel good about meeting other people; we can feel good about listening to their story and finding a space to tell them ours. And it makes no difference whether you're a seasoned professional artist or whether you're a nervous inexperienced service user. (Simon, 197–202)*

> *And then you know, more specifically, it, you know, brings communities together, it gives um ... people ... um an equality of status and belonging and all those things and I think everybody there recognised that, that's what that area needs. (Veronica, 63–8)*

> *I went to the pub last night. We had such a laugh! OK ... there was a lot of alcohol drunk and that may not be good for us but the sense of community was, so there was an intrinsic understanding that for life to be good we need to be having fun! (Simon, 323–7)*

Second Theme: Experiences and beliefs
Sub-theme 1: Personal experience

Five participants talked about their own experiences and how these experiences have shaped their views towards community arts and the project. These experiences were either 'mental health issues' or the power of creativity in people's own lives:

> *Because there's another issue actually, which has been very interesting throughout this whole project, which is about people identifying their mental health experiences or their past. And ... and I really didn't want to engage with that at all, because um ... I didn't well ... I don't really feel that qualified to talk about it. But for people who are using services, there's a big issue about that. And I just don't know if you ever really resolve that or ever really will. (Belinda, 380–6)*

And, you know, the thing is that would not have happened if there would have been light at the end of the tunnel for him, but there was no light, there was no way um ... we were going to get any further. (Clare, 376–9)

But alongside that there is a mental health motivator for me, but I didn't particularly want to reveal that to people because I didn't really think that it was enough for people and people would go 'Oh right'. But actually, you know, there is an issue in my family, there are things that I've experienced ... and ... but I didn't want that to be the reason. (Belinda, 402–5)

... one of my best friends at school was a, was a ... had a brother who was an artist, you know, and he was really, really good, and he was on the dole. And like, and I looked at his work and he was absolutely brilliant, you know, and I, and I, this is about, when I was about fifteen, and I thought, 'if Leslie can't get a job, I can't get a ... I got no, I got no chance, man', you know what I mean? And so that's when I sort of like, went broken-hearted, you know ... (Rupert, 193–9)

And, I started my healing process, really, in 1989, but I knew that I was uncomfortable, the way I was. So I had to keep moving and changing and, and adjusting and getting the therapy and getting the work, and stuff like that ... (Wendy, 1059–62)

... and I think to a greater extent we all have part of us which has a slightly sort of schizophrenic side and I think especially, I don't know, kind of within the arts there's also a kind of a hint because you know, we all have our black side and we all have our good side. (Clare, 520–3)

I think, though, that I have done some work, well, in two areas, really, one, when I was abroad, I did a little bit of work which was ... working through sort of post-trauma, people who had been bereaved through war, was, when I was in Beirut in the Middle East, and using the arts as a gateway to work some of those issues. (Roger, 330–3)

I think everyone who was there has their own personal experience of how it works and I think probably not just ... I mean a lot of it is professional obviously in terms of their work experience. (Veronica, 34–6)

Because that's obviously a significant factor I think. Um ... an understanding I guess that we all have mental health issues, that's I suppose the other obvious thing to say. I don't think any of us would have been there if we'd not thought that. (Simon, 110–14)

... psychiatric services are very, very bizarre. They really are. Um ... and I um ... I think, I think here I'm going to come down to my personal knowledge of them and my personal experiences of them. (Clare, 330–2)

Sub-theme 2: Belief in the work

All the participants professed their conviction for the vision and philosophy of the project:

> *I think, you know, having faith in that setup has got us to here, if you stick with something, yeah things are going to change ... (Belinda, 652–4)*

> *Well, yeah, I mean, like, I thought, 'right, okay ... let's, let's start trying to be that artist again', like, you know, opened a dream for me, again. (Rupert, 206–8)*

> *Yeah, I have a huge, I have a huge conviction in, you know ... a huge belief in ... knowing that people can grow and can develop and um ... you know within the arts, within again within mental health. (Clare, 81–3)*

> *... it was within the Art in Mind wanted to be something, we wanted to fulfil our own dreams as well. (Wendy, 248–9)*

> *... for me one of the most important things was ... um, in the initial process was that it was something that I believe in, because I won't do anything I don't believe in. (Clare, 32–4)*

> *It felt like that everybody was there, had an experience and a belief and an understanding that creativity is very important for all of us. (Veronica, 61–2)*

> *And I'm a firm believer in that anyway because I know it works. I can't always give a reason for why it works but I know it does work. (Clare, 71–2)*

> *Yeah. It's a feeling that everybody that was there, had a ... a ... deep ... quite a profound belief that the arts has a hugely beneficial effect on mental health. So that was part of it and partly fundamentally really! (Laughs) (Veronica, 22–4)*

Third Theme: Effective collaboration

Participants were encouraged to think about the significance of the working alliance of the original diverse group:

> *The artists ... have the potential to do really creative consultation work with people. They have an understanding of some of the issues, but I think they benefit greatly from working more directly with service users in planning services and planning arts events and activities, because there are people sitting round the table that they can just ask. (Belinda, 116–20)*

> *... we'd never been involved in a group where the actual process of the bid requires that the group itself develops its own life and identity and it was a very pleasant surprise I think. (Simon, 72–4)*

... you know, coming together with a group of partners quite often the end beneficiaries of a project may have been consulted or their views are in there through evaluations of past projects. Whereas, in this case, there has been this longer term development with service users directly involved with ... you know ... reading things and with approving things and talking about ethics and commissioning and um ... you know, different aspects of the project. (Belinda, 144–51)

... any sort of meetings I've been at have been very much more structured, where you've got a written agenda, and we're going to talk about this today. And, it wasn't like that, it was very much more open, which, I think, to me, initially, was a little bit threatening, because I thought, well, I, I quite like structure, I quite like to know where I'm going, but, there was a great sort of freeing element there as well, you know, where, you could drop anything in, you know, and nothing would be rejected. You know, everything was valid, you know, so, so that was sort of very, kind of, positive memories. (Roger, 110–19)

And what was lovely about the group i.d. there was no differentiation between those that express themselves as mentally ill or in need of mental health support and those that say they're doing it professionally. (Veronica, 58–61)

I think that's what Art in Mind has done, is ... there are certain people who are definitely stakeholders and owners of this project who traditionally would not be in that role. (Belinda, 198–200)

... everybody like tacitly says 'We're going to incorporate service-users' views and ideas', but unless you've got a base of people to consult upon, and a relationship with those people, you're never going to know what their ideas are. (Belinda, 266–9)

For me, like, just to, normal, like, sort of guy, walking off the street, like, there's all these professionals, they're all dressed quite well, like, you know what I mean? (Rupert, 74–6)

For the first, first time that we actually got influence and were actually part of something that we were important to, you know, it was like, wow, you know, to, to, to me, like, in sort of situation, wow, you know, this is a wild thing, it looks quite good actually. (Rupert, 1304–7)

We were just local residents, you know, trying to be artists, but, we weren't, I didn't feel like I was anything. In particular ... Yeah, we were kind of nothing. (Wendy, 84, 88–9)

... an extraordinary group, it's not an ordinary group, you know, the people involved in it are all, like, like I said before, like, y'know, the, they, they, they're in touch, they're emotionally in contact, y'know. (Rupert, 1314–26)

And responding to one another without having to necessarily fulfil a role of uh ... of being the professional, being the service user. There soon emerged a um ... a bit of a culture of sharing, having fun, being creative, knowing that um ... we were working towards putting together a bid that uh ... would be interesting, fascinating, perhaps ground breaking uh and useful in some ways so I think getting to know one another um ... was, was the thing that spurred it on in a sense. (Simon, 40–7)

Narrative and discourse

The findings from the research are synthesised and summarised and a collective narrative is identified. Of the seven participants, five were arts professionals. It is understandable therefore that the data contains much in the way of theory and philosophy. This is however contextualised in very personal accounts including beliefs and motivations driven by personal experience. There exists throughout the data, a language of theory in a context of life experience. Participants therefore offer theoretical constructs of the therapeutic benefits and healing potential of the arts, not necessarily based upon academic understandings but from their own experiences of working in the arts, collectively over many years. There also appears to be a mutual respect between the five professionals and the two non-professionals in the group. Ultimately, the group shared a vision for a community arts project that united those involved rather than created a forum for competitiveness. Whilst originally, the two local residents felt quite apart from the professionals, the potential divisions were articulated by both Wendy and Rupert:

For me, like, just to, normal, like, sort of guy, walking off the street, like, there's all these professionals, they're all dressed quite well, like, you know what I mean? (Rupert, 74–6)

We were just local residents, you know, trying to be artists, but, we weren't, I didn't feel like I was anything ... In particular. (Wendy, 88–9)

The group later claimed a blurring of roles and eventually an absence of an 'us and them' mentality. Wendy and Rupert (interviewed together here) put this down to the 'emotional intelligence' of the professionals:

There was an emotional intelligence about these people.
... probably, pretty like, sort of, successful professional people, but they'd actually sort of, like, had, had insight and awareness and, you know.

Mental health problems are seen as common, not in terms of frequency and morbidity but rather, common to both artists and people defined as 'service users'. Personal vulnerabilities are identified, not only for people who use services but also amongst the professionals themselves.

In summary, the group shared the understanding that participating in community arts is essentially good for people. Personal experiences are acknowledged as shaping people's beliefs, and those beliefs are responsible for the 'vision' and subsequent 'passion' that was evident to implement such a project. Thus, collaboration became workable because the group felt united by personal beliefs and motivations.

From vision to reality: Individual to a co-constructed narrative

The findings reveal the personal motivations behind the Steering Group's commitment to develop the programme. The group shared the belief that participating in community arts is essentially 'good' for people.

Reflections on personal motivations

As a member of the original group and researcher, it is inappropriate for me to separate myself from the participants; furthermore, it was I that brought them together for the purposes of developing a proposal for the New Deal for Communities. When I discuss the participants' beliefs, personal experiences and motivations, I acknowledge the similarities between theirs and my own. Therefore, before a discussion is further developed relating to the original Steering Group, I include extracts from my research diary to consider the ideological motivations and potential material benefits for this group. This extract from my diary reveals my belief that such a project could only function properly if it were to be located outside of the statutory system:

> I believed that mental healthcare could be better provided outside of statutory services. My observation was that it was the system that prevented good people from doing good. Nurses and social workers were mostly committed to client-centred ways of working but became drained, exhausted and burned out with mounting bureaucracy and reduced resources. I resolved that the system could not change, therefore it was best to work outside of the system. (17th September, 2004)

The ideological position I adopted was one of social justice based upon observations of practice within a psychiatric system that had long been accused of oppression. It was relatively easy for me to find people that shared this ideology. The belief that people with mental health problems needed creative approaches was a belief shared by people that I knew both in the arts world and in mental health services. There was also a strong sense of potential for people's recovery through healing and benefiting from positive human relationships. The prospect of securing large amounts of funding also drew the attention of such people. Whilst financial benefits or opportunities for work do not feature in the findings, such motivations are implicit. Personally, I have not materially benefited from my involvement in the project although I have benefited in terms of professional responsibility and development. I have enjoyed the kudos of being the visionary lead of a dynamic project and have had the opportunity to study for a PhD based upon its work.

I have reflected that the Steering Group participants talked about their vulnerabilities in their interviews. Perhaps this was because they were offered the safe space of research interview where anonymity could be ensured. However, this might also indicate that those in the voluntary sector have greater liberty to be wounded healers (Jung, 1966, 1989) than those in the statutory sector. I have latterly reflected that by bringing together the Steering Group and the people who would later form the Lost Artists Club (in the following chapter), I may in fact have been unconsciously bringing together different parts of myself.

Acknowledgements

The New Deal for Communities originally funded Art in Mind. The programme of work was delivered by City Arts, Nottingham. The programme manager at City Arts, Kate Duncan, was originally appointed to coordinate the project years ago, and the success of the work has much to do with her tireless patience, imagination, commitment and good management.

Some of the findings in this chapter have previously been published: Stickley, 2010a; 2010b; 2011; Stickley & Duncan, 2007; Stickley et al,. 2007.

References

Barthes, R (1977) Introduction to the structural analysis of narratives. In *Roland Barthes, Image–Music–Text* (trans, Stephen Heath) (pp. 79–124). Glasgow: Collins.
Brockmeier, J (2001) *Narrative and Identity. Studies in autobiography, self and culture*. Philadelphia: John Benjamins.
Carey, J (2005) *What Good are the Arts?* London: Faber and Faber.

Chase, SE (2005) Narrative inquiry: Multiple lenses, approaches, voices. In NK Denzin & YS Lincoln (Eds), *Qualitative Research* (3rd ed, pp. 651–79). London: Sage.

Czarniawska, B (2004) *Narratives in Social Science Research*. London: Sage.

Denzin, NK (2001) The reflexive interview and the performative social science. *Qualitative Research, 1*(1), 23–46.

Edwards, D (1997) *Discourse and Cognition*. London: Sage.

Edwards, D & Potter, J (1992) *Discursive Psychology*. London: Sage.

Gergen, MM & Gergen, KJ (2003) Qualitative inquiry: Tensions and transformations. In NK Denzin & YS Lincoln (Eds), *The Landscape of Qualitative Research: Theories and issues* (2nd ed, pp. 1025–46). London: Sage.

Gubrium, JF & Holstein, JA (2000) Analyzing interpretive practice. In NK Denzin & YS Lincoln (Eds), *Handbook of Qualitative Research* (2nd ed, pp. 487–508). Thousand Oaks, CA: Sage.

Harré, R & Gillett, G (1994) *The Discursive Mind*. Thousand Oaks, CA: Sage.

Jung, CG (1966) *The Spirit in Man, Art, and Literature*. London: Routledge & Paul.

Jung, CG (1989) *Memories, Dreams, Reflections* (recorded and edited, A Jaffé, trans, R & C Winston). New York: Vintage Books.

Labov, W & Waletzky, J (1967) Narrative analysis: Oral versions of personal experience. In J Helm (Ed), *Essays on the Verbal and Visual Arts* (pp. 12–44). Seattle, WA: University of Washington Press.

Mishler, EG (1986) *Research Interviewing: Context and narrative*. Cambridge, MA: Harvard.

Ricoeur, P (1981) Narrative time. In WJT Mitchell (Ed), *On Narrative* (pp. 165–86). Chicago: The University of Chicago Press.

Ricoeur, P (1984) *Time and Narrative, Vol 1*. London: University of Chicago Press.

Ricoeur, P (1991) *From Text to Action: Essays in hermeneutics*. London: Athlone.

Riessman, CK (1993) *Narrative Analysis*. London: Sage.

Riessman, CK (2004) A thrice-told tale: New readings of an old story. In B Hurwitz, T Greenhlagh & V Skultans (Eds), *Narrative Research in Health and Illness* (pp. 309–24). Oxford: BMJ Books, Blackwell Publishing.

Silverman, D (2006) *Interpreting Qualitative Data: Methods for analysing talk, text and interaction* (3rd ed). London: Sage.

Stickley, T (2010a) The arts, identity and belonging: A longitudinal study. *Arts & Health: An International Journal for Research, Policy and Practice, 2*(1), 23–32.

Stickley, T (2010b) Does prescribing participation in arts help to promote recovery for mental health clients? *Nursing Times, 106*(18), 18–20.

Stickley, T (2011) A philosophy for community-based, participatory arts practice: A narrative inquiry. *Journal of Applied Arts and Health, 2*(1), 85–7.

Stickley, T & Duncan, K (2007) Art in mind: Implementation of a community arts initiative to promote mental health. *Journal of Public Mental Health, 6*(4), 24–32.

Stickley, T, Merryweather, W & Leighton, P (2007) With art in mind. *A Life in the Day, 4*(11), 22–4.

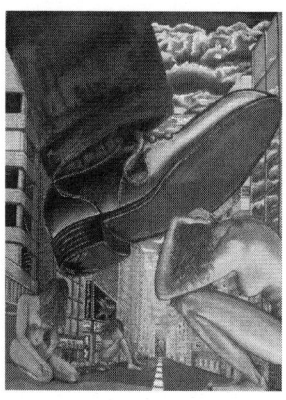

CHAPTER FIVE

Social Identity and Belonging: The Lost Artists Club

Theo Stickley

This chapter focuses upon research I conducted amongst members of the Lost Artists Club (LAC) in the East Midlands in the UK. Two of the participants in the previous chapter (Wendy and Rupert) were also included in the research for the LAC. The LAC was formed by them during the period of the development of the proposal for Art in Mind. Over the years, since that time, the LAC has attracted around 100 members. The LAC was a by-product of the Art in Mind organisation and later became independently constituted. During the setting up phase of Art in Mind (February 2002–December 2004) Wendy and Rupert, both members of the original steering group, decided not to wait for the funding of Art in Mind to come through and developed plans to commence their own original and democratic organisation which became known as the Lost Artists Club. The LAC has an inclusive policy and attracts people who live in the city, identify themselves as artists and who feel in someway or another on the margins of society. It is informally observed that the majority of the LAC have used or currently use mental health and/or addiction services. In the early years, the LAC remained close to the Art in Mind project, using its resources, including premises, and benefiting from advice and staff support. During 2006, the host organisation of Art in Mind was able to provide studio space to a number of the LAC members. The development of the studio space has been significant to a number of LAC members (this becomes evident in the findings of this research). Demographically, participants are reflective of the wider population of people attending Art in Mind over a two-year period.

The interviews were conducted over a period of about eighteen months (2005–2007). The findings from four participants are presented in this chapter. Three were interviewed three times and one person twice to provide a longitudinal perspective. For each research participant, a vignette is presented giving brief biographical information that became evident from the interviews and the subsequent text. Following each vignette an analysis is offered through the various analytic lenses.

Mike: A mental illness narrative

Vignette

Mike is a white male in his thirties. He came to the city in 2000 as a homeless person and was quickly in contact with statutory mental health services. Ten years previously, Mike had dropped out of an art degree course. He describes his past self as 'an angry young man'. Homelessness, a previously chaotic lifestyle, mental health problems and the arts, all feature strongly in his narrative across the three interviews: February and August 2006, and February 2007. Mike lives in the local area. He first came to the area because he was housed in a local hostel for people with mental health problems when he was discharged from an inpatient unit. Although on sickness benefits, Mike is engaged with the local community as a secretary of a local residents' association and has been actively involved in the running of the LAC. Each interview was conducted at the Art in Mind premises, and on each occasion, Mike had taken the time to show me his art work. Mike is quietly spoken, and some of the narrative was inaudible for transcription.

There is relational significance between Mike and myself as one of the inpatient units where he was previously living is where I worked prior to working full time at the University. Mike has acknowledged this with throwaway comments such as, 'As you will remember …'. This previous relationship has not negatively impacted upon the research process. If anything, Mike appears to enjoy relishing in his progress and appears to have enjoyed the opportunity to perform his narrative for me.

Analysis

Mike regards himself as *mentally ill*. Significantly, his illness has prevented him from working and he remains on sickness benefits. Mike's identity is tied up with his history of illness and he labels himself throughout the text:

> *I don't particularly look mentally ill as such, I think people can see through, beyond that, I think.*

> *[Concentrating on art works] ... is good for somebody who's mentally ill because they can take their mind off whatever crap's going off in their life and just concentrate on something.*

Mike challenges his long-established 'illness identity' however with the emerging 'artist identity'.

> *I think the recognition is good as well, I mean, everybody looks at me and thinks I'm an artist, anyway ...*
> *I've always considered myself to be an artist.*

One of the most difficult challenges to this changing identity is the difficulty that confronts him coming off sickness benefits:

> *... it would be great to be able to sell enough work to come off benefits but I've spoken to [Name] about this and I, I have a situation ... and it's the hardest things people like us, is to come off benefits.*

It became obvious throughout the interviews that Mike greatly appreciated the studio space available to him through the project. It was here he could find meaningful activity that reinforced his artist identity:

> *Well, it's got me working again ... I've sold work and I've learned new skills ... I've been offered the studio which is great, been there every day for about seven hours a day.*

> *But yeah, the recognition is good, I mean, quite, quite prestigious working here, I think being the first ones as well. Yeah.*

Contact with other artists has given Mike inspiration, support and friendship:

> *... It's, oh, you get influenced by other people. Sort of sharing ideas and things and it's quite interesting.*

> *Yes, I make new friends as well, I mean, yeah, that's good, yeah. ... went out for a drink on my birthday, that was good.*

Being able to exhibit and sell work is important for Mike:

> *I been sort of exhibiting for ... sort of mental health awareness fortnight will be a big fortnight for me. An ... exhibition ... there but, sort of Waterstones, yeah. There's a lot happening.*

In the first interview, Mike articulated a number of ambitions that included: getting back his driving licence, securing his own studio, getting back into education and succeeding as an artist. To some degree, he achieved all of these goals within the year. Ultimately, Mike would like to gain full employment although he recognises the difficulties he may encounter by sacrificing the security that benefits provide:

> *It's just the safety you feel, I mean, once you can like budget on what you get, it is quite easy.*

In January, 2007, Mike signed a contract for his studio away from the project. He continues to see his studio work as his vocation:

> *... there is a good kind of working atmosphere, we were, it's kind of, you know, it's kind of, you know, it's kind of work ethic, and just actually doing it and, and the kudos of the studio and things.*

Most poignantly for someone who has experienced homelessness and exclusion for a number of years is the sense of belonging that Mike's involvement in the project has provided. This sense of belonging is not confined to the people in the project:

> *I think umm it's given me confidence ... I've developed as a person, sort of, for my own confidence. I feel I can belong, I also, I used to do umm the, I'm chairperson and I do some secretarial jobs for the residents' group thing as well, it's, maybe I'm feeling a belonging.*

Mike's story is one of being lost and found. As an 'angry young man', Mike faced rejection and his natural development was interrupted through mental distress and being diagnosed with schizophrenia. This is most poignant in relation to having to quit his art college course. Mike has struggled socially and psychologically; his struggles have included cycles of hospital admissions and homelessness. It is only in recent years that Mike has found stability in his life. He attributes this to stable housing and appropriate support, new medication and developed social bonds. With these in place, Mike has been able to successfully express his creativity and resume social roles and responsibilities. Mike has realistic plans for the future that involve work and recreation.

Mike does not refer to childhood therefore it is hard to imagine the origins of his personality. As his narrative is located almost exclusively in adulthood from the time when he became unwell, his identity claims are bound up with being an artist and experiencing mental illness and its consequences. Mike's identity therefore is one of an artist who became ill, who became homeless, who became recovered, who became an artist again. Although a 'Lost Artist' Mike sees himself as an artist in society fulfilling a social role.

Sarah: Creativity to futility to artistry and identity (Interview 1)

Vignette

I interviewed Sarah twice: February 2006, and January 2007. Sarah is a white female in her forties. She decided on a career in the arts when she was at school and achieved a first degree in fine art. In her twenties, she had her own studio and went on to teach art in a secondary school. She was a teacher for 12 years, during which time she raised a family. In these early years, she experienced a minor breakdown, but has not enlarged upon this. Sarah describes experiencing an estrangement to herself over a period of 20 years that culminated in a major breakdown relatively recently. Following this experience, Sarah has been re-discovering her 'true self'. Much of this discovery is about establishing herself once again as an artist. Her involvement in the LAC is a significant part of this journey. During the period between the interviews, Sarah had made considerable progress in establishing her identity and role. The content of the two narratives are quite different and are therefore presented separately.

My first-ever contact with Sarah was in the context of the mental health NHS trust, perhaps a year previously. I did not recognise her from this context, but Sarah made a point of reminding me that we had previously met. It was apparent that she was proud of her progress and she delighted in talking to me and showing me her work.

Analysis of Interview 1

Sarah's personality and identity are inextricably bound up with her art and she narrates a childhood story of being a sensitive, expressive and creative child who was misunderstood:

> *But I think I was really quite young when I had my first depression, about eight. I know, when I was in junior school. And it was picked up because my position in the class had taken a dive in the exams and the teacher brought my mum and dad into school and said that I'd been falling asleep in the class, and they managed to get it out of me that I wasn't sleeping at night, I was lying awake at night till really late, and nobody asked me what I was lying awake thinking about, they just gave me some sleeping medicine and got my sleep back into a normal pattern and I got back to my school work and my position in the class went right back up again and I won the school prize for progress. But I hadn't really progressed. I'd progressed in the way that they saw as being progress. But I probably started to bury myself from that point.*

She felt almost punished and 'abused' for being creative, so much so that when she expressed herself creatively she became pathologised by others as ill and this has been expressed through her art work:

> *... but I've been shocked at the kind of images, you know, that have come out that are to do with my distress and I describe it as abusive and it's perhaps not in the conventional sense but I felt abused in my childhood because I wasn't allowed to be who I was. To me, that's how I define abuse.*

By conforming to social norms Sarah developed an estrangement to herself, leading a life to please others and neglecting her creative self:

> *So, I lost myself ... I did have ... I had a period of time working at [Name] studios ... I'd just really be starting to engage with my work but then other things seemed to take over and take me away from, from my work, you know...*

Following her major breakdown, Sarah lost the friends that she had:

> *When I had my breakdown, all my friends disappeared. And my family. All of them. Without a trace. And it became apparent to me that they were only interested in me when I was being that pretend person. And that the real me erm, well, they quite simply don't, don't want to hear about, know about, they think it's selfish, they think it's my mental health. They don't want to believe it's the real me.*

The sense of belonging that Sarah has experienced with the LAC has been of utmost significance to her:

> ... you know, and if we're having a particularly bad time, we can share that with like-minded people 'cos they know what that means.
>
> And now I'm part of this community and people recognise me through the merit of my work, you know, 'I've seen your work, I love it, you're (Sarah), are you?', and, and that, it's the nicest thing.

Sarah reflects upon missed opportunities and identifies what she lacked in her upbringing:

> ... if I could have grown up in a community that valued art, I'd be a very different person and I'd be a lot more healthy, mentally.

Apart from the social benefits, Sarah recognises the intrinsic therapeutic role of art in her life:

> I find, when I do art that it's as though I'm balancing my system, when I, when I'm working on a painting and I'm trying to decide is it finished, which bits need changing and which bits need developing and once I get that painting to where I want it to be, I feel very calm and very balanced myself. As though I've been balancing myself externally and then it comes back to me and to be able to give that gift, it's wonderful.

The identity that Sarah has now established completes for her, a cycle from childhood:

> Well, as though it was all there when I was little, and yet, the journey's just been so hard, just to, just to sustain what was already there from the beginning.

Sarah: The professional artist (Interview 2)

Analysis of Interview 2

At the time of Interview 2, Sarah was in the middle of conducting research for an Arts Council proposal. This had demanded much reading and writing. Much of this second interview therefore focused upon the use of words and how she had incorporated text in her art work. However, she describes the year as having two phases and the application dominated the second phase. The first phase related to how she had been imaging realisations from her psychotherapy and some of these realisations were shocking to the viewer:

I'd done a very ethereal-looking painting of a child's bedroom, all in pinks and pale blues and things, and then I'd written over the top, 'You just kept hitting me and you wouldn't stop and I was only little', and, I found conceptually the way that piece worked very interesting because people would see at first these pretty colours, the pinks and that, and then see the writing, go over and think, 'Oh, what does the writing say?' and when they saw what the writing said, they kind of stepped back from it, 'cos it wasn't what they were expecting.

She reflects upon alternative futures that she might have experienced had her upbringing been different, and that art might have become less significant to her if she had not experienced emotional and psychological pain:

I did, I did have this wonder about when I was a child and the way it went, that if it hadn't gone that way and if my dad had been the kind of dad who thought everything I did was wonderful and told all his friends, 'Oh yes, my daughter, she's going to art college and she's a fantastic artist and I can really see her potential and she's got a bright future ahead of her', what those kind of, what effect would those kind of messages have had on me? Would my life have taken a completely different path and would art have had less significance than it has actually?

Sarah's story is one of personal redemption through breakdown and creativity. She places herself as one who has discovered her 'true self' having struggled with her identity through childhood experiences and the subsequent compromises made in adulthood. The plot reveals the necessity of breakdown to facilitate redemption and identity integration.

Sarah narrates a coherent story from childhood to the present day. The story contains a psychotherapeutic interpretation within its commentary and I was expected to appreciate the psychological nuances of the plot. Sarah also appeared to enjoy showing me her art and talking about her work simultaneously. Sarah appeared to want to hear about my appreciation of her work.

In spite of telling such a deep story, Sarah's description of her nuclear family life remains unclear. There are roles played by influential characters that remain anonymous. Significantly, Sarah wished that her parents could have appreciated her artistic ability rather than having oppressed her for being creative. Sarah's description of herself as a dreamy, creative child is one that represents her authentic organismic self (Rogers, 1951). A self that became buried in order to please her parents and others. Much of Sarah's adult life continues with compromise yet she retained her desire to be creative by becoming an art teacher. Through life experience, and even breakdown, Sarah ultimately rediscovers this authentic self and transforms herself into becoming an artist.

Wendy: Recovery, identity and aspiration

Vignette

Wendy is in her early forties and lives in the local area. Similar to Rupert, Wendy has been involved in Art in Mind since the original meeting in 2002. She was instrumental in creating the LAC and during the period that the three interviews spanned (April 2005–August 2006), she took a leading role. During the interviews, Wendy had referred to abuse but never elaborated on the issue. However, much of her narrative focuses upon her recovery and how this is bound up with her identity as an artist. After completing an art degree some 10 years before the time of interview, Wendy commenced a journey of self-discovery that continued to the then present.

Analysis

Looking back to 2002 to the very first meeting, Wendy describes herself as a *'kind of nothing'* compared to the status of the professionals who were present. She goes on to explain that the driving force to form the LAC was to establish an identity:

> *We were just local residents, you know, trying to be artists, but, we weren't, I didn't feel like I was anything. In particular ... And, and, I wanted to find some identity, and I think that's where the Lost Artists, that's why we created the Lost Artists, because ... we didn't have an identity, we got, you know, this theatre company and this company and that company ... and then, we were just nothing.*
>
> *... it was like I was nothing, I had no concept of self at all.*
>
> *And surviving and that's all we were doing.*

Thus, identity features as a strong theme throughout the narrative. The period between leaving university and forming the LAC Wendy describes as a journey of self-discovery in the development of her identity:

> *... but there's been this whole journey of finding myself really.*
>
> *... I went into healing like, like you do a job really.*

Some of this journey has been discovering the need to trust others:

> *... for me it's a very long journey of trying not to be isolated and to trust people.*

Wendy describes an artistic barrenness between finishing her art degree and commencing the LAC:

> *Before I did the LAC, right, I had more time to do art, but couldn't do it ... But, as soon as I did the LAC, it's got my creative juices going, and the two things balance.*

Being a part of the LAC has given Wendy a sense of identity:

> *Now, people say, 'what do you do?' I say, 'Oh, I'm, you know, I'm part founder of a group called the Lost Artists Club', you know, it's all those kind of social things ... that you lose when you're in a workless ... it's given us an identity.*

This positive identity and role is in stark contrast to what preceded it that often left Wendy silenced by shame:

> *[People would ask] 'How do you make your living?' And because I was unemployed and on the sick and ... dealing with my emotional stuff, and it always fell back with, 'right now, I'm not doing much of anything' ... and, and ... you fall back to talking about your emotional traumas is very, very, you know, triggering. You know. And I end up with nothing to say.*
>
> *... I had an identity as a person on incapacity benefit living really in the gutter with a lot of people who are ill, addicted and stuff like that.*

The creation of Art in Mind was a significant event in Wendy's life:

> *Art in Mind gave us an anchor.*

The project provided a role for Wendy:

> *At one point, later on, we felt that we were really actually very essential, because of, and that made us feel more important. We felt that we were actually, I mean, all these professionals are important, but we felt that we were actually important in a different way, because it's for us and we were part of it.*

Wendy described how she had developed practical responsibilities organising creative gatherings, newsletters etc. Furthermore, Wendy spent time getting funding into the LAC. She saw her identity change to become both an artist and a businesswoman:

> *I changed identity, the moment I went on to the small business, despite still having the benefit ... I became the worker in the world, that changed again 'cos I know last time I talked, we talked about starting the LAC, now that gave us an identity.*
>
> *I like the identity of businesswoman, it's better than being thick or on the dole or mentally ill or something, isn't it, I mean, it's [laughs] you know, I like the, there is some kudos about running the group as well.*

Becoming this new person has tensions:

> *I've got loads of abilities, I know I have when I write them down. But it's still kind of, 'Wow, is that me?' [laughs] You know, where does all this come from? ... I can do Adobe, Photoshop and ... all that kind of stuff ...*

This emerging role challenged Wendy's long-standing commitment to the sick role:

> *How long can I stay on incapacity benefit? At that point, I'd had about ten years of therapy ... In the end, I want to be a functioning member of society.*

To accept a new role however means having to socially re-integrate:

> *Yeah. It's about learning how to be in the world, as well, especially when you've been isolated for a very long time.*
>
> *And now I'm one of the workforce, and that, I feel really different, you know, I feel incredibly valid.*

Having spent years as a recipient of the benefit system, Wendy revealed her inner feelings about visiting the Department of Work and Pensions:

> *You know when I've gone to the DSS ... I know, in the back of my head, that ... they can't look down on me as, as being the worklessness ... I have felt really crap and I've felt that the people who work there have got a value judgement of me, because I'm there but in the back of my head I knew I was doing this business and therefore they can't, and in the back of my head, I was going, 'Well, fuck you' ...*

Wendy does not wish to be seen as a *nobody:*

> ... you can't judge me because you can't just think ... that I'm one of these dossers, you know what I mean. So you don't realise how much that really affects you until you actually start to face it, until you start changing something, you can live with that kind of emotional squalor for decades, years, your whole life, really and not realise how much it deeply, deeply, affects you.

Wendy aspires to be an established and successful artist:

> When I dream about myself, I'm an artist with an easel, with a paintbrush painting, you know, and I want to sell my art and everything.

Having spent many years in therapy and recovering, Wendy acknowledges the potential for role conflict between the sick role and the artist/businesswoman role:

> I've never tried working and dealing with my emotional stuff at the same time, I've always separated it. So that's gonna be an interesting experiment.

Apart from the LAC benefiting her in terms of role and identity, Wendy also identifies the social benefits:

> And we, and we, in the summer, we went up to the Nine Ladies and spent a day sketching and we went to London ... that was group development, we went to see the Frida Kahlo exhibition.
>
> I've got a community of people I can talk to about art and I've got a studio.

In the final interview, Wendy described her development as an artist. This included acquiring studio space, completing a teaching course, public exhibitions etc. Most importantly however was her success with business funding that enabled her to come off benefits for the first time in many years. The future however remains uncertain:

> And it's kind of coming to terms with that, who I am as a person, what kind of person I am, erm, what are, what are the things that I would trip up on, you know, and it is mostly my emotional stuff, and, and I do wonder whether, you know, I don't know, if I run out of money or whether my emotional stuff will catch up with me. I've got until March, I can still go back on incapacity benefit, up until March, you know, if it all falls apart.

Much of Wendy's story is about *struggle*. Whilst Wendy recounts periods of progress, there are inevitable setbacks around the corner. Wendy's story includes her survival through difficulties and ultimately, her drive and determination to succeed in life. Throughout the three interviews, Wendy's language was introspective and she found self-disclosure easy. In this sense, the research interview was an opportunity for a confessional interaction. Wendy explained that she had experienced therapy of various kinds over the years and the interview process may have stimulated a counsellor/client transference which was acknowledged by Wendy at one point.

Much of Wendy's narrative is tied up with identity. Prior to the formation of Art in Mind and the LAC, Wendy and Rupert described themselves as being quite isolated as artists. Having spent years on a journey of self-discovery and healing, Wendy's identity has adjusted. Furthermore, this transformation comes to light through the telling of the story, i.e., the research process.

Rupert: An identity narrative

Vignette

Rupert is a white male in his forties. Along with Wendy, Rupert is a local resident who contributed to the original vision and development of Art in Mind. I first met him and Wendy at the original meeting of people in February, 2002. He has been a committed member of the Steering Group ever since. Rupert has also been involved with developing the LAC. In recent months, he has also been involved with further community arts projects that have been developed as offshoots from Art in Mind. He has studio space in the building; he paints and plays the saxophone. Rupert has probably been involved with more aspects of the project than anyone else. I interviewed Rupert three times; the first two interviews (April 2005 and February 2006) were together with Wendy. The final interview was with him alone in his flat in September 2006. Rupert has described himself as a long-term drug-user. He has serious health problems as a direct result of his drug use. He is an intelligent and articulate man although his speech was sometimes affected by either drug use or poor concentration. During the course of the project, Rupert has declared his cessation of drug use and directly attributes this to the effect that his involvement in the project has had on his life.

Analysis

Rupert describes an unhappy childhood and an unhappy life that precipitated his emotional and psychological problems that led to his subsequent drug use:

> ... you know, it was only when I left school and I found out that I couldn't function, in actual fact, I was pretty suicidal, that, like, you know, things started falling apart, you know.

Rupert offers a political critique of the period when he left school:

> Yeah, I don't, don't, don't think that leaving school when I did particularly helped and the political climate of the times ... I left school in '79. It was right, you know, the complete, you know, winter of discontent, the mass lay-offs, the mass unemployment, the complete, ... it seemed that maybe the system was on a breaking point, you know, and it did seem to be a very, very different time in spirit from now. ... I think that the key differences are now that the state is aware of the danger from within and has legislated, quite heavily, in its own favour, to basically, destroy civil liberties in this country and through the trickle-down effect, some, actually of the, the, 'cos it's not that the wealthy are any less wealthy, they're just so much more extremely wealthy than we can actually comprehend that some of that wealth is going down to the lower classes and they've been bought off.

Rupert continues:

> ... there is a power elite and they, they sit on top of the pile and they've worked out that if they just about give us enough to keep us happy, they can carry on doing what the fuck they like. You know. And, the history of this world being at war every year since the end of the Second World War and our chief manufacturing export being weapons, then, I think, like, you know, totally shames our country, shames our country.

Rupert soon felt an outcast from society:

> Yeah, I, I, I was, I mean, like, you know, I was really traumatised and like, you know, I mean, I didn't see myself as part of the outside world, and I still have trouble find- you know, doing that now, you know ...

Rupert has a well-developed critical analysis of how people become excluded and *underclass*:

> *And, and, and, and, and mental health. It's having a direct effect, you know, no wonder that so many people having breakdowns and shit like that. You know. I mean, I can't cope with the world as it is, just even being on the dole, you know what I mean, like, screws me up, like, sometimes, going out there and it's so fast and tch tch tch tch, you know, oh, ugh, you know, come back here shaking, you know.*
>
> *... they don't feel a sense of self-worth because society doesn't put any worth on them, so... they end up taking, like, loads of narcotics to fucking kill the pain, and they end up like, in some dirty fucking lavatory dying with a fucking syringe in their arm. You know? Durr! What a fucking life, you know!*

Rupert immersed himself into a world of drug-taking for many years, a world in which his identity became lost:

> *You know. And, I didn't have the support ... I had a lot of bad influences, you know, and that's really the story of my life, you know, in, in, in a nutshell. You know. If I'd, if I'd had, now I've been so damaged by the effects of my life, that it's hard to know where the damage starts and I finish, you know what I mean.*

One turning point in his life was the recognition that he was ill. Being awarded incapacity benefit rather than unemployment benefit somehow legitimised his experiences:

> *The big, the big change for me was a long time ago, was like, getting on to incapacity benefit in the first place because then, well, getting on to the disability, you know, that is like ... the DLA, it made me sort of like think, Okay, you know, I'm not just a lazy bastard, I've got problems so I can ... I can sort of relax a little bit, I can relax a little bit ... I don't have to be so scared of the world all the time, and I've been so terrified of the world. So I started to relax, I started to relax and as I relaxed more and more, I started finding that I needed the drugs less and less, I needed the other stuff less and less ...*

Furthermore, being in receipt of sickness benefits helped Rupert find an identity alternative to being a drug addict:

> *Well, I just, I just think that, like, I would love to have a more solid identity ... it's a delicate kind of situation like the, the, the, coming on the benefit, it made me more able to be who I really am, but at the same time, it's like comes along with that, who are you then? And to be quite honest, I don't ... I, in a lot of respects, I don't know, still, you know?*

> *I don't want to go back, you know, so it's like, and it, that, that, ... us all into the stuff of identity, who am I, what, what is my value as a person, like blah de blah, all very, very salient to the, to, it's a central issue, really, self-esteem.*

The sick role may have brought its material benefits for Rupert, but it also came with a price:

> *I really want the chance to take a bit of control of my own life because that, that is the most frustrating thing about being labelled err ... mentally ill or, you know, drug addict or both. You know, as in my case, it's a, you, you get so little actual personal power. You know. You, you, you are stripped away of any real human dignity, you know, you're at these people's beck and call and you know it. You know. And if you're not intelligent person then that's okay but I am intelligent person like, you know, I know that I'm at these people's beck and call. You know, they've got the power.*

When talking about the LAC, Rupert asserts that the group has provided him with a role:

> *That, that's helped a lot because that's gave me a bit of a role.*
>
> *... at first I found that, you know, yeah, I really enjoyed drawing and painting again, like, you know, that was something I'd forgotten, how much I enjoyed it. And then I realised I'd got ability in those areas and, I dunno, just having like stuff stack up you can feel like, feel good.*
>
> *... self-respect. Self-respect. Self-identity. Being able to say to somebody I do this. Being able to think, think to yourself, I do this. I am this. You know.*

Rupert recounts his experiences of Art in Mind as a journey of healing and growth; a journey from his old life to a new life:

> *You know, and there's a lot of demons that I've had to face over the last few years, but, like ... Yeah, I'm actually starting to face them, like, like, that, that, and that's, I don't think that would have happened without Lost Artists either. You know. Or, or, or the Art in Mind thing.*
>
> *I've sort of like, grown so far away from people that I used to know and I used to hang about with a lot, you know, and, that, and I don't really feel part of that world any more, and I don't want to feel part of that world any more.*
>
> *And what's good about the LAC is that you get such a mix of people that's like, you*

> *know, the arts is such a great umbrella because you know, it's not like a mental health group, it's an arts group, but like, you know, what we've found is so many people are like us, you know, have had histories that have like joined that group ...*

For the first time, Rupert has found a sense of belonging that does not depend upon substance misuse:

> *Yeah. [laughter] I mean, I feel that like, I, I have some small place in the world for the first time, you know? And that's really good, you know ...*
>
> *It's true though, man, it really is true, it's hundred percent, you know, that something that I can actually feel a bit of pride in, that I've been part of and it is good, ... good ...*
>
> *... the feeling that I actually belong, you know, that, that this is a society that I belong to. You know, that I am a part of which is something that I've never had, you know, and, and there's some things about society that I hate, but, like, I'd rather be hated from the inside and try and change it from the inside than ranting and raving from the outside which does nobody any bloody good.*

Rupert offers a personal evaluation of the impact of the project on his life:

> *Oh god ... it's been tremendous ... like, you know, being in Waterstones, I mean, Jesus, prestige, man, I mean, yeah, I feel quite humbled actually, ... like it's, it's such a prestigious venue, so yeah.*
>
> *And, yeah, you know, it is, it's been a great thing, I'm really glad that it's been there. With Lost Artists 'cos it's been a real great back-up, you know, and just, just the, the being part of that community group is a big lift-me-up, really is a big lift-me-up, you know, and being, being picked out of everyone to be chairman, just even though it was an informal vote was, was so flattering.*

Rupert's story is one of being a social victim and him subsequently dropping out. Rupert places himself in a sad story, with loss, misunderstanding and drug abuse. Rupert has always demonstrated warmth towards me. I have wondered if he sees me as the kind of person he might have become had circumstances been different. Rupert is articulate and his socio-cultural analysis is compelling. He has therefore elicited my respect, but also my pity.

Rupert claims that he cannot cope with the world and states that he experiences very low self-worth. His identity has been historically tied up with drug abuse and subsequent illness. His dependency on state benefits he finds degrading. Rupert knows that he is intelligent, however this has worked against him because he is aware of the hopelessness of his current situation in the same way he was aware of the hopelessness of his social situation when he grew up. Rupert makes strong identity claims of being an artist. This is possibly the most positive identity claim Rupert has made in his adult life.

A collective narrative of people who participated in the Lost Artists Club

I was never given an explanation of how the LAC acquired its name, however an examination of the data supports the concepts the name evokes. The use of the expression 'lost' indicates some form of historical loss of role as 'artist' that is mediated by the formation of a 'club' that retains art as its common focus. As with any club, members share common interests. Whilst membership of the LAC extends beyond the six participants, the data suggests the following commonalities: the Lost Artists interviewed are all white British, in their forties, identify themselves as artists, and for whatever reason, have felt excluded from mainstream society; there is a sense of being misunderstood or outcast for being who they are. Thus, 'Lost Artists' may also be paralleled with 'outsider artists' discussed earlier in Chapter One. However, not all have constructed an 'illness narrative' neither have all talked about using mental health services. There is some consensus that UK politics of the last 20 years since the participants left school has not supported creative people from lower social classes.

The collective narrative of the LAC is one where art is used to construct an identity whereby people may see themselves as artists. To some extent, the formation of the LAC has legitimised this identity claim. Additionally the provision of studio space and increased opportunities for exhibitions and therefore sales of art works has reinforced these claims. There is a common understanding that there are personal and social benefits of engaging in art activities. There is a sense of worthlessness attached to being in receipt of state benefits for many years. Creating art work that is valued by society brings with it a sense of personal worth. Furthermore, the creation of a 'Club' that brings together people seeking this kind of recognition has also provided members with a sense of belonging. Much of the data from the LAC is not only about their personal journeys and experiences but also about their relationships with one another (with their ups and downs). The identity claims therefore are not only personal but also collective. There is a sense that the lostness that is shared by the LAC members is recovered through finding one another. This is translated through a common theme of establishing social roles as artists and the value of friendships. The role of artist is the only apparent alternative to the sick role previously experienced. People are under no illusions though how difficult it is to earn a living as an artist, thus the role of the artist may be cultivated whilst retaining sickness benefits.

Social belonging and identity

The formation of the Lost Artists Club, over a period of time, enabled the potential for membership of a socially positive group identity compared with a negative and highly stigmatised identity as 'mental health service user' or 'mental patient'. Tajfel (1982: 2) placed emphasis upon the 'value and emotional significance' that people place upon their social group according to their personal identity. If one is a member of a group that increases self-worth, there is potential for personal affirmation and a sense of belonging. Tajfel and Turner (1986) further proposed that the group's quest for 'positive distinctiveness' creates a favoured 'in-group' that is referred to as 'we' and often, an 'out-group' is identified that is not 'we' or 'us' but 'them'. Further research would need to be conducted to find out if this becomes true of members of the LAC. Rupert acknowledges the need for identity at the time of setting up the LAC:

> And, and, I wanted to find some identity, and I think that's where the Lost Artists, that's where we created the Lost Artists, because ... we didn't have an identity.

In his final interview however, Rupert appraises the nature of developing a sense of social belonging in a society whose values he struggles with:

> ... the ... recognition ... the feeling that I actually belong ... that this is a society that I belong to. That I am a part of which is something that I've never had ...

Rupert imagines the possibility of becoming an insider artist:

> But, like, you know, I'm ready to take the step now to becoming an insider and trying to help things get, get better. In some small ways ... But maybe the Art in Mind, you know, has inspired me in that way ...

In his social treatise *The Sane Society*, Fromm (2002) connected the need for identity with the maintenance of sanity:

> As with the need for relatedness … this need for a sense of identity is so vital and imperative that man could not remain sane if he did not find some way of satisfying it. (Fromm, 2002: 59)

Furthermore, Fromm blamed the lack of social identity on the failure of modern society (Fromm wrote in the 1950s) to embrace the utopia of individualisation and its failure to acknowledge the place of the clan or the family in social identity. A strong sense of identity is developed in a culture where one feels a sense of belonging. What the Lost Artists have achieved is a sense of belonging to a group where individual members feel valued by other members of the group. As Mike expressed: 'I think it's given me confidence. I've developed as a person, sort of, for my own confidence. I feel I can belong.' Fromm (2002) further argued that unless a genuine social identity is formed, one is invariably forced into an identity of conformity. Thus the 'service user' or 'mental patient' identity, although it has benefits, invariably involves conformity to the socially constructed and applied identity that holds negative connotations. Although Fromm refers to this as a 'conformed identity' that is illusory, the social consequences of such an applied identity are anything but illusory.

It is interesting to note that Storr (1972) asserted that the motivation towards creativity is the need to assert one's identity. It is argued that while one is being labelled a 'writer', an 'artist', a 'poet' or a 'musician' for example, the person is not being labelled anything more negative such as 'mentally ill'. The artist identity implies that the person so identified is making a contribution to society, whereas the 'mentally ill' person may be regarded in a more negative light, both socially and economically. Storr (1972) also suggested that problems with identity formation are more likely amongst creative people as demonstrated by greater access to different parts of themselves when inspired or emotionally challenged. Extreme forms of mental ill health are associated with problems of identity and therefore, the causal relationship between identity, creativity and mental health problems is inevitable.

Goffman (1963) pointed out that the effects of stigma are inevitably deleterious to one's identity. However, stigma may be 'actual', that which exists in reality such as the stigma associated with physical disfigurement, or 'virtual', that which is created in people's minds through stereotypes and prejudices. Either way, the person is made to feel excluded because of their difference. Either the stigmatised person accepts their lot and exploits their position for secondary gains (and, in the process, self-stigmatises) or they may resist stigmatisation and attempt to rise above it. Either way, the result of stigma is increased feelings of worthlessness and loss of a positive social role.

In Goffman's (1963) theory of 'spoiled identities', people's identities become spoiled by society. While people may have to cope with experiencing mental health problems such as hearing voices and deep depression for example, these may be more manageable than the subsequent effects of stigmatisation and discrimination. Thus by creating a collective artist identity, a social answer is developed to counter a social problem. If it is society that can spoil a person's identity because of 'virtual' stigma, then collectively people with mental health problems can find a social answer to a social problem through redefining themselves as artists and therefore restore their identities. Not only are the Lost Artists enjoying a state of social belonging, they are also asserting their 'actual' social identity.

The limited demographic information I deduced from the research indicates that most of the participants reached adolescence when Margaret Thatcher was Prime Minister. It is Erikson who identifies the psychological tension in this developmental stage as 'identity versus role confusion' (Erikson, 1995: 234). These creative, intelligent people, mostly (from what I have deduced or speculated) from working class backgrounds, may well have felt misfits at a time when they should have been developing social roles and identities. Rupert's bleak picture speaks volumes of this period when he refers to the year he left school '… winter of discontent, the mass lay-offs, the mass unemployment, the complete, … it seemed that maybe the system was on a breaking point, you know'. And Sarah not being appreciated for being the artistic creative person she was: '… I felt abused in my childhood because I wasn't allowed to be who I was …'. Rupert has worked out for himself his own need for a respectable identity:

> … So, it's getting, so … like, you need an identity to present to people who are like, you know … Like, you know, you've got to have some kind of label other than unemployed or, or sick, … those ideas, you know, they been so dragged through the mud by the government …

Sarah's version of her identity being repressed is not dissimilar to Storr's account (Storr, 1972) of the experiences of Beatrix Potter who encoded her journal so that her parents could not discover (and so disapprove of) the true nature of her individuality. It is asserted that her 'secret world' was essential for the maintenance of her identity.

The subsequent stage to Erikson's (1995) theory of development is one of the tensions between intimacy and isolation. If the previous stage was interrupted by problems with identity formation, this stage is unlikely to be successfully completed. Whilst issues of loneliness are identified in the literature, one of the issues often ignored in the social inclusion agenda is the person's need for intimate relationships and sexual expression. It is noteworthy that several intimate relationships have been formed throughout the Art in Mind project. Further research would need to be conducted to establish the benefits of intimate relationships participants might enjoy whilst engaging in a community arts programme.

In the latter half of the last century, and building upon the foundational work of thinkers such as Erikson, Fromm and Tajfel, the concept of identity has become enshrined in social practices (Foucault, 1984; Fairclough, 1989; Phillips & Jorgenson, 2002). Together with widespread acceptance of constructionist concepts of self, people are seen to construct their identities as a continual process of development. Life events are considered significant in this process and people can perform or re-present various identities according to social roles.

As time progressed, the LAC developed a strong group identity. A number of members have rented studio space in a building away from the Art in Mind offices. Whilst this move was primarily for practical reasons, this relocation is a significant shift both in terms of social inclusion and in terms of the group's identity. Although they rent studio space individually, they have decided to relocate together. The formal link with a 'mental health promotion project' (Art in Mind) is now gone. Perhaps this group autonomy that retains a healthy interdependence is the greatest compliment the LAC could give to the project, that is, it is no longer needed. Ultimately, over a period of seven years, the LAC as a social group has been facilitated into existence, supported and now moved on and no longer dependent upon the project. Quite possibly, this is the best kind of community development there is – one that is not dependent on a system that helped set it up.

Acknowledgements

Some of the findings from this study have been previously published: Stickley, T (2010) The arts, identity and belonging: A longitudinal study. *Arts & Health: An International Journal for Research, Policy and Practice*, 2(1), 23–32 .

References

Erikson, EH (1995) *Childhood and Society* (2nd ed). London: Vintage.

Fairclough, N (1989) *Language and Power*. London: Longman.

Foucault, M (1984) On the genealogy of ethics: An overview of work in progress. In P Rabinov (Ed), *The Foucault Reader* (pp. 340–72). Chicago: University of Chicago Press.

Fromm, E (2002) *The Sane Society*. London: Routledge.

Goffman, E (1963) *Stigma: Notes on the management of spoiled identity*. New York: Simon and Schuster.

Phillips, L & Jorgenson, MW (2002) *Discourse Analysis*. London: Sage.

Rogers, CR (1951) *Client-Centered Therapy: Its current practice, implications and theory*. Boston: Houghton Mifflin.

Storr, A (1972) *The Dynamics of Creation*. London: Penguin.

Tajfel, H (1982) *Social Identity and Intergroup Relations*. Cambridge: Cambridge University Press.

Tajfel, H & Turner, JC (1986) The social identity theory of intergroup behavior. In S Austin & WG Austin (Eds), *Psychology of Intergroup Relations* (pp. 7–24). Chicago: Nelson Hall.

CHAPTER SIX

Interview as Generative Practice in Arts and Wellbeing Partnership Work

Julie Hanna & Polly Moseley

This chapter focuses on two specific pieces of action research and draws on practice which has formed part of Liverpool's city-wide Arts and Health programme.

Both authors bring multiple identities to this work, Julie as occupational therapist, counsellor, Arts and Health commissioner/producer and cancer patient and Polly as policymaker, Arts consultant, producer and renal dialysis patient.

In Polly's consultancy report for Liverpool Primary Care Trust in 2008 recommending how to improve the health and social gains generated by investment in the European Capital of Culture, she prioritised *artist-led research* as an area for development. At the time, Julie commented that research led by health professionals deserved equal status. The examples given and findings of this chapter seek to air the values and approaches to research that lead to a furthering and deepening of practice and understanding, in a field which demands constant interrogation of self and other.

Interview as relational rather than judgemental research tool

Both authors have used interviews as a way to explore the connecting principles behind the practice of artists and healthcare professionals, and hence to champion more humane and empowering interactions with patients.

The etymology of the word *interview* is in two parts: *between*, from the French *entre*, and *view* from the Latin *videre*, to see. The first use of the word in English dates back to the 1500s and the court of Henry VIII, where it was used to denote *a formal meeting*. Evidently, contemporary usage is often linked to a professional testing out of a person for a job or position. Both of these usages bring an implied asymmetry to the discourse through an imbalance of power: one party is the decision-maker while the other is the decided-upon. However, both in the case of the facilitated interviews which Polly conducted, and Julie's interviews with dancers, the premise was rather to bring out seldom-heard voices and to empower the interviewer and the interviewee in the process.

This process in itself can be regarded as an art form, and one from which clinicians, researchers and people living with an illness or undergoing treatment can learn.

Bakhtin's work is some of the best known on the art of dialogue. In his essay 'Discourse in the Novel' (Bakhtin, 1981) he talked about writing and the how the reader absorbs the thought processes of the characters:

> What is realized in the novel is the process of coming to know one's own language as it is perceived in someone else's language, coming to know one's own horizon within someone else's horizon. There takes place within the novel an ideological translation of another's language and an overcoming of its otherness – an otherness that is only contingent, external, illusory ... An artistic hybrid demands enormous effort: it is stylized through and thoroughly premeditated, achieved, distanced .... (Bakhtin, 1981: 5086)

Arts and Health partnership work is a hybrid form, existing in a space in-between – a space which can hold multiple standpoints, and which can result in empowerment and transformed perspectives, hence a shift in inequalities, behaviour and, ultimately, culture. In achieving this, the balance of power is redressed and those who are cast as artists or beneficiaries can influence policy and thinking.

In this chapter, we are seeking to reframe the underpinning research question, from 'Can arts and culture increase levels of wellbeing?' to '*How do the arts best increase levels of wellbeing?*'

François Matarasso interviewed a number of participants in arts projects during 2010, Liverpool's Year of Health and Wellbeing, and gives voice to their experience in his report *Telling Stories: Arts and Wellbeing in North Liverpool*. In his essay within this report, he asked us to reconsider the term *impact*, which, like interview, implies a one-way process and result, and asserts that,

> The arts in all their forms, at voluntary, amateur and professional level, are one of the richest routes people take to find themselves and to find others, telling stories of their experience as they go. (Matarasso, 2011: 28)

Within the field of mental health, be it at a public level, as in this project which took place in an geographical area where levels of depression and anxiety are high, or within an acute mental health facility, working with the arts demands that we question the social and clinical 'norms' and context. One of the most inspiring centres for arts practice which crosses psychological and institutional boundaries is 3bisf (www.3bisf.com) in Aix-en-Provence – a contemporary arts centre and artist residency space within an acute psychiatric hospital. Whilst there for a short placement, Polly translated their manifesto document, which includes the statement:

> Artistic practice does not define norms in advance because it brings with it a questioning which is unique to that time and place. It leaves space for the human question: do we close down the human question? Do we quieten/pacify it in our 'normality'? Do we leave space for it to become something, along with the pain and the risk involved? Doesn't art constantly need to ask again and again 'what do we mean by norms?'

This manifesto talks about management and security as being increasingly dangerous to innovation and the importance of leaving space for people to define and redefine their identities.

Due to the persistence of health inequalities in Liverpool, some city leaders have embraced the need for innovation and creativity to be brought to the fore in this field, a factor that has enabled Julie and Polly to use mental health and public health funds to commission and develop arts programmes.

The Liverpool context

Once a thriving port and the Empire's second city, Liverpool is now one of Western Europe's most striking examples of post-industrial decline. Historically, public health innovations have been driven by a challenging set of needs and inequalities. When slum housing conditions were getting out of control, the city decided to employ the world's first Public Health Officer (Dr WH Duncan, 1847–1863). At that time, not all public health initiatives were humane. *The Nightcatcher* was a man who would take children from houses considered to be overcrowded as a public health measure.

Liverpool City Region has certainly enjoyed a cultural renaissance in recent years, though statistically Merseyside continues to suffer with low life expectancy, high levels of chronic illness, depression and dependency on state benefits. Both the Liverpool City-region Health is Wealth Commission Report (2008, 2011) and the North West Mental Wellbeing Survey, (Deacon et al., 2009) draw attention to the key social and health issues which need to be addressed and suggest creative ways of tackling these issues.

Julie Hanna was the first Creative Health and Wellbeing Manager for any European Capital of Culture Team, working for the Liverpool Culture Company from 2004 to 2008, seconded from her long-term post as an occupational therapist and manager at Mersey Care NHS Trust. Polly Moseley worked for Arts Council England North West and the Regional Department of Health from 2003 to 2005 developing a regional strategy. She returned to Liverpool in 2008 to make recommendations for how the City's Primary Care Trust could commission arts and culture in a sustainable way, and delivered the cultural programme for the city's Year of Health and Wellbeing in 2010.

Building an Arts and Health narrative for Liverpool has involved ensuring that milestone reports, such as the Mental Wellbeing Impact Assessment for Liverpool's Cultural Programme (West et al., 2007) and the Joint Strategic Framework for Public Mental Health for 2009–2012 (Reynolds, 2009), flag up the arts as central. Alongside these publications, Polly and Julie have brought people together at a number of cross-sectoral events, such as the 2004 'Investment in Cultural Capital for Health' think tank at Alder Hey Children's Hospital, the 2008 Big Conversation (Lewis, 2011) and an artist-led 'Creative Conversation' in January 2011. Finding innovative formats for these events, which promote dialogue, has been integral to their success. Equally, choosing the interview, a dialogical method, as their way of collecting research data could be seen as contributing to the broader conversation happening about this work in Liverpool and beyond. By studying the form and quality of the interactions between artists and service users in more depth, Polly and Julie have attempted to bring more meaning to this multi-layered narrative, in order to generate a deeper understanding and a sense of progress.

Our dialogical process in writing this chapter

Given our shared agendas and passion for the transformational potential of the arts to promote wellbeing and social change, it may be fair to assume that we would have spent time together exploring the nature of this work. However, the process of collaborating on this chapter offered us the first real opportunity to exchange more deeply about the nature of this work, to see each other and to listen to each other in a different way. Whilst formulating the chapter we recorded and transcribed a conversation. This dialogical process highlighted some similarities in our approach: a shared need to interrogate our roles and learn from creative practice, as well as differences in our thought processes and ways of working. From this point onwards, extracts from this conversation are threaded through the chapter.

> *I've always worked in mental health since qualifying as an occupational therapist ... the Masters in Research has given me the opportunity to look at ... this particular piece of research from the artist perspective but with me as researcher with a health background ... (Julie)*

It is not easy to articulate clearly what we mean by effective Arts and Health engagement in the field of mental health; to describe transformation, connecting and finding meaning. After describing our individual studies, we will focus on three areas of agency that we conclude are key to sustaining participatory arts practice and improving mental health.

We both have insight into how the health system works from our own experiences as patients. Polly was diagnosed with glomerulae nephritis aged 19. A course of intensive drug therapies led to end-stage renal failure 14 months later. Since 1993 Polly has spent at least 16 hours per week in a hospital environment on dialysis. During this time she has pursued her career and continues to campaign for improvements to dialysis at a local and national level.

The planning of the Liverpool Capital of Culture *Waiting Programme* coincided with, and was partly inspired by, Julie's own experience of diagnosis and treatment of breast cancer, and the diary she maintained that chronicled her own experiences of waiting as part of her personal health journey, as she described,

> *I would say that there was very much of myself in there really, in the thinking that through and in my own subjective experience.*

Polly's appreciation of both the non-clinical, light environment and the openness of the staff at Maison de Solenn, described below, related to her own campaigning to improve the quality of dialogue with healthcare staff and the dialysis care environment. The role of observer and facilitator gave Polly some perspective which enabled her to recognise more fully the value in leaving her own negative experiences behind.

In Polly's research the young inpatients became the interviewers and researchers interrogating the health professional. Therefore, although the research was about understanding the other it was also about understanding the self, and recognising the universality of roles and experiences.

In Julie's research with dancers, artists talked about their own mental health and wellbeing. Humility of professionals in this work and the willingness of artists to identify with others' experiences are keys to empowerment. Therefore, Polly and Julie's own experiences of ill-health and subsequent treatment enable them to empathise with service users, perhaps accelerating the process of building trust.

Young patients interviewing psychiatrists at the Maison des Adolescents in Paris (Polly's research)

In 2006, I spent four months on a research placement at this new treatment centre for adolescents with eating disorders and other mental health problems. The ensuing research was published in the *International Journal for Psychiatric Nursing* and as part of the body of research from the Clore Leadership Programme (Moseley, 2007). This condensed account links some of what I learned there to some of the best Arts and Health practice in the UK.

The Maison de Solenn (or Maison des Adolescents) in Paris (http://www.mda.aphp.fr) is a mental health facility that makes a bold statement about doing health differently, not only in terms of its design but also in terms of embedding arts and cultural workshops into the treatment plan and fabric of the hospital. Each young person is prescribed a variety of cultural workshops delivered as a service called 'Les Soins Culturels', which translates as cultural care or healing.

Symbolically, the building, on the edge of the large Hôpital Cochin site, deliberately extends its two arms away from the hospital and towards the town. At all times of day from the busy Boulevard Port Royal you can see people walking the corridors of the second and third floors of this secure hospital for 11 to 19-year-olds. The location and the transparent frontage reflect the will not to hide away these young people as problems, but to give them a central place in the life of the city.

This was the structure of the floors:

Roof Terrace: Japanese landscaped garden; planned allotments
Third Floor: arts and cultural workshop spaces: dance, music, radio, visual arts and beauty studios; library/IT suite; kitchen, dining room and classrooms
Second Floor: accommodation for 20 inpatients in single suites; medical staff room
First Floor: mezzanine for administration and offices
Ground Floor: café; large open consulting and exhibition space ('Espace Santé)
Basement: putpatient consultation and treatment rooms

Great care was taken to ensure that the design of the building embodied its core purpose.

Bernadette Chirac, the ex-Prime Minister's wife and Chair of the Paris Hospitals Trust, has spoken out openly about her daughter's anorexia. As the Founder and a Patron of the project, she stated at its opening, 'I wanted a welcoming home for teenagers ... to help relieve families from some of the pain which we went through ... I wished for a light open space, drowned in greenery ...'

The entrance of the Maison des Adolescents, 2007

Mapping floor to function may have been a logical process, but with hindsight, the split between the second and third floors accentuated the split between cultural and medical staff, and there was definitely work to be done to link 'Les Soins Culturels' to the clinical care in practical rather than simply symbolic ways.

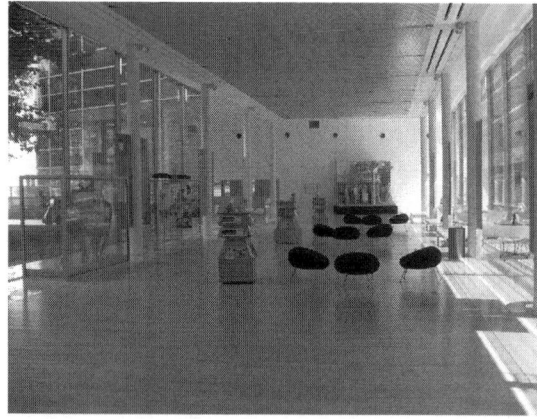

The Espace Santé, ground floor, of the Maison des Adolescents

After observing a good number of workshops, it soon became clear to me that the variance in background and facilitation skills of the staff had an enormous influence on the balance between learning, empowerment and therapy. A total of 21 workshop activities had been on offer over the first two years. The full-time cultural staff were either secondees from libraries, teacher training, sports centres, and schools, or part-time practitioners, such as a DJ and beauty therapists. Only one full-time member of the team was an artist, Catherine Couanet, a visual artist, as well as an arts teacher. Paintings, drawings and sculptures from the visual arts studio dominated the third-floor environment.

Catherine Couanet's visual arts workshop at the Maison des Adolescents
© Catherine Couanet

In this bilateral working environment, my challenge was to engage with the very busy medical staff. Rather than interviewing them myself, I decided to facilitate interviews with the young people taking the lead, so that the process could build bridges. The process for my research involved co-hosting two preparatory radio workshops: the first about English and French youth culture; the second was spent devising and testing out questions about the Cultural Care Programme (Les Soins Culturels). I then set the questions, recruited staff, set times for and facilitated the 12 interviews. Finally I transcribed and translated the interviews, wrote and shared a *Compte Rendu* (summary of findings) in French with the staff, which formed the basis for an Open Space to explore areas of cross-disciplinary development work.

Many of the young people, some of whom had been associated with the centre since its opening, were very insightful and keen to be involved in influencing decisions about the evolution of the service. They spoke of a newsletter and a blog, which had been stopped for reasons to do with patient confidentiality.

It was important that this motivation came from and remained with the individuals who were directly involved in the process. I found that it was when intentions to change others' behaviour dominated that the transformational potential was lost. From the young people's side, this was most evident in a case where two girls wanted to interview a young psychiatrist, and it became evident that they had a crush on him. They were giggling and pushing for personal information in a way which provoked a defensive response and detracted from the open nature of the dialogue. Equally, when healthcare staff stayed in their fixed roles as providers and talked too much about the beneficial nature of the cultural work in treatment terms, the conversations tended to get stuck.

One of the most successful interviews was with the Nurse Manager, someone who came across as most sceptical about my placement initially. The young woman who interviewed him was an 18-year-old who was going on to art school. The Nurse Manager really engaged, often asking for clarification and thinking time before coming up with interesting observations, such as when defining culture:

> *Culture can be thought of as a look* [un regard], *can't it? You can develop it by looking at things, and it is linked also back to the person. There are people who are more sensitive ... either intellectual or tactile or ... gastronomy is also part of culture. So it is a vast area. Of course it grows. It can be cultivated, culture is infinite, I think. ... I think that we can benefit from cultivating culture in hospitals. (translated interview, 2006)*

The point here about culture being directly tied to a subjective interpretation is interesting because this highlights a clear tension between artist-led research and clinical research. In starting the interviews by asking the healthcare staff about their most powerful cultural experiences as adolescents, I was deliberately getting them to bring their passions to the conversation, and, when these positive or nostalgic emotions triggered a connection with the young interviewer, the tenor of the conversation would completely change, becoming more open and relaxed.

In the case of this interview with the Nurse Manager, the fact that the young woman was artistically talented, and had found space at the Maison de Solenn to develop her confidence, as well as her arts portfolio, was important. Her genuine interest in his responses enabled him to question the practice of the centre more openly. In response to a question about the relationship between youth culture and the arts ecology of Paris, he replied:

> *There is a divide, but this divide is necessary, because culture in itself implies a divide, a journey, something we need to work at. And with this divide, I think, people are trying to please or to attract people ... to become more appealing ... that's what we're doing, which is happening more and more ...*

He is making the point that there is a trend for projects to aim too much for popularity by optimising the numbers of people getting involved or providing a purely pleasurable, easy experience, perhaps to meet the short-term bias of media or funders. This can eclipse the valuing of skills and craft behind the work or the importance of artists being wholly responsive and present in performance, thereby negating the quality of the art itself and compromising the interaction, and ultimately the transformative power of the work. By placing too much intention or trying to manipulate a shared space we limit creativity. This issue is well understood by Artist/Director Mark Storor, who directed the Four Corners programme in Liverpool in 2008 and the second iteration of the Wellcome Trust- and Arts Council-funded production 'For the Best' in Liverpool last year. Mark was very clear about his role as an artist in creating and protecting this space from an intention to 'do good' to people.

> It's the liminal space that's very important, once we're entering into it, but you can only create it, I don't think you can militate what happens in it exactly ... it's about keeping its fragility, and its authenticity in that moment, and to keep that authenticity everybody has to be a little uncertain, including the performers, which is why you need extraordinary performers. (Walsh, 2011: 38)

This work demands people who are willing to take risks and listen, who can follow their instincts, and who have a genuine will to create something new. This issue, raised by another senior clinician at Maison des Adolescents in her interview, showed her awareness that the training and roles no longer fit with the nature of the care provision:

> *Over and above treatment processes, we certainly need to learn about communication: how to listen to a patient; how to behave and present yourself before a patient; what a verbal exchange between two people can change; everything which is non-verbal.*

During my theatre placement, playing with bodily ways of expressing status and power in improvisation workshops, led by Phelim McDermott, from Improbable Theatre, and Keith Johnstone, made me acutely aware of the way in which some of the workshop facilitators asserted their authority in the Maison des Adolescents. In one music workshop warm-up, the girls were all lying on the floor with the male teacher walking between them, standing over them and telling them how to breathe. One of the long-term anorexic girls told me that she really liked this style of teaching. I reacted against this didactic approach, seeing it as reinforcing a potentially destructive culture of dependency. There is a well-versed argument in theatre that non-verbal communication cannot be taught, it is something, which needs to be learned through doing, through experiencing different situations with a sense of play and detachment. The successful 'Performing Medicine' programme asked the question:

> If we imagine that a doctor is 'performing medicine' how does his/her stage presence impact on the well-being of the patient and affect the dramatic narrative of the consultation? (extract from www.performingmedicine.com)

Marcel Rufo, Clinical Director of la Maison de Solenn, questioned not only the traditional role of the psychiatrist but also reframed consultations to become group workshops and weekly 'Groupe de Paroles' for all patients and a separate one for parents (Rufo, 2007). He facilitated one of these sessions; Véronique Poivre D'Arvor, mother of Solenn, who the centre is named after, the other. These people played an important role in the narrative of this centre and carried with them a celebrity identity, which both contributed to the initial development of this place, and perhaps weighed on some of the processes with staff and patients.

A total of 26 different workshops were regularly prescribed to the young inpatients and outpatients. I was privileged to experience many of these, even if the ones which I learned most from were not the most positive.

Towards the end of my research placement, I participated in a workshop led by a professional dancer in the studio lined with mirrors and found the workshop to be one of the most difficult and poignant which I had witnessed. The format was demanding and structured. The dancer demonstrated beautifully a sequence, all the time giving very clear direction as to what was right and what was wrong. However, her awareness of the social and psychological dynamics in the room amounted to poor facilitation, which unfortunately reinforced a disaffection and a sense of failure. The nursing assistant in the room only intervened when one of the girl's discomfort was physically manifested in her having a nosebleed. This workshop tipped the balance in terms of making demands which did not allow for self-expression or respond to the feelings in the room. It also emphasised the need for better cooperation between artists and nursing staff. In contrast, the dancers whom Julie interviewed had developed reflexive, movement-based techniques, which opened up space to respond to people, at the same time as teaching them.

'Listening to the voice of the dancer' (Julie's research)

'I have been saved from being a victim of depression ....' These are the words of a dancer working as a dance facilitator in community, hospital and other institutional settings. The dancer was interviewed as part of a small qualitative inquiry, to increase understanding about the artist's contribution to Arts and Health and to further knowledge about what makes Arts and Health effective, while I was studying for a Master of Research Degree. In my conversation with Polly for this chapter, I reflected that 'It's almost like they haven't got a place. It's very unusual for them to be able to talk about what they're doing. There aren't spaces to do that.'

I had carried out a mapping of predominantly unpublished Arts and Health literature during the years leading up to and including Liverpool's 2008 European Capital of Culture Year. The artist's voice featured rarely except as a reporter of events and outcomes. I sought to address this aspect in my research in order to contribute to a whole and shared understanding of Arts and Health.

Semi-structured interviews were carried out with three dancers and examples from two of the interviewees are included here. An Interpretative Phenomenological Analytical approach was taken to the study engaging with individual's reflections and seeking to make sense of those lived experiences that have particular significance for them (Smith, Flowers & Larkin, 2009).

Both dancers worked nationally and internationally as well as working locally in Liverpool with groups of people with different conditions and disabilities. Dancer 1 was an Asian British 65-year-old woman with experience working with older adults, including those suffering with dementia. Dancer 2 was a Black Caribbean 47-year-old man with significant experience working in schools with vulnerable young people.

The research process was subjective and reflexive, grounded both in the data and the experience of the researcher. As an occupational therapist who has worked in mental health services for more than 25 years I was interested in the impacts of dance on people's emotional and mental wellbeing. I used the new economics foundation (nef) *Five Ways to Wellbeing* (Aked & Thompson, 2008) to help in the analysis of the data.

As I listened and began to analyse the dancers' narratives, the data revealed the dancers' personal relationship with dance and its impact on their own wellbeing. Both dancers described powerfully the role of dance in their own lives and their belief that they would have suffered significantly more from mental distress if they had not engaged in the arts. Dance has increased their resilience and ability to 'survive', a word used by one of the dancers to mean health, suggesting that health does not mean an absence of illness but rather the ability to cope with difficulty.

> *... art has become an essential part of my life ... like breathing, it has given me life's force. (Dancer 1)*
>
> *I am proof of how the arts can help improve the quality of life of an individual. (Dancer 2)*
>
> *I have used my art ... as a tool ... to bring balance to myself. (Dancer 2)*

It can be difficult to access the lived experience of individuals participating in creative experiences and take time for individuals to assimilate the meaning of these experiences. As participants in dance themselves, the dancers' particular experience helps to illuminate something of the universal experience of participating in dance, as an art form, and the benefit on wellbeing.

The dancers linked their own experiences with their work of introducing others to dance. Both dancers are motivated to help others experience through dance what they themselves have experienced. In this way their work is rooted in their personal and lived experience of dance as illustrated by the quotes below:

> *I really feel that I have almost got a duty to share that joy and importance with other people. (Dancer 1)*

> *... you work on yourself and by doing that you automatically help to support others ... working on yourself brings ... such a sense of wellbeing ... you go out and want to enable others. (Dancer 2)*

Wellbeing is concerned with how people experience their lives (Foresight, 2008) and is desirable for the flourishing of individuals and communities as it correlates with increasing productivity, good relationships with others, good physical health and longer life expectancy. Nef's list of the five things that enhance wellbeing are: Be active; take notice; learn; give; and connect (Aked & Thompson, 2008). I focused on 'connect' as defined by nef as 'building links and relationships with others to support and enrich individuals' everyday lives'. This interpersonal aspect of connecting can be found in the interview narratives. The dancers also referred to connecting with the inner self, a different dimension of connecting, not included in the nef definition.

> *... it's that aspect of wellbeing that my work as an artist focuses on, tap into the inner self because that's where the work needs to be done. (Dancer 2)*

Jensen (2002) asserted that the arts are not good for us but instead they are an integral part of what it is to be human and are expressions of ourselves. Therefore the issue becomes how we as human beings engage in art. For some it can be helpful to spend time in the presence of those who can open up possibilities for them.

> *... people ... get the benefit of seeing somebody in comfort and that does help people ... that is what I have been told. (Dancer 1)*

The dancers are offering comfort to others, a sense of social integration and wellbeing described by Keyes (1998), through their own sense of wellbeing and wholeness gained through their engagement with dance.

Therefore in this way the dancer and participants connect with each other. Dancer 2 encapsulated the relationship in the following way:

> *I'm supporting them, they are supporting me and the work is supporting both of us.*

Talking about this point in conversation with Polly retrospectively, Julie reflected,

> *... dancers do have to practise – we have to practise learning to be resilient ... these things don't [just happen] we have to listen to ourselves, we have to keep learning to do things in a different way ... dancers bring a discipline ... in that there's quite a lot for us to learn ... (Julie)*

These dancers' narratives tell a story of how dance has increased their resilience and wellbeing and reduced their own mental distress and how sharing their own experience may help others to do the same.

Emerging themes and practice

We have found three key agents for change, which have a direct impact on the quality of the engagement, process and outcomes for partners and people involved in this work:

1. Collaborative commissioning: making time for processes which strengthen understanding and thereby partnership-working

The health sector needs to value curating and programming artists as a professional skill, whilst being clear themselves not only of the needs they are wanting to meet but in the qualities of artists which are best suited to the work. Where new partnerships are being formed, the processes for commissioning and delivery need to leave space for orientation and trust to be built. The benefit of commissioning work locally is that trust can be built face to face rather than through overly complex reporting procedures which can distance partners from the work.

Projects should be seen as parts of a longer-term journey, and outcomes defined clearly from the outset, in a way which allows space for innovation. As we write this (2011) Liverpool Primary Care Trust is embarking on a two-year Collaborative Commissioning programme to open up these processes.

Ideally service users and artists should be brought into the commissioning process early or made aware of the transparency of this at the outset of the project so that they learn about options and buy into the premise for the work, and, in time, can start to commission or partner in the commissioning of work.

2. Choosing forms for events and arts projects which promote equality and dialogue

There is a strong, emerging arts and research practice which inherently promotes democracy and inclusivity. Key to these forms of engagement is the understanding of responsibility which each player carries with them.

> ... the arts aren't good for us; they are us – expressions of us. We can't look to the arts to transform us, or to make the world a better place ... It's up to us, not art. (Jensen, 2002: 206)

Sonia Boyce is an artist whose process has been described as an 'act of dialogue (involving both verbal and bodily interaction)' (Boyce, 2010: 69). Her exhibition, *Like Love*, featured footage and work of people from Liverpool with learning disabilities and was the opening exhibition of Liverpool's Year of Health and Wellbeing. The first iterations of *Like Love* were produced with different groups in Bristol and Stoke, so the work in Liverpool had generated further content, contributing to 'a nomadic and accumulative form'. One participant said of her experience of working with Sonia, 'I wouldn't say that Sonia collaborated with me, it feels more like she interpreted my work.' In the book on this project Zoë Shearman describes Sonia's process in this way:

> Rather than entering into a communicative exchange with others with the goal of representing their 'selves' through already formed opinions, she has identified with them ... through empathetic insight ... Boyce's approach to working with others has not been to reinforce the supposedly organic body uniting hierarchised individuals, as is the case with much contemporary 'socially-engaged' art practice, but rather to provide a platform for their subjectivity, and her own. (Boyce, 2010: 69)

Professionals from institutions could learn much from this approach: how to be more transparent about their own subjectivity and use creative methods to reflect collectively on work and consult on policy priorities. Easily communicable frameworks such as the 'Five Ways to Wellbeing' (Aked & Thompson, 2008) can facilitate such dialogues by allowing different organisations and people to populate them with their own interpretations of how they can be applied.

The value of group dialogue can be enhanced by taking the time to embed forms such as 'Appreciative Enquiry' and 'Open Space'. Dr Arnold Mindell has promoted Open Space Forums through his work. His Worldwork techniques in process-orientated psychology are some of the most well-developed in terms of finding ways to listen and hear multiple roles and voices (Mindell, 2002).

3. Connecting, referencing and contributing to bodies of research

We believe that research can be a mechanism for connecting more bodies of knowledge and practice as well as for giving depth of understanding to localised work. Indeed, this is what this book is doing!

There have been recent articles in both the *British Medical Journal* and on the BBC website signalling more of an acceptance from the mainstream media about the power of Arts and Health, and The King's Fund (see www.kingsfund.org.uk) is coordinating a national marketing campaign to be driven by regional practitioners.

It is an exciting time for this work and incumbent on all of us involved to contribute to the bigger picture, whilst learning all of the time where our strengths lie as individuals and organisations.

> 2010's Vision and Objectives recognised the power of the arts as a mechanism for engaging with people experiencing low wellbeing and less likely to engage with health, social and educational opportunities and lifestyles as well as to support those with long-term conditions to manage them better, and to enable everyone to gain skills to provide resilience for the future. (Liverpool PCT, 2011: 23)

What is now needed in research terms is to connect the bodies of knowledge which exist over a longer time-scale. For this to happen we need to break down the culture of competition between academic institutions, and pool together research where synergies exist. In the 21st century we are operating in a networked society and to make the most of our technology and structures, we increasingly need to work across geographical and institutional boundaries.

Concluding thoughts

Following the theme of dialogue, we decided to end this chapter with an email exchange between us summing up our learning.

> *Julie: The experience of writing this chapter with you, Polly, has helped me to reflect on the difficulties of what is meant by an evidence base. Of course there are*

lots of different kinds of evidence for arts and mental health each bringing fresh perspectives and expanding our knowledge and understanding. It is important to weave these strands together to gain a fuller and more comprehensive picture. Focusing on the particular can have universal implications and I hope that our research might inform further quantitative research that utilises measures of equality, dialoguing and collaboration to assess the impact of the arts on mental health and wellbeing.

Polly: I completely agree, and collaborating on writing this chapter has been an interesting process in itself which has emphasised how to make a piece of work in partnership demands dedicated time and listening and care, and for all these things it has been a richer process. It has seemed important for us to record our learning as part of Liverpool's journey at a time when funding cuts are making this type of partnership-working more challenging, and at the same time more focused, making a longer-term vision and ambitious programming ever more important ...

Julie: Yes indeed, this work necessitates stepping out of our comfort zones and being able to move across organisational and professional boundaries ... I have learned myself that it is when I take risks and am vulnerable, with support, that I often learn the most. We need to develop a climate that supports experimentation and innovation, building on successes and learning from what doesn't work so well.

In the writing of this chapter we have used our subjective standpoints to throw light on the other. This has strengthened our conviction of what needs to happen in Liverpool as a city and in the wider ecology of arts and health practice. Opening up dialogue, be it through interviews or in introducing an artist to a group for the first time, demands *a will to listen* by both sides. Engaging with partners and service users is difficult to do in a competitive environment; it demands safe spaces where both statutory bodies and individuals can trust new processes, and embrace the unexpected *alongside each other.*

> In a dialogue no one is trying to win. Everybody wins if anybody wins. There is a different sort of spirit to it. ... a dialogue is something more of a common participation, in which we are not playing a game against each other, but with each other. In dialogue everybody wins. (Bohm, 1996: 7)

In his latest book, *Injustice: Why Social Inequality Persists*, Dorling takes this point a step further by pointing out the destructive effects of competition, advertising, and buying and selling healthcare, and directly attributing these to the shockingly high and rising levels of anxiety and depression in the UK, particularly amongst children (Dorling, 2011). All of us, whether artists, researchers, civil servants or NHS staff, have a responsibility to reverse this trend by working towards a more equal society, and part of this picture is defining the nature of work which embodies this change. The learning which comes through interrogating work in this context leads us to the definition of how Art can be relational and transformative by finding a universal language, by bringing forth unheard voices and by embodying a more fundamentally democratic society than the one we live in.

Acknowledgement

We would like to thank the passionate protagonists and participants who continue to contribute to the rich ecology of Arts and Health work in and across Merseyside. Without you none of this would have been possible.

If you would like to contact either Polly or Julie about this work please send emails to: pollymoseley@mac.com julie.hanna@changeintheweather.co.uk

References

Aked, J & Thompson, S (2008) *Five Ways to Wellbeing*. New Economics Foundation. Retrieved from: http://www.neweconomics.org/projects/five-ways-well-being

Bakhtin, MM (1981) *The Dialogic Imagination: Four essays* (University of Texas Slavic Press Series) [Kindle edition for Mac].

Bohm, D (1996) *On Dialogue*. Oxford: Routledge Classics.

Boyce, S (2010) *Like Love*. Berlin: The Green Box.

Deacon, L, Carlin, H, Spalding, J, Giles, S, Stansfield, J, Hughes, S, et al. (2009) *North West Mental Wellbeing Survey 2009*. Liverpool: North West Public Health Observatory, Liverpool John Moores University.

Dorling, D (2011) *Injustice: Why social inequality persists*. Bristol: The Policy Press.

Foresight (Cooper C, Field J, Goswami U, Jenkins R & Sahakian B) (2008) *Foresight Mental Capital and Wellbeing Project 2008 Final Project report*. London: The Government Office for Science.

Jensen, J (2002) *Is Art Good for Us? Beliefs about high culture in American life*. Lanham, MD: Rowman & Littlefield.

Keyes, CLM (1998) Social well-being. *Social Psychology Quarterly, 61,* 121–40.

Lewis, S (2011) *Positive Psychology at Work: How positive leadership and appreciative inquiry create inspiring organisations*. Chichester: Wiley Blackwell.

Liverpool City-region Health is Wealth Commission (2008). *Health is Wealth Report*. Liverpool: Liverpool City-region Health is Wealth Commission.

Liverpool City-region Health is Wealth Commission (2011). *Health is Wealth Report*. Liverpool: Liverpool City-region Health is Wealth Commission.

Liverpool Primary Care Trust (2011) *2010 Year of Health and Wellbeing Evaluation Report*.

Liverpool: Liverpool Primary Care Trust.

Matarasso, F (2011) *Telling Stories: The arts and wellbeing in North Liverpool.* Commissioned by LARC (Liverpool Arts & Regeneration Consortium). Available at http://www.larc.uk.com/wp-content/uploads/2011/05/LARCTellingstorieswebjob.pdf

Mindell, A (2002) *The Deep Democracy of Open Forums.* Charlottesville, VA: Hampton Roads Publishing Co.

Moseley, P (2007) A home from home for adolescents: Integrating cultural expression with treatment-based therapies at La Maison des Adolescents. Research in brief. *Journal of Mental Health and Psychiatric Nursing, 14,* 816–22.

Reynolds, C (2009) *Everybody's Business: The Joint Strategic Framework for Public Mental Health 2009–2012.* Liverpool: Liverpool Primary Care Trust. Retrieved from: http://www.liverpoolpct.nhs.uk/Library/Your_PCT/Publications/JSFMH.pdf

Rufo, M (2007) *La Vie en Désordre: Voyage en adolescence.* Paris: Éditions Anne Carriere.

Smith, JA, Flowers, P & Larkin, M (2009) *Interpretative Phenomenological Analysis.* London: Sage.

Walsh, A (2011) *For the Best.* Retrieved from: http://annaledgard.com/wp-content/uploads/report_final_online_SP.pdf

West, H, Hanna, J, Scott-Samuel, A & Cooke, A (2007) *Liverpool 08 European Capital of Culture: Mental well-being impact assessment.* Liverpool: IMPACT, Division of Public Health, University of Liverpool.

CHAPTER SEVEN

Movies, Movements and Moving Moments: Connecting film, user involvement and student learning

*Mick McKeown, Russell Hogarth,
Fiona Jones, Mark Edwards, Keith Holt, Sarah Traill,
Jane Priestley, Garry Watkins, Michael Hellawell,
John Lunt & Lisa Malihi-Shoja*

Introduction

This chapter develops thinking about participation in different but connected initiatives concerned with mental health, the arts and humanities. These are located in a university community engagement context developed with participatory action research methods. Particular themes at play include: the filmic depiction of madness and its relationship to wider social representations; the motivating zeal of service user participants and the potential for this to be understood as part of a wider movement for change; and the extent to which these can touch or move an audience of learners. We will draw on participant accounts arising from the course of the action research project and a number of purposeful focus groups and interviews relevant to the experience of (i) developing and managing a mental health film festival and (ii) participating in a mini-project to produce video/re-usable learning objects, in effect service users making their own films to support practitioner education. These participant experiences arise from within the Comensus initiative, at the University of Central Lancashire, which organises service user and carer involvement in the work of the university. This includes involvement in teaching and learning and associated research in the field of health and social care, together with other more strategic involvement in decision-making committees (Downe et al., 2007, McKeown et al., 2010).

The setting: Service user involvement in universities

Service user and carer involvement has become a growing part of the education of health and social care practitioner groups, with some variations in its extent or quality (see Wykurz & Kelly, 2002; Felton & Stickley, 2004; Basset et al., 2006; Beresford et al., 2006; Lathlean et al., 2006; Repper & Breeze, 2007; Brown & Young, 2008; McKeown et al., 2010). There has been a concomitant demand for service user involvement in research partnerships and knowledge production (see Church, 2005; Hanley, 2005; Involve, 2007; Frankham, 2009), so much so that levels of participation are now typically appraised as part of grant approval processes. Such trends can be seen as part of a burgeoning policy rhetoric and state interest in public involvement, encompassing national and local government and with a particular emphasis on health and social care services (DH, 2004, 2005; HM Government, 2007). Arguably, the politics of expanding participation are beset with ideological contradictions where consumerism clashes with the radicalism of social movements (Crossley, 2006; Spandler, 2006; Brown & Zavetoski, 2005; Williamson, 2008).

Various well-placed commentators have questioned whether service users' transformative goals can ever be realised within institutionalising or incorporated systems of involvement. In this light service user involvement faces significant challenges to move beyond tokenism to achieve genuine empowerment, autonomy or control for participants and greater authenticity of expression. Associated with these concerns have been efforts to calibrate different levels of participation (Arnstein, 1969; Tew et al., 2004) which idealise true partnerships over minimal or tokenistic forms. Despite prevailing incorporation and co-option hazards, perhaps university settings represent a serendipitously advantageous environment for enacting involvement (McKeown et al., 2010). Tutors and researchers working in universities with a background in clinical practice remain somewhat protected from direct association with statutory power or service provision. The fact that this may be more symbolic than actual does not deny the possibility that the academic role might afford more potential for nurturing trust between staff and service users than may exist in, for example, service settings.

Creative arts, health and practitioner education

There is a lengthy tradition of creativity in learning and the use of creative arts in particular to support the education of mental health practitioners (see Staricoff, 2004; Warne & McAndrew, 2009). Here we are most interested in the thoughtful use of filmic material in teaching about concepts and communication skills relating to mental health and empathy with the lived experience of mental distress. We focus on two examples from our own experience that draw upon movies. The first is our annual 'One in Four' Mental Health Film Festival,[1] which brings together students, service users and the wider community to debate issues of mental health stigma and discrimination. This initiative is firmly located in that phase of our work which exemplifies a shift towards service users being in control of the planning and management process. The second focuses on the service user contribution to development of videos to support the education of practitioner learners, with a specific interest in mental health nursing students addressing communication skills. There has also been interesting synergy between the two examples.

For the last four years we have successfully hosted the week-long 'One in Four' Film Festival aimed at consciousness raising and challenging stigma around mental health. We have the use of the university cinema and the event is open to the public. Selected movies are followed by facilitated discussion and debate; there are introductory talks by invited guests; and the festival also showcases local music and other art. The presentation of films towards these ends is not unusual. On a larger scale, the Mental Health Foundation has organised the Scottish Mental Health Arts and Film Festival also aimed at tackling stigma (SMHAFF, see http://www.mhfestival.com; Quinn et al., 2011). Similarly, Creative Personalities is a collaborative initiative in the Yorkshire and Humber Region co-organised by a user group for people diagnosed with personality disorder; they have run a community arts festival and currently organise a cinema club (*The Guardian*, 2010).

Since its early development, film has probably always found a place in pedagogy, and more recently, in education for mental health work. A number of lecturers and service users in the School of Health at the University of Central Lancashire (UCLan) have to greater or lesser degree been utilising

---

1. The UCLan 'One in Four' Film Festival is an annual event taking place in the week of World Mental Health Day. It was first conceived of in 2008 by Phil Blundell, a mental health nursing lecturer in the university, and showcases movies that illustrate themes relevant to discussion and debate about mental health in society and tackling stigma. The film festival is a collaboration between the university, Comensus and local community groups; it is now completely user led.

film, literature, or other works in their teaching. We were also inspired by attending the Mental Health in Higher Education (mhhe) and Keele University workshop on art and the humanities in the mental health curriculum (mhhe, 2009). The active participation of students in the film festival led to spontaneous requests from them to use more film in the mental health nursing course. We responded to this when planning a new pre-registration nursing module: *Working with People with Mental Health Needs*. This module aims to help students to develop the core skills, knowledge, attitudes and behaviours essential for creating and sustaining therapeutic relationships. Module content includes notions of recovery, alliances, communication skills and empathy.

In a context of small-group work, students engage in exercises that explore the intersection between self-awareness and reflection on both personal biographies of service users and the dramatic realisation of relevant themes in movies such as *Snow Cake, Birdy* and *Elling*. The films precipitate student discussion and debate of issues relevant to notions of recovery and social inclusion. This and other exercises (which involve reflections on selected poetry) lead to interesting contemplation of the process of empathic responding. In the course of this the students are encouraged to identify aesthetic 'objects' of their own (e.g., films, songs, poems, novels) which touch them emotionally and describe these impacts for the rest of the group. Latterly, we have also been involved in the production of our own films which depict relevant personal experiences of health or community groups and peer support.

Service users are also directly involved in live teaching sessions, relating aspects of their personal stories relevant to the learning objectives. Service user and carer involvement in the mental health module extends to identification of desired communication skills and interpersonal style which people would like to see in nurses. Carers and service users also have a facilitation role in the group work, and bring forward their own reflections, together with those of the students, in the subsequent discussions.

Student and service user feedback has been overwhelmingly positive. The relationship with participants in the wider Comensus initiative allows us to make connections between the very personal way in which people are moved by reflections on art to the political turn of making changes to education and practice, which is the goal of a social movement. The personal becomes the political; and the goal of better mental health practice is sought through the small but profound changes brought about in individuals' learning and emotional experiences.

Mental health in the movies: A resource for teaching and learning

As might be expected with any subject, there is a great plurality of coverage of mental health themes in the cinema and this interest is truly international (see Bhugra, 2006; Kelly, 2006; Mangala & Thara, 2009; Menon & Ranjith, 2009). Over the years, movies have portrayed individuals with a range of different psychiatric diagnoses or exhibiting the sort of behaviour which typically would lead to the attachment of such labels if a psychiatrist were in attendance. Thus we have cinematic presentations of all of the recognised categories of mental illness (Hyler, 1988), psychiatric commentary on these movies (Robinson, 2009), and critical sociological reflections (Roberts, 2011). Other commentators have restricted themselves to analysis of filmic portrayals of single diagnoses such as depression (Magos, 2009), psychopathy (Hesse, 2009; McKeown & Stowell-Smith, 2006) or schizophrenia (Rosenstock, 2003). This depiction of different experiences of mental ill health is matched by various representations of psychiatric practitioners and different types of treatment (Gabbard & Gabbard, 1987; Orchowski et al., 2006; de Carlo, 2007; Greenberg, 2009; McDonald & Walter, 2009). Some clinicians have suggested that the movie treatment can be influential on the public's expectations of care and therapy (Orchowski et al., 2006), and others describe sometimes using cinema as part of the therapeutic process (Winship, 1999; Gelkopf et al., 2006; Greenberg, 2009).

Commentators have noted an association with themes promoting a 'social message' including a direct, on occasion, challenge to the stigma attached to mental health. Other movies have garnered criticism for their casual deployment of stigmatising imagery, or the failure to keep up with progress in clinical practice or even social policy (Cape, 2003). Torrey (1994) pointed out that stereotyping mental ill health in terms of homicidal dangerousness dates to the silent era, noting an early example, *The Maniac Cook*, as far back as 1909. Critique of negative representation extends to films and cartoons produced for children, where the power to denigrate the mentally unwell is linked to the early socialisation of youngsters and prevailing negative stereotypes of mental ill health (Lawson & Fouts, 2004). In this sense, the movies are of a piece with much of the mass media, having the potential to reproduce both positive and negative portrayals of mental health (see Wahl & Lefkowits, 1989; Philo, 1996; Gleeson, 1991; Hyler et al., 1991; McKeown & Clancy, 1995). The potential of arts and the media has been recognised by mental health activists and used to powerful effect in community engagement (Chung et al., 2006) and other arenas for activism.[2] Corrigan and colleagues (2001) propose a model of social relations whereby stigma and social distance are closely linked to familiarity with mental health problems. These authors report that 90 per cent of the people they surveyed in the US reported learning about mental health problems from the movies and go on to argue that more progressive portrayals would help to challenge stigma, reduce public fears of dangerousness, and promote social inclusion. In a study of the impact of the Scottish Mental Health Arts and Film Festival there was an increase in positive attitudes, for instance relating to recovery, but no decrease in negative attitudes especially relating to perceived dangerousness (Quinn et al., 2011).

Notwithstanding critique of the various depictions of madness to be found in the movies, they can undoubtedly present a powerful medium for teaching future generations of practitioners (Fritz & Poe, 1979; Raingruber, 2003; Sierles, 2005; Akram et al., 2009; Datta, 2009; Bhugra, 2009; Cape, 2009; Magos, 2009). An interest in the filmic portrayal of different categories of 'mental illness' more often than not focuses on notions of 'accuracy' of depiction of particular conditions or mental states and the value of this for teaching about psychopathology (see Hyler, 1988; Parry, 2009; Powell, 2009; Robinson, 2009; Wedding et al., 2010; Atkinson, 2011). Roland Atkinson, Emeritus Professor of Psychiatry at the University of Health and Science, Portland, Oregon, has developed a fairly comprehensive website to this end, listing and reviewing films which in some way depict mental disorder (Psychflix: http://www.psychflix.com/title_index.html). For some, the perceived inaccuracy of filmic treatments of mental disorder are reason enough to refrain from utilisation for teaching (Greenberg, 2009), though Hyler (1988: 195) has suggested that a number of films are so good in their portrayal of specific diagnoses they are 'prototypal'. This concern with exactness is reflected in Atkinson's reported involvement as a special advisor to moviemakers.

Of course, those who have misgivings about the value of psychiatric categories, or even the whole categorical approach to organising mental healthcare, may be equally averse to bringing this in to their appreciation of film. Arguably, if mental health is seen in the round, then many films which do not purport to address categories of mental illness but instead deal with the range of human emotions and experiences can be useful for teaching mental

---

2. David Reville and colleagues in Toronto have infiltrated Ryerson University to deliver a Mad History curriculum which deploys movies and activist-made films as an important part of their pedagogy. Similarly, the Scottish 'Oor Mad History' group are also interested in film and are active supporters of the Scottish Mental Health Arts and Film Festival.

health practitioners. Moreover, this might especially be the case where the focus is upon relational aspects of mental healthcare, such as the expression of empathy (Raingruber, 2003). Efforts to artistically characterise the extremes of mental health make for acute drama but also have most worth in connecting with more general insights into the human condition or appreciation of the fuzzy boundaries between socially constructed difference and a common humanity in shared experience. Greenberg (2009) argues that student practitioners may learn more from films without an obvious *psychiatric* agenda.

Methods

The Comensus initiative was initially conceived as a modified participatory action research study (Reason & Bradbury, 2000; Kemmis & McTaggart, 2003). Arguably, the philosophical underpinnings and inclusive practices of participatory research methods render them highly suited to developing and evaluating user involvement initiatives (Frankham, 2009; McLauglin, 2010). The involvement activity in Comensus has included numerous intersections with film and filming. We have links to service users with formal training and experience in movie-making and have helped to showcase their productions[3] and we have developed links to national and international survivor groups who also have made films that record examples of user movement activism[4] and embrace the value of film for teaching about mental health. Comensus participants have engaged in a number of filmmaking or digital technology projects that have explored the value of these technologies for education or peer support[5] and also utilised participatory methods.

Typically action research involves a number of repetitions of planning–action–observation–reflection–planning cycles (Lewin, 1946). Claims are made that the implicit democratisation of forms of this research process are empowering and emancipatory for participants and traditional boundaries between researcher and research subjects are blurred in the pursuance of collective development goals (see Freire, 1971, 2004). Our project is best

---

3. David McCollum is a media studies graduate of UCLan who is now self-employed as a filmmaker. His own biographical film was showcased in 2007, winning the festival prize which was awarded by Ken Loach (see http://www.dmcmedia.org.uk/).

4. Staff and mental health survivors associated with Ryerson University, Toronto have collaborated to support and develop a number of community businesses and resources; these include filmmaking with progressive messages for mental health, including the award-winning *Working Like Crazy*.

5. These include the Bradton project to develop user-made film clips as part of e-learning, a collaboration with staff and service users from Bradford University.

described as a modified form because the initial planning phase to secure funding was mainly organised by university academics, albeit informed by previous engagement with community partners. From there on, the framing of the project was as fully participatory as we could make it. The project thus sought to make changes to practices in a single university directly where the action took place. Though action research is most concerned with the actual changes wrought in the course of a project, the focus on a single university setting ought not to preclude thinking about the potential generalisability of insights from the change process for other similarly situated universities.

We describe the methodological approach taken in more detail elsewhere (Downe et al., 2007). In broad terms Comensus has progressed through three meta-cycles of action and analysis. The launch phase involved thorough engagement with community partners to frame the project, ending with the recruitment of the first Community Involvement Team (CIT) (January 2004– February 2005). The second stage of development covered the maturation of the CIT (March 2005–June 2006). The CIT is a diverse group of service users and carers operating as the decision-making forum for Comensus and linked in to a panoply of affiliated community groups and individuals interested in becoming involved in the university. Thirdly, the current phase is notable for developing the growth of increasingly autonomous user-led practices in the CIT.

For action research projects almost anything which occurs or is produced in action is data. In our project this has involved minutes of meetings, actions and observations, reflective diaries, formal reports, talk between participants, recorded interviews and focus groups. Early on, we had funding for a research assistant who observed Comensus activity, made field notes, and at intervals debriefed and interviewed participating service users, carers and staff. More recently we have continued with regular moments for reflection and annual debriefings of individual participants. Thus there is a continuous process of collecting individual responses to questions such as, for example, what has been happening? how do we make sense of it? what are our priorities? how do we feel? what motivates or sustains activity? and what could be done better and how? On occasion we convene specific rounds of interviews or focus groups to inquire more deeply into specific examples of activity, such as, for example, the involvement in making film or video clips.

We have a commitment to write reports and scholarly papers as collectively as possible, which included producing a book focused on service user and carer involvement in universities (McKeown et al., 2010). Efforts concerned with writing together and sharing in authorship reflect the emancipatory and participatory ideals of the action research approach, and the writing process mirrors the research cycles. We include people's contributions to the writing enterprise pragmatically and eclectically depending on particular states of preparedness, confidence and experience – some write fairly independently, some prefer a process akin to amanuensis. We also meet together in small groups for collective reflection (often recorded), writing, review and redrafting and prefer to use collective language and personal pronouns unless there is a need to indicate individual attachment to a sentiment, idea or piece of biography, for example.

In this chapter we present various participant reflections on involvement in the production of film for use in student teaching drawn from interviews and focus groups convened specifically for the purpose of gathering these particular views. Some of the interview data included relate to the Bradton project which involved participants in making short DVD clips to be uploaded into a virtual 'community' e-learning environment. This project covered a range of health and social care perspectives; we have limited ourselves here to data provided by those participants who identify with mental health service use. Data analysis proceeded using simple thematic analysis (Holliday, 2002) and emergent analyses are considered collectively. The following themes emerge from analysis of seven semi-structured interviews with individuals and two focus groups.

Making sense of making movies

Telling stories, making a difference

Participants highly value opportunities to be involved in the process of filmmaking associated with teaching. These enthusiasms and motivations are linked to implicit fulfilment in the act of being involved, positive feelings towards the finished products of their efforts, and typically connect with more fundamental objectives of user involvement in this context: essentially driven by a desire to make a constructive difference to practitioner education, and hopefully the quality of real-world clinical practice. This can be about righting wrongs, improving on negative experiences of poor practice:

> ... *as you know, I've survived the mental health system ... and when you've gone through that, living in fear for year after year ... and I don't want that to happen to anybody ... when you've experienced things for so long, and you know its wrong, somebody has got to stand up and say its wrong, and when other people are saying it – there must be something that needs to be changed.*

Alternately, the contribution can be about celebrating good practice and persuading students to maximise this. Both perspectives are ultimately about changing practice for the better:

> Its about the value of this for student learning and practice change.
>
> I feel as though I'm helping people to create better services ... things come up and you can talk them through with people, help them to see different sides.

With reference to the impact on self and students, the making and use of film can have multiple benefits:

> I'm glad I've done it ... I know I've made some changes somewhere ... when students say that it has made an impact ... makes me feel what I'm doing is worthwhile.

Telling stories is a significant element of user involvement in teaching and learning, and user-made film is seen as one vehicle for supporting such storytelling. The use of one's own, or colleagues', films as part of face-to-face teaching sessions can add value to ordinary teaching opportunities, increasing the impact of personal stories. Service user participants are interested in communicating their messages in an accessible way, or offering students access to complexities of experience which can only be conveyed authentically by people who have had these experiences:

> When I tell my story – the audience is accessing my internal world – what's going on inside – which isn't usually readily available to them.

Film can open up possibilities of reaching a wider audience, often linked to other technologies such as the Internet, and this is seen as a welcome development (though, for some, it can equally raise anxieties about people's degree of control over their stories and privacy, see below).

Discussion of personal motivations quite commonly reveals altruistic values, wanting to make a difference for the benefit of others rather than being primarily motivated by material rewards:

> I feel people ought to talk about their experiences because this is a part of making the world a better place ... if as many people as possible can get a bit of a feel for as many other people's experiences then that should lead to better decisions being taken.

This altruism is the antithesis of any narcissistic aspects of appearing on film; it is not about calling attention to self:

... not about me being on film

Though, there is a fundamental concern with the importance of communicating the subjective, which is seen as at the heart of user involvement in education:

It is about the essence of me, and communicating it.

Patterns of motivation that reflect an altruistic disposition extend into concerns regarding the potential for filmic storytelling to provide a legacy beyond one's active involvement in a project. This connects with a desire to maximise capacity to reach the potential audience. A few of our number have been diagnosed with life-limiting conditions on top of their mental health problems since becoming involved in Comensus, many others have variable levels of energy or confidence and their mental wellbeing can ebb and flow:

... if I were having a bad day and couldn't come, I know I can still be involved.

Committing a personal contribution to film which can be utilised beyond one's active engagement in the project or at times when individual circumstances militate against active engagement with students in a classroom, or in some cases anticipating the end of one's life, can be a tangible legacy or gift for future students. This is the case for one person who sadly received a diagnosis of lung cancer but has continued to be involved and has spoken movingly of the legacy effects pertaining to these filmic and other artefacts developed in the course of their involvement. As an aside, this person joined Comensus on the basis of being a carer for his elderly mother, later identified with his mental health experiences (joining the local user forum through connections made in the Comensus group) and got involved in teaching mental health practitioners. He has carried on with this and now has also contributed to teaching nurses and others working in cancer care and end of life care. In these special circumstances the notion of legacy assumes quite profound and poignant value for participant and students alike. Whatever the personal circumstances, the filmic representations made by service users can be seen as extending their capacity to reach the student audience; the mission to 'make a difference' can continue even if the particular individual is unable to bodily attend the classroom.

Controlling the story

For most of the participants, control over how their film is to be used and trusting the process is paramount, and specific anxieties connect with views on various technologies and sensitivities about the personal aspects of storytelling. Concerns abound about how the reusable learning objects will be used, with an expressed desire to retain control over how the films will be used in the classroom:

> *I might lose control of my story.*
>
> *Fear that the tutor may use in non-intended way.*

There is some fear of being replaced in the scheme of things. Interestingly, these anxieties connect with the suspicions of some professional lecturers around how their work may be reorganised with the advent of new technologies. Will the advent of service user films become wrapped up in the sort of cost-cutting substitution exercises that eventually limit opportunities for face-to-face teaching? Ultimately this boils down to a concern that technology might result in being done out of work and role as a service user educator:

> *... not a Luddite but do have concerns about it ... we don't need people because machines are doing it.*
>
> *... if there is a video, would I still be needed?*

Other people are more concerned with losing out on the element of interaction with students; this face-to-face contact is highly valued:

> *When things come up you can discuss it – you don't get that interaction with a video.*

These worries contrast with the aforementioned view that use of film can maximise, albeit in a disembodied, virtual way, connecting the story with a student audience. This perspective acknowledges that the reusable nature of film clips can actually expand the reach of service user influence into teaching. For instance, for those lacking in confidence to face a room full of students, or where energy levels or physical illness or variations in mental wellbeing are a barrier to lengthy or repeated involvement in the classroom – in these circumstances, the film may become a welcome substitute for face-to-face involvement, or partially so – with individuals accompanying their film into the classroom, thus maximising their control over its use with students. This is mirrored in the use of film clips in other media, such as distance learning using web-based learning environments e.g., the Bradton initiative, which has been utilised in a context of face-to-face classroom teaching, or service users can retain involvement with virtual teaching by actively engaging in live web forums as part of the learning experience. These 'hybrid' approaches allow service users to retain some degree of control over how their material is used whilst keeping hold of an element of personal interaction with students.

The 'legacy' view (above) can maximise 'reach' or frequency of student contact with one's story/film, but need not necessarily compromise control as long as people have the opportunity to negotiate or stipulate how their film is to be used. This sets up interesting examples of teaching whereby an individual's film may be used in a teaching session in which they are not personally present, but it is being used by other service users who are leading the session.

The Internet and e-learning modalities further muddy the waters when thinking about control and can amplify anxieties and trust issues:

There are some people who prey on vulnerable people; it could be used to make peoples' lives a misery.

The Bradton project was initially a 'closed-access' e-learning environment for the use of students on specific courses in the collaborating universities. Later on in the project, the participating service users discussed the possibilities of this becoming an open access resource and this was eventually agreed. Arguably, the commitment to maximising 'reach' overrode concerns about vulnerability and loss of control over online access:

... if it is for the benefit of all then I don't have a problem.

These discussions included some general mistrust of the Internet but also included reference to various misgivings about the application of 'technology' and whether it squeezes out the personal or relational dimensions of user involvement in teaching.

In a more positive and proactive approach to control, certain participants have suggested that specific films need not be seen as the final word on any individual's story – and people may wish to add to or update their films. Examples include returning to a recorded biography to emphasise changes such as progress on personal journeys of recovery.

An interesting aspect of participants' reflections on issues of trust and control features articulation of views concerning the difference between embodied 'face-to-face' contact with students in classrooms and the more 'virtual' presence of one's story in a film. Some of these concerns relate to the actual 'authenticity' of expression or impact, and whether this might be diminished by use of film alone. Many participants, hence, advocate that committing their stories to film needs to be seen as part of a teaching process whereby they, or peers, remain in control of how these films are used, and ideally in some way accompany the film into teaching sessions. Conversely, the power of film to bring people's voices into the classroom is valued, and ranked higher than teaching and learning that does not involve service users:

Reading it is one thing, seeing someone in the flesh is another thing – it is true authenticity.

That is, in this sense the 'virtual' is an adequate substitute for face-to-face contact with learners.

In summary, any misgivings about the use of film are associated with perceptions that participants may lose control over the films. Conversely, affinity for the use of film involves the extent to which it can offer personal control over one's involvement, opening up opportunities that were previously closed due to various impediments such as degree of confidence or capacity to fulfil teaching opportunities.

Storying selfhood

Being involved in communicative acts via film raises important issues of identity for participating service users: the telling of biographical stories opens up the potential to refashion one's identity through the interaction between presenting stories and the audience reception. This 'storying' is felt to result in changes in how people view themselves and how they perceive others see them. There is a powerful feeling that participants are engaged in a direct attempt to 'challenge attitudes'. Many positive features of identity are thought to accrue from being involved; these include feelings of prestige, respect and being listened to, shedding negative aspects of identity:

I can do this, this is what I'm about – contradicts other people's negative views of me.

When I'm in the town centre ... people walk past me and laugh ... when I'm here people listen to me and are interested in my opinion; that feels good.

Assuming a more positive sense of identity involves the adoption of new roles and purpose in the act of filmmaking and presenting films. Interestingly, a feature of this is a view of these forms of participation as meaningful activity or 'work':

> *I'm doing something worthwhile ... otherwise sit at home but I have an interest and focus in my life.*

This opens up the potential to obtain the sort of social value attached to positive aspects of work and also the sociability of relating to work colleagues:

> *I've met people I wouldn't have met otherwise and it has helped me understand their take on things.*
>
> *I lead an isolated life and it's great to have those sorts of relationships.*

For some, these valued experiences are contrasted with previous negative experiences of employment or difficulties in social interaction:

> *I've got social phobia, I find it difficult to go into social situations, so this is ideal for me because I find it easier to come here ... it is a structured situation, it has a purpose and a focus.*

Participants also report that these identity issues also connect positively with a perceived impact on personal health and wellbeing:

> *... it's helping me with my mental health problems; it's therapeutic.*

Movements and moving people

There is a scholarly debate regarding the extent to which participatory methods are truly authentic or emancipatory (Frankham, 2009; McLaughlin, 2010). Regardless of the resolution of such debates, incidental to the interviews in our project have been participant reflections on the research and development approach which in some way connect with a commitment to empowerment. People very much appreciated the opportunity to pause and reflect, and that this was not merely an academic exercise – their views would be fed back into the development process. This was seen as more than just routine debriefing: the value of a 'helicopter view' was remarked upon positively, bringing together everyone's thoughts and being interested in each other's stories. The social dimension was also commented on, with appreciation for the process of being involved in groups, in active production, cooperating with each other, where personal agency can be expressed in creative alliances and relationships.

Reflections from the Comensus action research show similarities between this form of involvement and the narratives of participants in movements for social change. Commentators have remarked that organised mental health service users can be viewed as part of a wider social movement (Brown & Zavetoski, 2005; Crossley, 2006; Williamson, 2008). Analysis from our research highlights primary motivations as the desire to make a difference, stressing the importance of relationships within the collective. This altruistic desire to make a difference or right wrongs in the system may be voiced in the context of filmmaking here but is arguably quite a general sentiment in the wider context of user involvement.

The teaching provided by Comensus participants brings people's lived experiences to bear on learning objectives relating to the professional development of health and social care practitioners. In its simplest sense this involves people relating certain aspects of their biography or experiences in receipt of care for reflection and discussion with students. At the interpersonal level of contact with learners, we can pick out key moments where students and teachers are personally moved within the learning experience. Participants in initiatives like Comensus report wishing to see tangible changes in the world of clinical practice and services. The jury is out on whether this is being achieved, or even if we could measure such impact. At the personal level however, there is growing evidence for a positive impact on students, and they certainly appreciate this form of teaching as witnessed in module evaluations and wider feedback. What we would like to emphasise here is the profundity of small changes at the interpersonal level, and personal comments and connections that arise in the course of this teaching and learning. In this sense the *personal is the political* and we square the circle back to the idea of involvement having features of a social movement.

Clearly the reported concerns over trust and control are of significant importance to participants. The wider support structures surrounding Comensus were reported as one of the most valued elements of the initiative in its earlier stages (Downe et al., 2007), yet did not figure too much in the data presented here addressing filmmaking. Perhaps in this context, as Comensus has matured, wider support was taken for granted and not dwelt upon in reflections, or individual agency and autonomy have come more to the foreground. Nevertheless, the ethics of trust and control demand a commitment to properly supporting user involvement and developing robust infrastructure to deliver such support and establish people's rights regarding control of their stories and other contributions to teaching and learning.

Those of us who are service users have also been involved in curriculum design and development of new modules and courses, some of which are completely user led. In these instances reference to personal experience also figures, but there is also a focus on learning about the context and practice of user involvement or more democratic care systems, and this includes lessons about the politics of the user movement and critique of the extent to which 'involvement' can be thought of as akin to 'movement' practices. These turns in education have led us into contemplation of relational aspects of involvement and the notion of prefigurative politics, whereby participants model the world as they would like to see it, on their journey to achieving it. Other existential concerns arise regarding the complexities of the relationship between participants and the university, and whether alliances with university personnel can transcend models of co-option and what this might mean for a more radical academic identity (McKeown et al., 2010).

The university setting for our purposes brings together two domains of activity, the arts and academic practices, which have been the basis for some interesting critical analyses and commentary. User involvement in embodied teaching on the one hand, and filmic representations of selfhood on the other, open up possibilities of thinking critically about different sorts of social space in a university and mental health context, and the different ways in which personal and political goals can be realised (see Parr, 1997). A notable collection of authors have wrestled with ideas surrounding the public role of staff in academia, specifically with regard to their potential for supporting the advancement of a radical agenda for social change. Over the years, at least some of this thinking has focused on the idea of public intellectuals arguing for a transformative politics and/or the role of arts and humanities in the amelioration of forms of human alienation endemic in advanced capitalism (see Marcuse, 1991; Freire, 2004; Reitz, 2000).

Charles Reitz (2009: 2) draws upon the critical social theory of Herbert Marcuse and reflects upon the role of art and academia in society to make a case for university academics to become more critically engaged in the service of their communities and the furtherance of radical political objectives:

> Marcuse contends that artists and intellectuals (especially) can find in their own personal estrangement a critical impulse to serve a future emancipation of self and society. Art and philosophy (i.e., the humanities) can, by virtue

of their admittedly elitist critical distance, oppose an oppressive status quo and furnish an intangible, yet concrete, telos by which to guide personal growth and emancipatory social practice … Neither art nor higher education, on their own, can fulfill the promise of liberation, yet in Marcuse's view, the insights provided by study of the humanities furnish the intellectual precondition to any political transformation of alienated human existence into authentic human existence.

Various commentators have applied similar reasoning to the field of user politics and movements. Cresswell and Spandler (2011) build upon Gramsci's distinction between 'organic' and 'traditional' intellectuals to highlight a valued positioning wherein university personnel can assume both an academic and activist role at one and the same time. These authors have also persuasively argued for using ideas from Sedgwick's (1982) text *Psychopolitics* as a point of departure for a new politics of mental health, better suited to supporting creative alliances and solidarity between those situated as practitioners or academics and the mental health survivor movement.

Conclusions

Both the mental health film festival and bringing film into teaching and learning, including the use of user-made films, have the power to move students and other participants at an emotional level. These individual or small-scale collective 'moving moments' (in the classroom or cinema) are not the grand, transformative shifts in power or consciousness demanded by the wider user movement, but are, nonetheless, profound in their own way, and may, indeed, be part of working towards larger scale social change. Alternately, the involvement of service users inside university bureaucracies raises the possibility of engaging with the politics of the wider user movement, mainly situated externally to the academy but possibly now infiltrating into classrooms and research activity. As such, the contribution of service users to the work of universities connects with other progressive agendas: amongst these are the humanising of curricula and student experience through the contribution of creative arts and humanities in a context of user involvement and the related opportunities this affords for expression of a radicalised academic identity, engaged with local and global politics of change. Using film in teaching practices, whether produced by artists or user activists, may be one way in which such ends can be arrived at.

References

Akram, A, O'Brien, A, O'Neil, A & Latham, R (2009) Crossing the line: Learning psychiatry at the movies. *International Review of Psychiatry, 21*, 267–8.

Arnstein, S (1969) A ladder of citizen participation. *Journal of the American Institute of Planners, 35*(4), 216–24.

Atkinson, R (2011) Book Review: 'Movies and Mental Illness: Using films to understand psychopathology' (3rd ed), D Wedding, M Boyd & R Niemiec (2010). *Journal of Psychiatric and Mental Health Nursing, 18*, e6–e8.

Basset, T, Campbell, P & Anderson, J (2006) Service user/survivor involvement in mental health training and education: Overcoming the barriers. *Social Work Education, 25,* 393–402.

Beresford, P, Branfield, F, Taylor, J, Brennan, M, Sartori, A, Lalani, M, & Wise, G (2006) Working together for better social work education. *Social Work Education, 25,* 326–31.

Bhugra, D (2006) Mad tales from Bollywood. *Maudsley Monographs 48*. Hove: Psychology Press.

Bhugra, D (2009) Editorial. *International Review of Psychiatry, 21*, 181–2.

Brown, K & Young, N (2008) Building capacity for service user and carer involvement in social work education. *Social Work Education: The International Journal, 27*(1), 84–96.

Brown, P & Zavetoski, S (Eds) (2005) *Social Movements in Health*. Oxford: Blackwell Publishing.

Cape, G (2003) Addiction, stigma and movies. *Acta Psychiatrica Scandinavica, 107,* 163–9.

Cape, G (2009) Movies as a vehicle to teach addiction medicine. *International Review of Psychiatry, 21*, 213–17.

Chung, B, Corbett, C, Boulet, B, Cummings, J, Paxton, K, McDaniel, S et al. (2006) Talking wellness: A description of a community-academic partnered project to engage an African-American community around depression through the use of poetry, film and photography. *Ethnicity and Disease, 16*(1 Suppl. 1), ss67–78.

Church, K (2005) Conflicting knowledge/s: User involvement in the field of knowledge. In S Tilley (Ed), *Field of Knowledge of Psychiatric and Mental Health Nursing* (pp. 181–5). Oxford: Blackwell.

Corrigan, PW, Green, A, Lundin, R, Kubiak, M & Penn, D (2001) Familiarity with and social distance from people with serious mental illness. *Psychiatric Services, 52,* 953–8.

Cresswell, M & Spandler, H (2011) *The Engaged Academic: Academic intellectuals and the psychiatric survivor movement*. Published conference papers for the Alternative Futures and Popular Protest, 16th International Social Movements Conference, Manchester, April 18–20.

Crossley, N (2006) *Contesting Psychiatry: Social movements in mental health*. London: Routledge.

Datta, V (2009) Madness and the movies: An undergraduate module for medical students. *International Review of Psychiatry, 21,* 261–6.

De Carlo, K (2007) Ogres and Angels in the madhouse. Mental health nursing identities in film. *International Journal of Mental Health Nursing, 16,* 338–48.

Department of Health (2004) *NHS improvement plan: Putting people at the heart of public services*. London: Department of Health.

Department of Health (2005) *Commissioning a patient-led NHS*. London: Department of Health.

Downe, S, McKeown, M, Johnson, E, Comensus Community Involvement Team, Comensus Advisory Group, Koloczek, L et al. (2007) The UCLan Community Engagement and Service User Support (Comensus) project: Valuing authenticity making space for emergence. *Health Expectations, 10,* 392–406.

Felton, A & Stickley, T (2004) Pedagogy, power and service user involvement. *Journal of Psychiatric and Mental Health Nursing, 11*(1), 89–98.

Frankham, J (2009) Partnership Research: A review of approaches and challenges in conducting research in partnership with service users. *ESRC National Centre for Research Methods Review Paper. NCRM/013.* London: ESRC.

Freire, P (1971) *Pedagogy of the Oppressed.* Harmondsworth: Penguin.

Freire, P (2004) *Pedagogy of Hope: Reliving pedagogy of the oppressed.* New York: Continuum.

Fritz, G & Poe, R (1979) The role of a cinema seminar in psychiatric education. *American Journal of Psychiatry, 136,* 207–10.

Gabbard, K & Gabbard, G (1987) *Psychiatry and the Cinema.* Chicago: University of Chicago Press.

Gelkopf, M, Gonen, B, Kurs, R, Melamed, Y & Bleich, A (2006) The effect of humorous movies on inpatients with schizophrenia. *Journal of Nervous and Mental Disease, 194,* 880–3.

Gleeson, K (1991) *Out of Our Minds: The deconstruction and reconstruction of madness.* Unpublished PhD thesis. University of Reading.

Greenberg, H (2009) Caveat actor, caveat emptor: Some notes on some hazards of Tinseltown teaching. *International Review of Psychiatry, 21,* 231–44.

Guardian, The (2010) Public Service Awards. Winners and Runners-Up 2010. http://www.guardian.co.uk/publicservicesawards/winners-2010

Hanley, B (2005) *Research as Empowerment? User involvement in research: Building on experience and developing standards.* York: Toronto Seminar Group/Joseph Rowntree Foundation.

Hesse, M (2009) Portrayal of psychopathy in the movies. *International Review of Psychiatry, 21,* 207–12.

HM Government (2007) *Putting People First: A shared vision and commitment to the transformation of adult social care.* London: HM Government.

Holliday, A (2002) *Doing and Writing Qualitative Research.* London: Sage.

Hyler, S (1988) DSM-III at the cinema: Madness in the movies. *Comprehensive Psychiatry, 29,* 195–206.

Hyler, S, Gabbard, G & Schneider, I (1991) Homicidal maniacs and narcissistic parasites: Stigmatisation of mentally ill persons in the movies. *Hospital and Community Psychiatry, 42,* 10.

Involve (2007) *Good Practice in Active Public Involvement in Research.* Eastleigh: Involve.

Kelly, B (2006) Psychiatry in contemporary Irish cinema: A qualitative study. *Irish Journal of Psychological Medicine, 23*(2), 74–9.

Kemmis, S & McTaggart, R (2003) Participatory action research. In NK Denzin & YS Lincoln (Eds), *Strategies of Qualitative Inquiry* (2nd ed, pp. 336–96) Thousand Oaks, CA: Sage.

Lathlean, J, Burgess, A, Coldham, T, Gibson, C, Herbert, L, Levett-Jones et al. (2006) Experiences of service user and carer participation in healthcare education. *Nurse Education in Practice, 6,* 424–9.

Lawson, A & Fouts, G (2004) Mental illness in Disney-animated films. *Canadian Journal of Psychiatry, 49,* 310–14.

Lewin, K (1946) Action research and minority problems. *Journal of Social Issues, 2*(4), 34–46.

Magos, T (2009) *The Lacemaker*: Helping clinicians identify the depression-prone profile. *International Review of Psychiatry, 21,* 278–80.

Mangala, R & Thara, R (2009) Mental health in Tamil cinema. *International Review of Psychiatry, 21,* 224–8.

Marcuse, H (1991) *One-dimensional Man: Studies in the ideology of advanced industrial society* (2nd ed). Boston: Beacon Press.

McDonald, A & Walter, G (2009) Hollywood and ECT. *International Review of Psychiatry, 21,* 200–6.

McLauglin, H (2010) Keeping service user involvement in research honest. *British Journal of Social Work, 40,* 1591–608.

McKeown, M & Clancy, B (1995) Images of madness: Media influence on societal perceptions of mental illness. *Mental Health Nursing, 15*(2), 10–12.

McKeown, M, Malihi-Shoja, L & Downe, S (Eds) supporting The Comensus Writing Collective (2010) *Service User and Carer Involvement in Education for Health and Social Care*. Chichester: Wiley-Blackwell.

McKeown, M & Stowell-Smith, M (2006) The comforts of evil: Dangerous personalities in high security hospitals and the horror film. In T Mason (Ed), *Forensic Psychiatry: The influences of evil* (pp. 109–34). Totowa, NJ: Humana Press.

Menon, K & Ranjith, G (2009) Malayalam cinema and mental health. *International Review of Psychiatry, 21,* 218–23.

mhhe (2009) *Experiencing Madness: How the humanities can enhance understanding of mental illness/distress*. Workshop help at Keele University, May 19, 2009.

Orchowski, L, Spickard, B & McNamara, J (2006) Cinema and the valuing of psychotherapy: Implications for clinical practice. *Professional Psychology: Research and Practice, 37,* 506–14.

Parr, H (1997) Mental health, public space, and the city: Questions of individual and collective access. *Environment and Planning D: Society and Space, 15*(4), 435–54.

Parry, W (2009) Diagnosing an *American Psycho*. *International Review of Psychiatry, 21,* 281–2.

Philo, G (Ed) (1996) *Media and Mental Distress*. London: Longman.

Powell, L (2009) Science fiction or reality. *International Review of Psychiatry, 21,* 273–5.

Quinn, N, Shulman, A, Knifton, L & Byrne, P (2011) The impact of a national mental health arts and film festival on stigma and recovery. *Acta Psychiatrica Scandinavica, 123*(1), 71–81.

Raingruber, B (2003) Integrating aesthetics into advanced practice mental health nursing: Commercial film as a suggested modality. *Issues in Mental Health Nursing, 24,* 467–95.

Reason, P & Bradbury, H (Eds) (2000) *Handbook of Action Research: Participative inquiry and practice.* London: Sage.

Reitz, C (2000) *Art, Alienation and the Humanities: A critical engagement with Herbert Marcuse.* Albany, NY: State University of New York Press.

Reitz, C (2009) A new Marcuse: Educational theorist for a new generation. Conference paper. Third Biennial Conference of the Herbert Marcuse Society: *Marcuse and the Frankfurt School for a New Generation,* York University, Toronto. October 29–31. http://sites.google.com/site/marcusesociety/charles-reitz-2009-conference-paper

Repper, J & Breeze, J (2007) User and carer involvement in the training and education of health professionals: A review of the literature. *International Journal of Nursing Studies, 44,* 511–19.

Roberts, R (2011) *Real to Reel: Psychiatry at the cinema.* Ross-on-Wye: PCCS Books.

Robinson, D (2009) Reel psychiatry. *International Review of Psychiatry, 21,* 245–60.

Rosenstock, J (2003) Beyond *A Beautiful Mind*: Film choices for teaching schizophrenia. *Academic Psychiatry, 27,* 117–22.

Sedgwick, P (1982). *Psychopolitics.* London: Pluto.

Sierles, F (2005) Using film as the basis of an American culture course for first year psychiatry residents. *Academic Psychiatry, 29*(1), 100–4.

Spandler, H (2006) *Asylum to Action: Paddington Day Hospital, therapeutic communities and beyond.* London: Jessica Kingsley.

Staricoff, R (2004) Arts in Health: A review of the medical literature. *Research Report 36.* London: Arts Council England.

Tew, J, Gell, C & Foster, F (2004) *Learning from Experience: Involving service users and carers in mental health education and training.* Nottingham: Mental Health in Higher Education/NIMHE.

Torrey, E (1994) Violent behaviour by individuals with serious mental illness. *Hospital and Community Psychiatry, 45,* 653–62.

Wahl, O & Lefkowits, J (1989) Impact of a television film on attitudes towards mental illness. *American Journal of Community Psychology, 17,* 521–8.

Warne, T & McAndrew, S (Eds) (2009) *Creative Approaches to Health and Social Care Education.* Basingstoke: Palgrave Macmillan.

Wedding, D, Boyd, M & Niemiec, R (2010) *Movies and Mental Illness: Using films to understand psychopathology* (3rd ed). Cambridge, MA: Hogrefe Publishing.

Williamson, C (2008) The patient movement as an emancipation movement. *Health Expectations, 11,* 102–12.

Winship, G (1999) 'Screen memories': The role of film in the therapeutic milieu. In D Waller & J Mahoney (Eds), *Treatment of Addiction: Current issues for arts therapies* (pp. 106–16). Florence, KY: Routledge.

Wykurz, G & Kelly, D (2002) Learning in practice – developing the role of patients as teachers: Literature review. *British Medical Journal, 325,* 818–21.

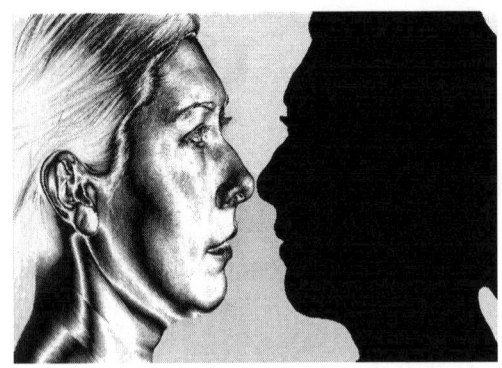

CHAPTER EIGHT

Working with Artists to Promote Mental Health and Wellbeing in Schools: An evaluation of processes and outcomes at four schools

Edward Sellman with Alma Cunliffe

Introduction

This chapter explores how collaboration between artists and schools can promote mental wellbeing and the ways in which such approaches can be evaluated. Research undertaken with targeted groups of students at four schools is then shared, showing how working with an artist on a group project for 8 to 12 weeks helped develop friendships, social skills, increased confidence and resilience. It will help readers think critically about the relationship between schools and mental wellbeing and how arts-based projects and their impact can be theorised.

Art and mental wellbeing in schools

Critical starting points: The nature of schools

Some people will reflect on their days at school as amongst the happiest of their lives. For them, schooling was 'protective' and prepared them for adult life – it was either a safe haven or a place to flourish or both. Schools also serve a reproductive function (Bourdieu & Passeron, 1990), so those pupils already 'rich' in cultural capital, or fortunate enough to obtain cultural capital through schooling despite disadvantage, are also those most likely to gain a 'good' education, which in turn is linked to greater socioeconomic security and wellbeing in later life (Rogers & Pilgrim, 2003; Seligman, 2003).

This is not everybody's experience of schooling of course. At the opposite end of the spectrum, there are others who experience schools as harrowing places – a stressful environment both academically and socially, hierarchically organised with punitive measures in place for transgression of its rules and norms. A place that constrains experience, rather than accepting and nurturing diversity and freedom of expression. Many students will bring issues (e.g., difficulties at home, poverty) to their school experience, which will potentially hamper their engagement, development and mental wellbeing (Atkinson & Hornby, 2002; Cowie et al., 2004).

To illustrate this point, Harber (2004) described schools around the world as damaging places, where:

- attendance is compulsory not voluntary
- vertical organisation of power and authority are standard
- movement is restricted
- assessment is routine
- individualism and competition are commonly promoted
- knowledge is often compartmentalised and performance within each subject scrutinised against normative performance criteria
- the experience of learning for many is exclusionary, the curriculum taught doesn't reflect every pupil's experience, and
- incentives and punishments are often used to 'shape' behaviour.

Whilst some security can be derived from clearly defined roles and routines, these begin to sound more like the description of a prison than a school, better suited to producing obedient citizens than free-thinking and expressive individuals. The implications of these points are that often we make uncritical assumptions that schools are natural environments and nurturing places for children. Such a contention has often been made by the work of Foucault (e.g., 1995), who has drawn our attention to how modern institutions such as schools operate along principles of near total observation and make judgements about people's development and mental states in comparison to what would be viewed as a typically developed person at a particular biological age. Under such apparatus, the individual is constructed as unable to cope with the institution rather than the institution failing to meet the needs of its pupils.

Many policymakers and school leaders have attempted to resolve the tension between a school's reproductive and emancipatory potential, and their performative and pastoral roles, by trying to both have their cake and eat it at the same time. A range of policies were introduced in the UK prior to a new government in 2010 to balance striving for academic standards with humanistic goals like inclusion, enjoyment and empowerment. Examples of the latter include the Every Child Matters agenda (DoE, 2003), which attempted to coordinate all children's services in orientation to five broad common goals and curriculum initiatives such as Citizenship, and Social and Emotional Aspects of Learning. The arts have benefited too from a broader view of education and how to enhance it through projects such as creative partnerships, which encouraged relationships between schools and artists to work together on development goals. At the time of writing, many of these initiatives face an uncertain, if not gloomy immediate future. However, despite the well-meaning intentions of these initiatives, writers such as Slee et al. (1998) had pinpointed a number of policy contradictions anyway. For example, to raise standards it may be necessary to permanently exclude challenging students from schools, yet such practices clearly run against any social inclusion goals. The academic discourse of schools remains dominant, often meaning that humanistic curriculum goals and other activities receive lower status and risk marginalisation.

So what does this all mean for the prospect of a school working with an artist or arts organisation on social or health-related goals? An initial critical standpoint is warranted, which includes not making the assumption that a school may be the ideal place for mental wellbeing to flourish, even though this can happen and readily does. One then has to ponder whether the 'intervention' is a complementary part of a holistic approach to student development or whether it represents a period of respite from the rest of school life, which may be stressful, even harmful? Will the art form planned therefore sit comfortably within the school's value system and educational approach or will it risk raising challenging issues that may require a response? Furthermore, any arts project has to be set against what can be realistically achieved and how this will be evaluated.

How art can support mental wellbeing in schools

The UK Government prior to 2010 had begun to recognise the role art can play in health; both the Department of Health and the Arts Council for England (DH/Arts Council, 2007), alongside scholars such as Staricoff (2004) and White (2006) referred to a sizeable and growing body of evidence, alongside examples of good practice showing tangible benefits. This was set against a rising political interest in an inclusive society with the Social Exclusion Unit (2004) also identifying that engagement with arts projects can combat social exclusion for different age groups. Much momentum gained is threatened at the time of writing by sweeping cuts to the arts and public services that will inevitably squeeze the gains previously made, regardless of emerging evidence.

Much of this evidence was case-study based and hence sometimes attracted criticism (e.g., Mirza, 2006) about the claims being made. In response, White (2006) argued that measuring the therapeutic benefits and social gains for individuals and groups involved with the arts is complex, with what normally constitutes quality 'scientific evidence' often being beyond the reach of small-scale Arts and Health projects seeking to be responsive to individual and group needs, as well as emphasising process over content and outcome. Perhaps the research world of education enjoys a little more freedom, with growing acceptance of the role that qualitative methods, even visual methods and participant-led research, can play in generating meaningful data (Thomson, 2008).

It is therefore worthwhile thinking about the kind of data that could represent, regardless of how collected, evidence of social and health impact. As a potential starting point, Servan-Schreibner's *Healing Without Freud or Prozac* (2005) identified several proactive and non-medical approaches to mental wellbeing that enjoy a good or emerging evidence base, including:

- breathing, cardiac coherence and eye movement exercises
- waking to light
- acupuncture
- omega-3 food supplements
- *regular exercise*
- *deep and meaningful relationships*
- *positive communication/effective conflict resolution*
- *contributing to something bigger than oneself.*

Whereas some of these strategies involve applying routines or new habits to daily life in an attempt to affect physiology, the final four points (shown in italics) can all be achieved through the arts, noting that regular exercise works because whilst someone is doing this it's difficult to think about the stresses of life, so similarly, absorption into an art form could substitute for regular exercise.

Aked et al. (2008) have identified five ways to wellbeing that demonstrate remarkable similarity and overlap:

- connecting with others
- being active
- noticing things
- maintaining learning
- giving.

Again, the arts can play a substantial role in achieving each of these elements. Some of the key ways in which the arts can make this contribution are now discussed.

Connecting, being listened to, sharing ideas and resolving conflict

'Creative partnerships' afford different ways of working between adults and young people (Sellman, 2011a) and much of the literature on the benefits of Arts and Health projects refers to an impact on social connectivity and resources, so this section warrants detailed discussion.

Taylor and Houghton (2008) described the relationships forged between artists and participants as fundamentally different to those forged with other adults, a point reinforced by participants in the research reported in this chapter. The young people involved are trusted and respond positively by honouring that trust. As a consequence, the project work is very different from work with teachers and usually centres on what Heenan (2006) calls a 'safe space'. Artists are clearly not a homogenous group and may enact multiple roles within a group, but nonetheless O'Brien (2004) described those with appropriate experience, training and expectations as possessing attributes ideal for effective working with marginalised and vulnerable young people. Participants are given greater freedom to ask questions and discuss issues. There may also be greater emphasis on process, instead of an instrumental focus on the production of outcomes/products. In such environments, young people are less likely to be told what to do and are thus offered different possibilities for ways of engaging and thinking. As a consequence, young people report a sense of enjoyment, achievement and wider community engagement (Hadland & Stickley, 2010), can demonstrate greater levels of motivation and improved self-esteem (O'Brien, 2004), and greater self-awareness and resilience (Coholic, 2010).

Stickley and Duncan (2007, 2010) are amongst many researchers (White, 2006, 2008, 2009 notably) highlighting the social benefits of arts engagement and stress how community networks forged through arts engagement build 'social capital' for their participants. For White (2006), the shared experience is important and he draws upon the work of Putnam (2001) as amongst the first to apply the term of social capital to Arts and Health. The concept emphasises the sense of community cohesion that can be created through both improved bonding within the group (increased frequency of contact amongst those geographically close to one another) and bridging (less frequent but meaningful contact with people beyond their geographical area) that can be enhanced through community arts. There may also be the added benefit of greater awareness of the social, health and cultural resources and services available to them within the local and regional area, and a greater degree of trust in these services and resources (Thomson et al., 2011).

Thiele and Marsden (2003) modelled the potential of arts projects to achieve such cultural and social outcomes through the concepts of possibility, animation, critical engagement and imagination, re-represented and explained in Table 8.1.

	Outcome	**Potential evidence**
Possibility	A space to explore what life has to offer and alternative pathways.	Changes in language, appearance, acquisition of new skills, hobbies and/or means to meet their needs.
Animation	The ability to be personally, socially, culturally and politically active.	Enhanced self-confidence and trust in others/services, improved self-management and social skills, greater self-direction and/or group orientation.
Critical engagement	The ability to suggest rules, values and ideas in relation to reflection on project and broader context.	Negotiation of group process, expression of points of view (and evidence for these), positive responses to feedback/criticism and personal development.
Imagination	Innovative capability applied to personal and collective purpose and fulfilment.	Articulation of problems and responses, anticipation of future challenges and strategies.

Table 8.1: *Potential outcomes for collaborative arts and likely evidence (adapted from Thiele & Marsden, 2003)*

Thiele and Marsden's (2003) concepts and suggested forms of evidence may thus provide the kind of coordination required by the field of Arts and Health, as well as the seeds of an evaluation framework helpful to researchers seeking to map the social gains clearly made by a number of arts projects.

Being active

As previously discussed, being active is good for health in general and it's a good stress reliever because whilst someone is 'doing' something, they are focused and less likely to be thinking of something else, including their troubles (Servan-Schreibner, 2005). The arts as a form of activity can go further than this; in a therapeutic sense they can become an outlet for the expression of pent-up emotions and ideas (see Griffiths, 2008, Liebmann, 1990 and McNiff, 2004 for good introductions to this topic). They can also provide a channel for energy that results in a deep engagement and absorption in a task, in addition to the natural enjoyment and pleasure that can be gained through arts and particularly participatory arts. Csíkszentmihályi (2002) has famously used the concept of 'flow' to describe this level of deep engagement. It describes a subjective state where the ability to concentrate is enhanced, a distorted sense of time is experienced, as well as a loss of self-consciousness, with the added benefits of stress relief, alongside a greater sense of self-control and purpose. Anybody who has experienced a sense of flow through sport or the arts will know how powerful and therapeutic it can be.

Learning new skills throughout the lifecourse

In addition to the arts serving as a vehicle for acquiring artistic and technical skills that may form the basis for new and lifelong interests, the arts can also be used to open up sensitive issues for discussion. Essler et al. (2006) discuss how arts approaches in schools can be used to raise awareness of mental health issues and challenge stigmatising attitudes with small but noticeable effects. Their study also acknowledges that such work isn't solely about working with individuals but involves challenging the context and social groups in which individuals find themselves located. The arts can also be used to enhance, extend and open up the curriculum in creative ways for those who would otherwise struggle to access its content, particularly if it's delivered in a traditional didactic manner (Sellman, 2011a, describes a number of case studies exemplifying such approaches).

Giving/contributing to something bigger than oneself

There is good evidence that those with religious faith/spirituality live longer and often happier lives (Seligman, 2003; Servan-Schreibner, 2005) and this is probably more to do with a faith in a cause greater than oneself that gives life a sense of purpose and meaning. When understood in these terms, voluntary activity, significant hobbies, active membership of organisations such as Greenpeace or other social movements can stand as substitutes for religion. Those working with community arts on collaborative projects also refer to this sense of giving/contributing, which is well represented by the case studies shared later in this chapter.

A word of caution: How art can diminish mental health

If the arts have the power to heal and transform lives through positive experiences, it is also the case that negative experiences can damage lives. Hence a great deal of responsibility is placed in the artist's or organisation's care to manage the process responsibly.

The 'lifespan' of any group created will be a key consideration. In relation to community arts projects, Thiele and Marsden (2003) modelled these as phases of:

- initial research and development
- an introductory phase
- a time for nurturing connectedness, and
- a period of disengagement.

The initial phase includes questioning the relationship of the project to its context in ways previously described. It will also be helpful to consider how the needs of a group will be matched to the attributes of the facilitating artist(s). Do they have relevant experience and an appropriate personality for the group? The selection of the group to work on the project also needs careful consideration, especially if it is a selected or targeted group. How this process is communicated to the group is important, as any possibility of colluding with a stigmatising label or stereotype should be avoided. Assumptions should also be challenged. Frequently, students experiencing different difficulties are attributed the label of low self-esteem as a 'catch-all' term. However, this 'low self-esteem' may only exist in the mind of the teacher and applies more precisely to esteem in relation to class-based activities or behaviour that may not have been fully understood. Finally, Thiele and Marsden's (2003) disengagement phase also warrants careful management as when projects inevitably come to an end there may be a grieving stage in recognition of the closure of the group, and this raises some ethical issues that will be discussed later in the chapter.

There are several further ways damage could occur:

- The artist sets young people a poor example through, for example, unreliable time management.

- The arts project is poorly planned and doesn't adequately reflect the group's entry level of experience, skills and confidence. Some participants may have had negative experiences of the arts previously and start a project with anxiety.
- Group dynamics are not managed well and there is a lack of group contract or exit strategy.
- Individual contributions are negatively evaluated by the artist, or more likely, by other peers.
- The artist intentionally or unintentionally colludes with stigmatisation by reinforcing judgements that have been previously made about the group.
- Obstacles and setbacks are not anticipated and have a detrimental impact on the project when encountered.
- The outcomes of the project are themselves disappointing.

Another way in which damage could occur is through over-direction or manipulation of students' work. As well as failing to take advantage of the potential of the arts to encourage freedom and growth as previously discussed, this can communicate to pupils that there are only fixed ways of doing things and consequently fixed possibilities for creative identities. This is well illustrated by Daniels (2001), who has done extensive research into the nature of social regulation in schools and how these are communicated pedagogically, through communication specifically – both spoken and visual. Contrast the types of display below, particularly the two images on the left against the two on the right.

On the left, there are clearly defined right and wrong procedures resulting in firm boundaries for identity and voice, a straight-jacketing of possibilities, compared to those on the right, which allow and reflect greater diversity.

Cases studies: Working with artists at four schools

This chapter now turns its attention to four case studies, which illustrate many of the themes previously discussed. A little background about how the projects were funded, then initiated through student and staff consultation, and evaluated is provided first.

Figure 8.1: *Institutional regulation, art and identity (originally published as separate images in Daniels, 2001, pp. 164–7)*

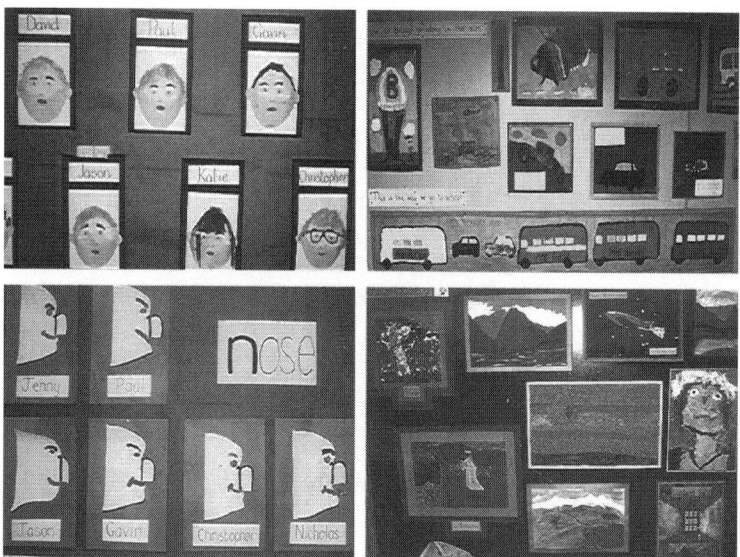

Background

Targeted Mental Health Services in Schools (TaMHS) Nottinghamshire and Arts Partnership Nottinghamshire (APN) funded City Arts, an arts organisation, and the University of Nottingham to organise and evaluate collaborative arts projects in three Nottinghamshire secondary schools with a specific focus on 11 to 13-year-olds and one primary school with a focus on 10 to 11-year-olds. The schools were pre-selected by TaMHS according to regional priorities and their own assessment of need, which had already been undertaken prior to project commencement.

City Arts is a voluntary-sector organisation, and is funded by a variety of trusts and foundations, as well as the Arts Council and Nottingham City Council. It is a participatory arts organisation working with many different members of the community: children, young people and adults; people with disabilities; refugee and asylum seekers; and members of the wider community. It is particularly experienced in working with people with mental health difficulties. Denholm (2008) described its work in schools, and case studies featuring City Arts are also reported in Stickley and Duncan (2007, 2010).

Consultation

The philosophy and approach of the projects and their evaluation were underpinned by a commitment to student voice. Sellman (2009) and Hall (2010) stressed the value of such an approach, highlighting that such processes can yield mature and informative insights to decision-making processes that have been traditionally reserved for adults. They also highlight how the outcomes of projects are more likely to be meaningful and sustained when informed by key stakeholders.

Therefore, prior to the arts projects being commissioned, a group of students was selected by a teacher from each school to participate in a consultation exercise. Each school was asked to seek volunteers from the relevant age groups, with a balance of male and female students, who represented a cross-section of students from the given year groups (i.e., both confident and less so, vulnerable and not so etc.).

During the exercise, each group was invited to:

- share their views of what constitutes 'mental wellbeing' in schools
- give a guided tour of the school highlighting spaces associated with positive and negative emotions/experiences whilst taking photographs of these spaces, and
- de-brief about the tour and put forward ideas for possible art projects that could improve environmental spaces or address some of the issues identified earlier in discussion.

Both discussions were digitally recorded and detailed notes taken. Their ideas were then taken to a staff consultation exercise to discuss practicalities and to what degree these suggestions aligned with school development priorities. There were no objections or obstacles raised by any of the schools other than at one of the secondary schools (School D). This school had been let down in the past by being promised a new school build, which also involved pupil consultation, only for the project to be abandoned, leaving staff and students feeling dejected and disappointed. They were understandably keen to protect their students and thus did not grant permission for this exercise to take place initially, which did cause a delay to the project starting as several issues needed clarifying first. The process did eventually take place a little later.

The consultation identified the following priorities in each school:

	Pupils' comments about mental wellbeing at their school	Pupils' ideas for arts projects
School A (primary)	It was important for students to feel safe and welcomed, to celebrate who they were and their connection with the wider community. The school has also been partially rebuilt and thus has large spaces, both inside and outside, which appear dull. They felt that the school could give a better first impression on arrival.	1. To create sculptures with natural materials that improved the appearance of the entrance to the school, walled garden and playground area. 2. Undertaking an art form (such as mosaic), which would celebrate the mining heritage of the school and brighten up the entrance hall. This could also be used to forge stronger links with the community, through artistic research into the local area.
School B (secondary)	Concern over the poor state of the building, treatment of displays by other students, its impact on the mental wellbeing of students at the school and the negative ways in which outsiders and visitors viewed the school. They also felt members of staff did not fully appreciate some of the difficulties faced by students and could show greater awareness and sensitivity at times.	1. To transform a space that was currently not being used into a bright and cheerful space, which could be used as a 'chill-out room' for distressed students. 2. To make posters and/or a DVD celebrating the positive aspects of the school. 3. To use arts-based workshops to explore sensitive issues.
School C (secondary)	Pupils wanted to feel safe in school and felt that awareness about the damage of alcohol and tobacco could be increased. They felt that the school environment was very dull and lacked clearly visible information to guide students around school, which sometimes meant they did not know where to go. They also felt the school was invisible to the community and wanted to change this.	To create signage for the school, which: • are more colourful • give more information about the school • highlight specific areas around the school • communicate safety rules • reflect and represent the school positively.
School D (secondary)	The project represented a second chance to improve elements of the school environment but on a smaller scale.	Use of large-scale art forms to transform outside spaces, possibly using recycled materials.

Table 8.2: *Summary of the consultation exercise at the four schools*

Common themes

Pupils at the schools were all eager to create work that would improve the appearance of the school environment. Generally the pupils reported a sense of pride in their schools and communities and wanted to challenge any negative stereotypes of either. One should not be surprised by the links made by the pupils between mental health and a sense of place. White (2008) cited research where this is a common finding. Drawing upon the concept of 'salutogenesis' (literally, health creation), he suggested that it is often a priority to search for coherence and security in the environment as a natural human trait. Many of the students consulted felt that the prospect of a community arts project was an ideal opportunity to create more cheerful and supportive physical spaces.

Commissioning of artists

Informed by the consultation exercise, APN and City Arts released a brief and call-out for artists, who were initially long-listed. This was important as it was felt essential that only artists with relevant experience and evidence of successful projects in the past were suggested to the pupils. Their proposals were then shown to the students who took part in the initial consultation and they made the final decision about which artists would be employed.

In summary, the following projects were commissioned:

School A – collaborative arts with the Forestry Commission, involving an initial visit to open and natural spaces to make environmental art and then willow sculptures back at school for the spaces previously identified.

School B – transformation of a space into a chill-out working with a theatre designer.

School C – creative work with two artists, a mosaic artist and a stained-glass artist, to create a variety of signage for the school to help new students and brighten up the environment. Students will also create stained glass art to take home.

School D – collaboration with a sculptor to create several large-scale pieces using a variety of materials to be positioned in the school grounds. The project would also incorporate a visit to a sculpture park.

Planning for meaningful evaluation

One of the obstacles facing the Arts and Health research field is the ethereality of the kinds of evidence that can be collected. White (2006, 2008, 2009) argued that one of the challenges facing community arts-based work, particularly as it becomes increasingly seen as an asset to social and educational objectives, is to assess a range of potential outcomes encompassing therapeutic improvement, social inclusion and empowerment, whilst no established protocols for evaluating such projects exist. He cited three alternatives to a medical model's emphasis on intervention delivery and accompanying randomised controlled trial so far employed in the field: (1) health-based approaches that usually seek to evidence improvements in concepts such as self-esteem based on self-reported questionnaires, (2) sociocultural processes focusing on social impact, and (3) community-based approaches examining impact on social capital. A further challenge here is the need to translate macro-level indicators of concern that often inform the commissioning of such work (e.g., promoting outcomes for young people not in education and employment, reducing behaviour likely to be harmful) into realistic evaluation criteria for projects that are often short term and small in scale (Thomson et al., 2011).

Both Woolf (1999) and Dewson et al. (2000) discussed how the results of interventions involving elements of support, guidance and training often produce 'soft' outcomes that can be difficult to measure, including: personal, interpersonal, coping, organisational and analytical skills such as raised confidence, awareness and motivation. They recommended clear phases for planning, collecting evidence and sharing findings, incorporating in-depth reflection during and after the intervention supported by recorded observations of individual and group activities. Dewson et al. (2000) also recommended a variety of creative strategies to collect such data; including games, the use of 3D evaluation tools (e.g., sliding scales), self-awareness cards and visual images. These are seen as particularly useful for gauging the experience of young children and those with less confidence and expressive language. Thomson (2008) also described a number of visual approaches to engaging young people in research, including video, photos, drawing, video diaries, as ways of making participation more authentic.

To meet these requirements, the approach to evaluating the impact of these projects adopted a two-fold strategy.

- The making of a documentary *video* of the projects, incorporating footage of individual and group engagement throughout the process alongside recorded interviews with pupils, artists and teachers.

- The use of *visual methods* to encourage young people to talk about the projects and their impact.

Haw and Hadfield (2011) suggested that the use of video in social science research can be understood in relation to five functions: observation, reflection, provocation, participation and projection. Although the films produced included extensive observation, they can't really be described as video ethnography (Pink, 2007) as the footage captured was only recorded at the beginning, middle and end of each project and included some staged footage (such as interviews). However, they did include ethnographic elements. Examples of this include: long periods of filming students engaging with the work; talking naturally and attempting to capture what the project was like for them. The films also included opportunities for pupils to influence the direction of the films (participation), to share their thoughts concerning the impact of the projects (reflection) and offer their ideas about mental wellbeing in schools (projection). Although they were encouraged to be open and honest, there may have been fewer opportunities for them to be extremely critical of school-based practices (provocation) on film as the end product would render their comments highly visible.

The latter point raises a number of ethical issues specific to film that go further than those considered by traditional approaches to research, also well discussed by Pink (2007). Given the visibility of their contributions and the fact that students wanted to project a positive image of their schools by releasing the finished film to a wider audience, the emphasis of the footage was on reflection rather than provocation. To ensure all participants were happy with the process, all children filmed gave their permission to be filmed/published, were allowed to say whether they were happy with the footage as it was taken, did not have to appear in front of the camera if they did not wish, and have been edited responsibly and favourably. The edited footage was also shown to the participants involved for feedback about whether it accurately captures their experience. They will also get to keep a final copy.

In addition to interviews with pupils, teachers and artists at the beginning of the project focusing on hopes and aspirations for the projects and informal interviews throughout the filmmaking to reflect on process and impact, the same participants were interviewed at the end of the project. A teacher closely connected with the project at each school and the artists were asked to reflect on the following open-ended questions:

- the strengths and weaknesses of the project
- any challenges experienced and how they were approached
- what they perceived to be the peak experience
- any observed changes in pupils
- the overall contribution of the project to a mental wellbeing agenda, and
- what will happen next, how will the project be sustained?

Five or six pupils from each school were also interviewed at the end of the project and to aid this process, a visual image (see Figures 8.2 and 8.3) was used as a stimulus to encourage reflection. The image selected, a feelings tree (Figure 8.3), had been developed to encourage young people and those with less developed communication skills to talk about quite complex or potentially intrusive matters, such as feelings and social engagement (Wilson & Long, 2009). Each student was asked to select a position on the tree that represented how they felt at the beginning and end of the project and what, if anything, had caused any change.

Figure 8.2: *Two students pointing at a 'Feelings Tree' (Wilson & Long, 2009) on film*

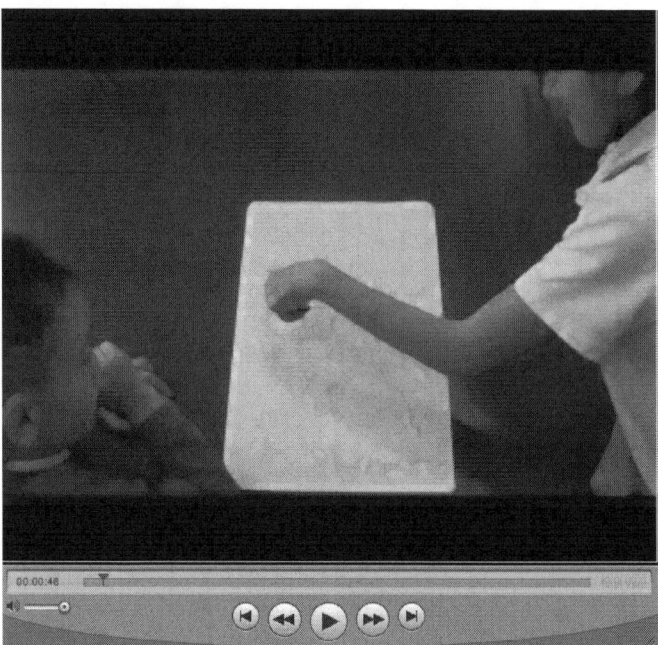

Impact on mental wellbeing

The perspectives of young people, teachers and artists have been captured throughout the course of projects whilst making a documentary DVD featuring the four schools and undertaking formal/informal interviews. All of the data gathered hence is qualitative in nature, the visual data captures the process, outcomes and level of engagement with the work and the interviews conducted capture participants' perceptions of the projects' success. All of the projects appear to have had a positive impact and this can be categorised under the following themes taken from the initial literature review, which are illustrated with visual material and quotes from a cross section of participants.

Growth in confidence and pride in the art-form produced

Figure 8.3: *'Blob Feelings Tree' Analysis*

Key: School A (Black), B (Dark Grey), C (White) & D (Light Grey)
Ring = position at the beginning of the project
Circle = position at the end of the project

Figure 8.3 shows the positions on a feelings tree indicated by pupils at the beginning of the project (shown with rings) in comparison to the end of the project (shown with shaded circles) at the four different schools. The image clearly shows two trends: (i) a general movement up the tree, with the three figures standing proud at the platform halfway up the tree or higher, being the most common positions chosen at the end of the project, and (ii) some other movement from isolated figures to figures with companions. Feeling proud, achieving something beyond their expectations, growth in confidence and making new friends were the reasons given by the pupils to explain these changes. Only one student reported not moving, who started and stayed on the platform halfway up the tree.

This feedback appears realistic as these observed changes are supported by interviews with all participants (pupils, teachers and artists). Also, this movement isn't often a simple case of a move from the very bottom to the very top of the tree – often the movements were more subtle and considered than this. Three students from two schools reported a change from a contented figure to a figure that was now upset but each said this was because the project, which they had both enjoyed and benefited from, had now come to an end, so this can be interpreted positively too.

The overwhelming majority of students reported feeling 'proud' of the project, which was linked to high-quality outcomes (e.g., Figure 8.4) that exceeded expectations, supported by working with an artist, for example:

I feel proud because I didn't know we could actually do the things we've done, the courtyard was used for nothing and now there's sculptures. (pupil, School A)

I'm impressed by it [a mosaic tree], I never thought it would be that good. (pupil, School B)

It has been a privilege to work with a top artist! (pupil, School B)

I feel like I've produced something significant. (pupil, School C)

On one hand, pride and growth in confidence was credited to ownership of the work, as this artist identifies:

The ideas have come from the students so they have real ownership of the work, they feel really proud and bring their friends up at lunchtimes to show them and say we've done this today ... you can see it in their faces, bubbling over to tell people what they've done. (artist, School B)

Figure 8.4: *Sculpture made of recycled cups at School D*

And on another hand, this was also linked to the ways in which each artist worked with the group, the process involved and the dynamics created:

> *They've become more confident as they've met up with students in other tutor groups, they've had to listen to other people's points of view and had to work as a team. (teacher, School D)*

> *I think it's important for the children to see something from start to finish and have something 'concrete' in school that can be celebrated. (teacher, School A)*

The pupils' sentiments of pride owe much to a process that culminated in the group producing something higher in quality than they expected, which will also be sited prominently at each school for many people to see for many years to come. In this sense, they feel they have contributed to something bigger than themselves. This was reinforced at each school through the organisation of a grand opening and celebration event that was well attended by the school community, parents, visitors and local press. As well as incorporating the opportunity to celebrate success and mark the end of a project into the overall plan, this feedback also highlights the importance of working with high-quality artists, who are able to guide students towards a successful outcome which is of high quality, as these elements were identified as key ingredients of improvements in confidence and esteem.

Absorption and engagement

Figure 8.5: *Pupils at work on mosaic signage at School C*

All students interviewed about the art work they have been producing, with only one exception, have commented about how enjoyable they have found the work. For some, this provides a degree of absorption (e.g., Figure 8.5) and respite from the stress they may experience in other areas of school life, as this pupil indicates:

> *Doing it is cheery, it makes you happier than doing anything else. (pupil, School B)*

Interestingly, this same student is the subject of reflection by the artist when interviewed at the end of the project:

> *One student was very interested in drugs and drug culture and was leading, well just bringing it up a lot while chatting about ideas and that's just now gone, he's just more interested in the project, drawing out floor plans and coming to me to say I've done this design and I've got this idea and what about this shade and colour for this wall and he just became more engaged in the art work, perhaps leaving other stuff behind. (artist, School B)*

This change in behaviour is also clearly documented by video evidence collected for the accompanying documentary. At the beginning, any ideas for transforming the room at School B made reference to smoking cannabis or the iconography of that culture. By the halfway stage, he gave the filmmaker a guided tour of the work produced so far and where it was going to go; he was clearly already proud and more fully engaged. By the end of the project, he was still eager to share his ideas but all his recorded references are to the process of transforming the room. If nothing else, the project has been a welcome distraction, though whilst it is beyond the evidence collected, tentatively it appears that an identity shift or maturation has taken place.

One student reported feeling bored at times. This may well be because the projects require sustained engagement over a period of weeks, which is an unusual experience at school. Although this doesn't appear to have happened for this student, it is precisely this way of working that allows other positive aspects reported here to take place.

Social capital

The most common impact theme in both adult and student interviews was how the projects had afforded greater group cohesion and improvements in social skills for many participants. Students at each project have reported making new friends and for some this has improved their wellbeing at school, as well illustrated by the quote below and the subsequent quote:

> *Two girls now have a blossoming friendship from the group, beforehand they were the target for some name calling, bullying and had low self-esteem; now they've formed a friendship they're able to support each other, they're more likely to seek help and are coming more to things like after-school art clubs. (teacher, School D)*

Some of this success could be credited to the formation of groups specifically for these projects, which also included students who were less familiar to one another. With some similarity to points already made, this student talked about how pleased they had been with the project but the fact that the students 'owned' the project was key to him and a group identity is clearly apparent in his own terms of reference:

> *I feel happy because WE* [pupil's own emphasis] *did it, the teachers helped us a bit with buying stuff but we mostly did it, we painted the room and its kind of life changing for us because we've done it, we didn't think we could do anything like this ... (pupil, School B)*

This would represent a growth in the sense of possibility as conceptualised by Thiele and Marsden (2003) and other students also talked about greater hope for the future and the likelihood of taking up new hobbies. There was also evidence of increased 'animation' or growth in social skills and capital, as suggested by this artist's reflection on conversations with pupils:

> *At the beginning a lot of them were very quiet and verbally wouldn't share their ideas or share them with the group but by the end of it they were saying 'oi – don't put that there' and really interacting with one another ... conversation opened up over the weeks, there was a lot more talking and making friends. One student said he's been able to chat to other classmates more and if he's stood in the dinner queue he'll turn round and talk to other people he doesn't know and he's found himself opening up to people a lot more ... (artist, School B)*

The artists involved all worked in different ways to most teachers, being more attentive to process and allowing students greater control in making decisions, and this was acknowledged by two of the four teachers interviewed and by several pupils. The learning environments created offered a safe space for students to share any view and have this respected with a realistic chance of this informing both the process and outcome, as these two comments suggest:

> *Instead of shouting at you, she [the artist] helps you a bit more, they were like more relaxed than lessons rather than forced on to you ... you were able to choose if you wanted to do the tree or the painting ... I feel more confident and able to speak up, speak up because usually you just get pushed to the side and everybody else chucks their ideas in, so we've all had a chance to get our ideas in. (pupil, School C)*

> *He [the artist] comes very prepared, he inspires them rather than forces them ... he understands dynamics and how to form a group too. (teacher, School D)*

At School A, an important link was made to the Forestry Commission, a recreational space close to the school, which was under-used. This element, described in the next section, can also be seen as improved awareness of social and cultural resources available in the area.

Partnerships

One positive outcome in terms of longstanding partnerships has been the relationship forged between the Forestry Commission and School A, which will result in a sustained relationship. One of the rangers will revisit the school to maintain the sculpture and further visits and work should also take

Figure 8.6: *Working on willow sculpture with the Forestry Commission at School A*

place. This is an important success for the project as one of the aims was to show how natural and open spaces, alongside engagement with nature, can also contribute to mental wellbeing, a point made by Berger (2006) and Cameron (2002), who both described how contact with nature and related creative activities can serve as a therapeutic medium for students and artists. It is therefore significant that shared activities between the two organisations will be periodically repeated.

Schools B and C have also explored how the artist can extend and continue the work done, though some of this is, as ever, dependent on funding/budgeting. Those schools able and willing to forge relationships with artists and arts organisations are likely to fare better in replicating the successes of the projects reported here, and all schools involved need to identify longer term and more systematic planning in order to achieve this. Establishing a long-term relationship will hence be a challenge hanging over some of the work reported here and this itself may have ethical implications which are discussed towards the end of this chapter. Steps are planned; a DVD, a resource pack, staff training, artists training and the potential of follow-up projects to ensure much of the work has a legacy at least.

Developing resilience

Figure 8.7: *The process of transforming a space into the 'chill-out room' at School B*

The project at School B, whilst ultimately successful, had to cope with an artistic setback, which actually served as an exemplary model for promoting mental wellbeing in general, and resilience and problem-solving more specifically. After the 'chill-out' room was painted to the students' initial ideas, they didn't like it and with the artist's guidance they went back to the drawing board to start afresh. This is a noteworthy achievement by itself, as it demonstrates the group's efficacy in identifying a problem, which also requires a good degree of confidence and self-awareness. Here is a pupil's and the artist's account of what happened:

> *The first design was like too childish, no one really liked it, it had rainbows going all around the room, it looked too babyish and the room was meant to be for teenagers and adults ... I felt we were in a tight spot, I felt a bit iffy 'cos I didn't know I'd be able to do it, and [pupil's name] said 'c'mon we can do it ...'. (pupil, School B)*
> *I thought that was one of the real strengths of the project, that they were able to say halfway through, that they had the confidence to actually say this isn't how we wanted it to look, we didn't feel it would be suitable for older students, it looks too young, and I was really pleased that they could say that and they had the confidence*

> *in their own colour schemes and patterns to say 'no' ... I don't think I would have had the confidence at their age to say to a member of staff what we're doing is wrong, let's start again, you might just go along with it. (artist, School B)*
>
> *They [the pupils] were initially disappointed then worried whether they would have enough time, enough paint and so they needed reassurance on practical levels that you can start again, this isn't something that has to stay like this, let's talk through how we can change it and make everybody's ideas fit together. (artist, School B)*

Artists are used to dealing with such setbacks and unanticipated outcomes. Yet, children and young people who are either vulnerable or experiencing mental health difficulties may find it difficult to navigate such obstacles. In this case, the artist was able to model problem-solving skills and communicate that it is perfectly normal to experience such setbacks but success is still possible. She was then able to guide them to a successful outcome. Such lessons are invaluable – Seligman's (2003) classic text on happiness shows us that what we think makes us happy (watching TV with a glass of wine, for example) often doesn't, and in fact can be linked to a mild and momentary dip/depression. Instead, greater happiness in the long term is often achieved by overcoming challenges and achieving things that are more difficult (like learning a new piece of piano music). Two students (Schools B and C) did discuss the difficulty of some of the things that they had done but this only seemed to enhance their feeling of worth at the end, as the process had been long and included technical feats. Hence, it could be a recommendation of this evaluation that artists working on projects with social and health goals deliberately incorporate 'planned setbacks' into their project design so students experience how to manage this process.

Some things to bear in mind

Although each project had successful elements and can be seen to have successfully contributed to a mental wellbeing agenda, there were also examples of practices that warrant further and careful attention.

Selection of targeted groups in schools

If project work of the type reported in this chapter is targeted, care needs to be taken with regard to how the school selects these groups and how this process is communicated. At one school, same-age peers attended a celebration of the art works and could have easily posed questions about why they were not involved and how others were; they could have felt excluded. It is not clear how decisions were communicated to students, both selected and not selected, but any classification of a group warrants caution as this could reinforce stigma. Schools should perhaps consider offering similar or comparable projects to all.

Individual behaviour management

One student was excluded from one of the projects for showing his friends the art form being produced during a lunch break and taking some biscuits that had been left out. This appears counterproductive, if not directly harmful. In the post-project interview, the artist involved reflected about how she felt she could have challenged the school more about this issue – it was her only regret. Such practices do need challenging from a mental wellbeing agenda and remind us that the cultures and polices of schools may not always be complementary to the aims of an arts/health project.

Sustainability and institutional critique

There is substantial evidence that any school-based intervention needs to be high profile, well supported and culturally compatible to enjoy a long-term impact, and several strategies can be employed to support this (Sellman, 2011b). Scott (2011) discussed the danger of what he calls, 'show and go', where collaborative arts projects are not incorporated into long-term planning and/or teachers or students are left feeling inadequate afterwards when faced with the daunting prospect of replicating or extending the work unaided. Hadland and Stickley (2010) went further with this and question how sustainable, even ethical, are arts projects that temporarily boost confidence and self-esteem, if these elements are lost when the project comes to an end.

Heenan (2006) related these challenges to the attributes of much of this type of work, which is often small in scale, time delineated and too frequently seen as marginal to the dominant activities of schools. Such a critical point was made by Hall and Thomson (2007), who problematise the emphasis placed on enjoyment and participation in school-based work with artists rather than social, cultural or institutional critique. Consequently, the transformative potential of such work is marginalised in favour of weaker forms of social inclusion that may only be short term. These points are not made in criticism of the valuable work undertaken and reported in this chapter, rather they are included as a reminder and challenge to the field of the shortcomings of such work in terms of transforming schools into places where mental wellbeing is a central feature of their culture.

Conclusion

The projects reported here, although time delineated, appear to have had a significant impact on the friendships, confidence, social skills of all those involved, and resilience for pupils from at least one school. The use of documentary filmmaking to evidence the processes and outcomes involved in achieving these outcomes was useful and may serve as a powerful means of both recording valuable evidence and raising challenges for the field in the future.

Acknowledgements

The authors would like to acknowledge the funders of the research: Department for Education, TaMHS and APN, and also Kate Duncan (City Arts) & Theo Stickley (University of Nottingham) who advised on the bid preparation.

Special thanks go to Anthony McCourt, the documentary filmmaker who worked with Edward during the evaluation and production of DVDs.

Gratitude is also expressed to all participating pupils and teachers at the four schools, and the following artists: Karina Thornton and Amy Chandler (both Forestry Commission, School A), Angela Connors (School B), Anna Dixon and Stella Chadwick (School C), and James Sutton (School D).

All photos copyright of Edward Sellman, except Figure 8.1 (Harry Daniels/Routledge, adapted by Edward Sellman), Figure 8.2 (Anthony McCourt and Edward Sellman, Figure 8.3 (Pip Wilson and Ian Long/Speechmark Publishing Ltd, adapted by Edward Sellman) and Figure 8.6 (Alma Cunliffe/City Arts, enhanced by Edward Sellman).

Figure 8.3 is Copyright © Pip Wilson and Ian Long from *Games without Frontiers* ISBN: 0-551-01554-3 published by Marshall Pickering imprint of Harper Collins Publishing. Not to be published without written permission from: pip@pipwilson.com <mailto:pip@pipwilson.com> www.blobtree.com <http://www.pipwilson.com/>

Websites

City Arts: www.city-arts.org.uk
Anthony McCourt/Push Media, filmmaker: www.pushmedia.org.uk

References

Aked, J, Marks, N, Cordon, C & Thompson, S (2008) *Five Ways to Wellbeing*. London: New Economics Foundation.

Atkinson, M & Hornby, G (2002) *Mental Health Handbook for Schools*. London: Routledge.

Berger, R (2006) Using contact with nature, creativity and ritual as a therapeutic medium with children with learning difficulties: A case study. *Emotional and Behavioural Difficulties*, *11*(2), 135–46.

Bourdieu, P & Passeron, JC (1990) *Reproduction in Education, Society and Culture*. London: Sage.

Cameron, J (2002) *Walking in This World*. London: Rider Books.

Coholic, D (2010) *Arts Activities for Children and Young People in Need*. London: Jessica Kingsley.

Cowie, H, Boardman, C, Dawkins, J & Jennifer, D (2004) *Emotional Health and Wellbeing: A practical guide for schools*. London: Paul Chapman Publishing.

Csíkszentmihályi, M (2002) *Flow*. London: Rider Books.

Daniels, H (2001) *Vygotsky and Pedagogy*. London: Routledge.

Denholm, A (2008) *City Arts Goes to School*. Nottingham: City Arts (available from: http://www.city-arts.org.uk/userfiles/pdf/Back%20to%20School%208pp.pdf).

Dewson, S, Eccles, J, Tackey, ND & Jackson, A (2000) *Guide to Measuring Soft Outcomes and Distance Travelled*. Brighton: Institute for Employment Studies.

Department of Education (2003) *Every Child Matters*. Retrievable at: http://www.education.gov.uk/consultations/downloadableDocs/EveryChildMatters.pdf

Department of Health (2006) *Report of the Review of Arts and Health Working Group*. London: Department of Health.

Department of Health/Arts Council for England (2007) *A Prospectus for Arts and Health*. London: Arts Council.

Essler, V, Arthur, A & Stickley, T (2006) Using a school-based intervention to challenge stigmatizing attitudes and promote mental health in teenagers. *Journal of Mental Health*, *15*(2), 243–50.

Foucault, M (1995) *Discipline and Punish*. London: Vintage.

Griffiths, S (2008) The experience of creative activity as a treatment medium. *Journal of Mental Health*, *17*(1), 49–63.

Hadland, R & Stickley, T (2010) A community arts project for excluded teenagers. *Mental Health Practice*, *13*(6), 18–23.

Hall, C & Thomson, P (2007) Creative partnerships? Cultural policy and inclusive arts practice in one primary school. *British Educational Research Journal*, *33*(3), 315–29.

Hall, S (2010) Supporting mental health and wellbeing at a whole school level: Listening to and acting upon children's views. *Emotional and Behavioural Difficulties*, *15*(4), 323–39.

Harber, C (2004) *Schooling as Violence: How schools harm pupils and societies*. London: Routledge.

Haw, K & Hadfield, M (2011) *Video in Social Science Research: Functions and forms*. London: Routledge.

Heenan, D (2006) Art as therapy: An effective way of promoting positive mental health? *Disability & Society*, *21*(2), 179–91.

Liebmann, M (1990) *Art Therapy for Groups: A handbook of themes and games*. London: Routledge.

McNiff, S (2004) *Art Heals: How creativity cures the soul*. Boston, MA: Shambhala.

Mirza, M (Ed) (2006) *Culture Vultures: Is UK arts policy damaging the arts?* London: Policy Exchange.

O'Brien, A (2004) Teacher, mentor or role model? The role of the artist in community arts work with marginalised young people. *Change: Transformations in Education*, 7(2), 74–88.

Pink, S (2007) *Doing Visual Ethnography*. London: Sage.

Putnam, R (2001) *Bowling Alone: The collapse and revival of American community*. London: Simon & Schuster.

Rogers, A & Pilgrim, D (2003) *Mental Health and Inequality*. Basingstoke: Palgrave Macmillan.

Scott, M (2011) Working with creative partnerships. In E Sellman (Ed), *Creative Learning for Inclusion: Creative approaches to meet special needs* (pp. 42–54) London: Routledge.

Seligman, M (2003) *Authentic Happiness*. London: Nicholas Brealey Publishing.

Sellman, E (2009) Lessons learned: Student voice at a school for pupils experiencing social, emotional and behavioural difficulties. *Emotional and Behavioural Difficulties*, 14(1), 33–48.

Sellman, E (2011a) *Creative Learning for Inclusion: Creative approaches to meet special needs*. London: Routledge.

Sellman, E (2011b) Peer mediation services for conflict resolution in schools – What transformations in activity characterise successful implementation? *British Educational Research Journal*, 37(1), 45–60.

Servan-Schreibner, D (2005) *Healing Without Freud or Prozac*. London: Rodale International Ltd.

Slee, R, Tomlinson, S & Weiner, G (1998) *School Effectiveness for Whom?* London: Routledge.

Social Exclusion Unit (2004) *Mental Health and Social Exclusion: Social Exclusion Unit Report*. London: Office of the Deputy Prime Minister.

Staricoff, R (2004) Arts in Health: A review of the medical literature. *Research Report 36*. London: Arts Council for England.

Stickley, T & Duncan, K (2007) Art in Mind: Implementation of a community arts initiative to promote mental health. *Journal of Public Mental Health*, 6(4), 24–32.

Stickley, T & Duncan, K (2010) Learning about community arts. In V Tischler (Ed), *Mental Health, Psychiatry and the Arts: A teaching handbook* (pp. 101–10). Abingdon: Radcliffe.

Taylor, B & Houghton, N (2008) *Inspiring Learning in Galleries*. London: Engage.

Thiele, M & Marsden, S (2003) *Engaging Art: The Artful Dodgers Studio – A theoretical model of practice*. Melbourne: Jesuit Social Services.

Thomson, P (2008) *Doing Visual Research with Children and Young People*. London: Routledge.

Thomson, P, Hall, C & Sellman, E with Vincent, K (2011) *An Evaluation of Arts Projects Working with Young People Not in Education, Employment or Training: Project report*. Nottingham: University of Nottingham.

White, M (2006) Establishing common ground in community-based arts in health. *Journal of the Royal Society of Health, 126*(3), 128–33.

White, M (2008) Are we there yet? Towards an international exchange of practice in community-based Arts in Health. In A Lewis & D Doyle (Eds), *Proving the Practice* (pp. 96–107). Fremantle, Western Australia: DADAA.

White, M (2009) *Arts Development in Community Health: A social tonic.* Oxford: Radcliffe.

Wilson, P & Long, I (2009) *Big Book of Blob Trees.* Milton Keynes: Speechmark Publishing Ltd.

Woolf, F (1999) *Partnerships for Learning: A guide to evaluating arts education projects.* London: Arts Council England.

CHAPTER NINE

Art, Autoethnography, and the Use of Self

Brendan Stone

The 'I' has no story of its own that is not also the story of a relation – or set of relations – to a set of norms. Although many contemporary critics worry that this means there is no concept of the subject that can serve as the ground for moral agency and moral accountability, that conclusion does not follow. The 'I' is always to some extent dispossessed by the social conditions of its emergence. This dispossession does not mean that we have *lost the subjective ground for ethics.* (Butler, 2005: 8)

In this chapter I will describe my experience of designing and leading what might loosely be called an art and community project in which long-term users of mental health services, and undergraduates taking a degree in English, work together to produce a variety of creative representations of contemporary life and identity in a major British city. The project is called *Storying Sheffield* (2011), and its design emerged both from my research interests and my own story. My research interests centre around the representation of 'mental illness' in contemporary culture, with a particular focus on narrative and its links to human identity; my story includes my own experience as someone who has been using mental health services for 35 years.

I will say a little more about myself here, because the knowledge I have accrued through personal experience, refracted through the lenses of critical scholarship and conversations with friends and colleagues, has been important in informing the development of *Storying Sheffield*. I will also briefly discuss the way in which my own attempts at autoethnography using both video and text have influenced my thinking and practice.

My relationship with 'mental illness', or as I would prefer, madness and distress, has been marked by a growing understanding that the terms in which the self is defined and by means of which it is understood are vital orienting factors in determining how I am able to negotiate my own life and experience. To summarise briefly, and this is simply to describe a personal insight for which I make no claims to universality, I have moved over many years from thinking of myself as someone who is inherently dysfunctional – biologically or neurologically flawed in some fundamental manner – towards an understanding that my own madness and distress have causes rooted in experience, history, and oppression. I am now better able to articulate and understand where distress is rooted, and the purposes it served and serves. To coin a phrase, my journey of understanding has taken me from a model of the self as inherently deficient, to one in which: '… *bad things happened and drove me crazy*' (Read & Haslam, 2004). What is important for the purposes of this discussion, however, is not the particular *content* of this model of understanding, but that it represents a way of thinking about the self which I find easier to live with, a way that is enabling rather than disabling.

This journey towards a model of understanding, or a story, which I can inhabit comfortably, has not been an easy one, and here I can move from the purely personal to an observation which has, I would argue, wider implications. I have written elsewhere (Stone, 2010) of the way in which the dominant model of understanding madness and distress – that is to say, the biomedical story of 'mental illness' – may colonise distressed individuals' self-conceptions. We may come to know ourselves through this story alone, which because of its dominance, its authorisation by powerful and often vested interests, can occlude and silence alternative understandings (Beresford, 2005). However, in emphasising a narrative colonisation in which the terms of self-description are imposed rather than chosen, I am certainly not suggesting that it is illegitimate for an individual to frame their experiences by means of the medical model of illness. What I do wish to argue for is the necessity of individuals being helped to understand that they have a choice in how they conceive of their distress. It is the absence of *choice*, rather than which particular model of understanding an individual chooses, which I want to highlight as deleterious here. Yet, even though I am arguing that an individual's choice to understand their distress by means of the medical model must be respected, my argument is still contentious, and possibly controversial to those with much invested in declaiming the scientific legitimacy of the medical model. The paradigm I am outlining here draws heavily on a model of human identity as narrative in nature, and owes much to the work of theorists such as Paul Ricoeur (1984, 1991, 1992) and Anthony Kerby (1991). By describing the medical model as only one of several narratives which an individual might choose to live within, I am implicitly disputing its scientific basis and emphasising the contingency and plurality of narrative understanding.

In addition, and in terms of self-representation, those of us who have used services for many years are well used to 'giving an account of ourselves' (Butler, 2005), yet the terms in which the account may be outlined are often to varying degrees delimited. We will probably be well accustomed to accounting for ourselves to our general practitioners, psychiatrists, psychologists, social workers, occupational therapists, benefits advisers and others; and the call for a narrative to which we respond will contain various powerful subtexts, often unspoken, the chief of which is a demand that we describe the extent of our dysfunction, the nature of our deficit. It is not surprising, then, that we may come to think of ourselves in these terms, come to describe ourselves, even *to* ourselves, in the language of lack, trouble, inadequacy, and failure.

Given the pervasiveness of stories which emphasise deficit, and the cultural dominance of a single story through which to interpret madness and distress, it is by no means straightforward for individuals to achieve a critical distance in order to examine these narratives, consider whether they are helpful and achieve a narrative 'fit' with their experience, and possibly engage with, perhaps even adopt and inhabit, alternative narrative paradigms for conceptualising the self. Yet, if one works within a narrative model of human identity there are possibilities for individuals to shift the ground of self-definition. Central to Ricoeur's work is the idea that narrative identity proceeds by way of 'innovations' – new models of understanding embodied in narrative forms and content. In this, the potential for agency and change is contained in this paradigm of identity: the individual is able to create new stories and ways of storytelling through which to understand the self, and by means of which, to live. However, and critically, Ricoeur (1991: 25) also stresses that 'the work of imagination does not come out of nowhere'; innovation, he asserted, 'remains a rule-governed behaviour … tied in one way or another to the models handed down by tradition'. The reader will be able to see in this qualification that a narrative model of identity negotiates a path between the polarities of subjectivity as either 'sheer change [or] absolute identity' (p. 33). The self is conceived neither as 'an incoherent series of events', as outlined in 'hard' versions of postmodern theory, nor, as in traditional accounts of selfhood, as an 'immutable substantiality, impervious to evolution' (p. 32). Rather, selfhood is conceived as an event, achieving identity through the dynamic processes of narrative composition.

Ricoeur named the 'models handed down by tradition' 'sedimentation', and it is the sedimented accumulation of past narratives and narrative forms from which innovation emerges. Moreover, sedimentation itself comprises material which had once been innovative, but came in time to be accepted and integrated into tradition. Notwithstanding the power imbalance between, for instance, the biomedical story and alternative modes of understanding distress, we can nevertheless see in this dialectic a model for changing not only the individual narrative, but also the narrative field on which innovations can draw. My own journey from one model to another came about precisely through exposure to alternative explanations; these included the trauma model of distress (Herman, 1992), but also my contacts with other survivors who had learned to critique the medical model and develop their own frameworks of understanding. It was through such contacts and study that I came to formulate a story which not only fitted with my experience, but also had the effect of freeing me from a uni-dimensional approach to selfhood in which I only defined myself in terms of difficulty and disability. After all, if we become acutely distressed because people do bad things to us, or because of the cultural oppressions which surround us, then there is a real sense in which our supposedly dysfunctional behaviour is in fact a mark of our sanity. Moreover, if we understand our 'symptoms' as evidence of distress rather than an inherent flaw, then we may feel more able to see ourselves as intensely 'normal', part of the continuum of normal human existence in which we understand that oppression, trauma and discrimination produce distress.

Before moving on, it is important that I stress one further implication of the narrative model of identity. Because creation *ex nihilo* is impossible, at the heart of this framework is the recognition that in charting identity, the individual needs others. Others' stories and insights, both written and verbal, informal and formal, and alternative accounts of the world and existence, form the resources on which we can draw. This model of independence achieved through *inter*dependence (Brison, 2002), through, indeed, dialogue and interaction, perhaps challenges some of the implicit ramifications of the medical model, which emphasises the *singularity* of the dysfunctional self. Rather than interdependence, the medical model could be seen as inculcating dependence – on the expertise of others, on authoritative stories which must be introjected wholesale. And of course, because of the dominance and power of the medical model in Western culture, alternative understandings are less available to us.

It was through engaging in artistic endeavour that I discovered the insidious nature of the dominant understandings of mental illness, and how, despite what I saw as my own more critical insights, these continued to influence my personal worldview. A few years ago I made a short film entitled *SCH!ZO*. The film is 'artistic' rather than a documentary, narrative, or discursive artefact: it included poetry, music and imagery designed to signify aspects of my experience of living with madness and distress. It was originally made as a teaching aid. I was teaching some social work students on a course which involved students meeting with and learning from a variety of service users, including individuals who used mental health services. My colleague and I wanted students to hear how individuals represented and understood their own experiences, and to use this knowledge alongside more traditional forms such as those encountered in textbooks and lectures. I would identify myself as both academic and service user in the hope that this might encourage students to question divisions between those who use services and those who provide them.

The process of making the video, however, became something more than just constructing a teaching aid. To undertake an 'artistic' endeavour one tends to employ a way of thinking which is different to that which is used in intellectual work. In artistic work, one may find that 'deep' narratives which usually lie underneath conscious awareness because they are so ingrained become more 'visible'. When I had finished the film and watched it, I began to realise that it showed me things about my self-conceptions which I had not previously understood. While the film was intended to be a critical tracing of where the self and culture meet (see, for example, the ironic title), in other words, a creative manifestation of autoethnography (or of *autoethnographic poetics,* to borrow from Denzin, 1997), I saw that other, more obscure, stories were told by the film, which I had not consciously intended to place there. The most significant of these insights emerged from noticing that I am completely on my own in the film. The film centres on repeated images of a solitary self, for the most part sitting alone in a darkened room watching his own image in a mirror. There are no images of others included, and while the poem in the film included references to a wider cultural context, the overall impression I received from watching my own production was of an extremely isolated individual, with his 'illness' linked mainly to a dysfunctional self rather than to any other factors. In addition, the film centred solely on the manifestations of distress. Why, I asked myself, did I limit my self-conception in this way? It was true that I had set out to make a film about distress, yet in its relentless focus, its complete lack of reference to the broader textures of my life, relationships, and interests, viewing it evoked an artistic version of the accounts given in clinical encounters, in which the patient-narrator is only authorised to frame their experience within a limited set of perspectives. It was as if I had internalised this frame of reference, had acted as an authoritative arbiter of what was and wasn't permitted to be represented.

I began to show the film at events and conferences, but I also included a commentary in which I discussed the implications of this solitary self-image, and added to the artistic representation some critical material about the ways in which dominant narrative modes can insinuate themselves into our understanding. What is interesting to me now as I think back to this moment, is that if I had not made the film I would not have realised that this was true for me personally. If I had been asked to present to a conference on my own self-conception using traditional academic forms, I would not have understood what I now see to be a central truth about my own development and life story – the belief that I existed in a solitary realm and that my so-called dysfunction and symptoms were a function of the self, rather than linked in any way to my culture and history. This lack of insight perdured, despite my having had various therapies over a number of years, some of them excellent in their own ways. Yet, and equally important I think, is that, having made the film, I was then able to critically interpret the film, and to articulate that critique, as a result of my knowledge, academic training, and research. What resulted, in the presentations of the film along with the critical commentary, was indeed a form of autoethnography, a form which was continually being reinvigorated by discussions with audiences including other survivors.

It was shortly after making this film that I began to explore the possibility of developing what eventually became *Storying Sheffield*. The insights I had gained through research, conversations with and the work of other survivors, my own academic writing, artistic endeavours, and personal experience, all of these informed the project, but perhaps some of the most important lessons I had learned were those gleaned in the making of *SCH!ZO*. It is also true that, as with that film, the design of the course revealed some of its origins and influences *post facto*, which is to say, that while my account here may seem to imply a project which had been consciously tailored according to a number of insights and imperatives, in fact the influences behind the course seemed to have often operated at a more intuitive level.

Storying Sheffield was born from a University of Sheffield initiative called The Inclusive Learning and Teaching Project.[1] This initiative is concerned with issues of inclusivity, diversity and equality within the curriculum; in my own university department we identified a need to try and diversify the student body, and to engage meaningfully with local communities. *Storying Sheffield* was envisaged as an elective credit-bearing course which would form part of the undergraduate degree in English but would also be open to people from the city, particularly people from groups underrepresented in UK Higher Education. Because of my research interests, and my contacts in mental health, we decided that the course would concentrate on recruiting long-term users of mental health services. Of course, the well-documented chronic social exclusion experienced by many service users meant that this group of people fitted with the brief for the project; however, I was also well aware of this personally. Having left school at 16 when distress first made a significant impact in my life, I subsequently spent nearly 20 years unemployed, on disability benefits, or in casual or menial short-lived jobs. In my mid-thirties I took a part-time access course and it was this return to education which eventually helped me to create a more fulfilling life.

The focus of *Storying Sheffield* is learning about, and then creating, artistic representations and narratives about everyday life, and lives, in Sheffield, with an emphasis on both identity and place. Service users are registered as (short-course) students of the university, and study and work together with undergraduates (long-course students). In the first half of the course, seminars typically include a presentation by an academic or artist on a variety of related topics, which then leads participants into working creatively, usually in small mixed groups, with the ideas outlined. In the particular course I am discussing here, sessions included presentations on Sheffield film; the history of the imagination; personal maps; the sociological and cultural significance of objects; and novel writing. In the latter stages of the course, as participants' ideas become more developed, seminars are increasingly devoted to collaborative workshops in which a variety of artefacts are finalised in preparation for a public exhibition of the work produced. There is no requirement for short-course students wishing to take the course to have any particular level of educational attainment or artistic experience. In introductory meetings it is stressed that the course was designed to draw out and help participants present the textures of everyday lives and histories, with part of the role of the long-course students being enablers – working with short-course students on the creation of artefacts. Indeed, potential

---

1. http://www.sheffield.ac.uk/lets/projects/inclusivelandt

participants are told that they would contribute to the course as much as they would take from it, with this emphasis intended to highlight their expertise in their own lives and experiences.

There is no reason why the course could not work with other individuals and groups, as there was no focus on issues around mental health in its planned (or actual) content. Indeed, this absence was critical in the conceiving of the course – and, I would hazard, to its success – in that, and referring back to the previous discussions, I wished to avoid as far as possible giving any signs that the course was authorising or calling for particular kinds of stories. A central idea behind the course, influenced by the work of theorists such as Michel de Certeau (1984), is that everyday life – and lives – are worthy of attention, study, and artistic representation, and that the everyday physical spaces we inhabit can be re-imagined, or re-narrated perhaps, in a process which de Certeau described as a form of tacit resistance to inimical spatial and narrative paradigms. Thus, while the project actively recruits service users, and helps participants to create representations of their lives and their city, there is no emphasis placed on illness, dysfunction, or treatment. Participants choose how they represent their lives, and which aspects of their experience they wish to highlight. In the course reported here, some short-course students did indeed produce powerful artefacts engaging with their experience of distress and mental health services, but others chose to depict other aspects of their lives and identities: holidays, giving birth, their neighbourhood, their aspirations. In addition, some short-course students included in their work mention of their experience with distress and services, but with this implied and outlined as only one small facet of a life.

The emphasis on place – the 'Sheffield' in *Storying Sheffield* – remained central to the course, and to the thinking behind it. Perhaps this does not immediately appear significant, but I would argue that it orients the focus of the course away from a paradigm in which inwardness and the autobiographical impulse are unanchored in material reality, and towards an engagement with the way in which self, space, and culture interanimate each other. Given what I have said above about the tendency for the distressed self to be isolated from culture by and through dominant discourses about mental health and illness, it will be clear why this strand of the course was important as a counterweight, and to help produce a range of representational options from which participants could choose to imagine personal experience. Consonant with work in cultural geography, therefore, participants were encouraged to engage in creative and critical ways with the spaces they knew and inhabited, that is, to quote Roland Lippuner (2004), to explore how '... people in their everyday life understand the geographical world, and how they represent it to themselves and to others'. A variety of exercises and activities included the drawing of maps of the areas in which students lived, in which places of personal importance were highlighted and annotated. In addition, small mixed teams of students drew maps of the city collaboratively, again annotating them, with the result that different pictures of the same geographical space were produced in a single artefact. Small teams of long-course students were sent to randomly allocated areas of the city, chosen because of their unfamiliarity to most undergraduates, and tasked to deliver a creative representation of their journeys and explorations to the whole class. Tyrone, a short-course student, worked with two long-course students, Jess and Kate, on a film in which he returned to the suburb of Arbourthorne where he had previously been a youth worker, and soundtracked the film with a reflective and moving commentary on both memory and physical space.[2] In all of these activities and others, the city was, in differing ways, defamiliarised or re-imagined. Moreover, in bringing these varying representations and perspectives together, in both the classroom and then in the end-of-course exhibition, an effect was created which was greater than the sum of its parts, in which the city and its spaces were re-envisaged in multiple and diverse ways, yet with these pluralities seeming in some unforced manner to cohere. This whole might be imagined as a 'discordant concordance', as Ricoeur designated the way in which plot weaves together disparate events into a recognisable and meaningful entity, or, in de Certeau's terms (1984, p. 93), as a 'manifold story' composed from '… networks of … moving, intersecting writings … shaped out of fragments of trajectories and alterations of spaces'.

Emphasising the focus of the project on connection and collaboration, several art works were displayed to which all or most participants contributed, with this motif also offsetting, perhaps, the individualising tendencies of both traditional autobiographical work, and also of the biomedical story. These works included a wedding dress decorated with images of participants and staff; a cabinet of spoons, each contributed, personalised and decorated by participants; a display of mugs, each one again contributed by individuals, and with each mug containing a text or image fragment representing an aspect of personal identity; and a hanging mobile decorated with text and image fragments in which participants meditated on Sheffield. Moreover, individual works, which ostensibly represented aspects of a single life, were also collaboratively produced to varying extents. All participants on the course – both short- and long-course – cooperated and were co-producers of the work and the exhibition, with this focus facilitating a subtle but important

---

2. http://www.storyingsheffield.com/video-fragments

critical element to the work produced, in which initial creative impulses were afforded the space and time to be re-examined and perhaps reworked.

The public exhibition of the artefacts produced during the course was a remarkable success, but it also embodied several key elements to the project, namely: the highlighting of connections and echoes between individual narratives; the sense that participants' creations were all contributing to a single web or tapestry of diverse representations; the central role of collaborative working relationships; and the agency and responsibility given to students to take charge of the direction of the project. The exhibition exemplified what had been gradually built up during the workshops; the sense that the project had created a distinct identity, made up by and embodied in the diverse stories of and relationships between the participants. What had been produced was both a series of art works and stories, and, to use another of Ricoeur's concepts (1984: 246), 'a cloth woven of stories told'. That this had emerged according to the vision and motivations of the participants, rather than by way of directives from those who worked on the course, lent the whole an authenticity which undoubtedly captivated many of the people who viewed it.[3]

It is interesting to note that those short-course students who did choose to represent distress often produced work with a highly critical sensibility, in which the experience of distress was set against or within the context of broader sociocultural or political considerations. Thus, for instance, Paul's paintings wittily depict bizarre landscapes and scenes in which madness is exemplified in, and the product of, oppressive or violent actions and policies;[4] while Kathryn's installations and objects frequently critique the services with which she has had to negotiate, while also maintaining an ironising and cutting stance serving to emphasise the craziness of the mental health system.[5] Both these artists' work contain elements of autoethnography, in that they bring together representations of intensely personal experience with an analysis of how the personal is inflected with and refracted through – perhaps constructed by – culture. Kathryn produced a suite of work, using objects, food, text, and video. While some of her work engaged directly with the mental health system, she also made pieces which represented aspects of her family history such as the moving short film *The Ordinary House*.[6] Taken as a whole, Kathryn's work effects a nuanced engagement with identity and

---

3. http://www.storyingsheffield.com/exhibition http://www.storyingsheffield.com/exhibition-feedback
4. http://www.storyingsheffield.com/paul-art
5. http://www.storyingsheffield.com/objects-page-2; http://www.storyingsheffield.com/food
6. http://www.storyingsheffield.com/video-fragments

culture, and the sense of a life critically examined and imagined. Working with Matt, a long-course student, Paul also produced a film, the extraordinary *Institute Dentamental*, in which he wittily interrogated his own prejudices and the stigma against people with mental health problems.[7] The film was set in the day centre Paul uses, and it featured performances by staff and other service users. While *Institute Dentamental* is focused on a different subject to that which I addressed in *SCH!ZO*, it is still instructive to note some of the differences. Paul's work focused on specific geographical contexts – both the day centre and the city itself – and it had as a central dramatic component Paul's relationships with others. Moreover, the creative impulse behind the film was directly focused on exploring the crucial issue of self-stigmatisation, whereas *SCH!ZO* only revealed to me the mechanisms of self-stigma *after* it had been made. While Paul's film conveyed isolation, it managed to do this from a critical distance, in part by the incorporation of a framing narrative.

Other work which focused on distress or the use of services included Helen's remarkable art and writing, in which Biblical and mythical imagery and motifs played an important role.[8] Helen's work was arranged in the form of a display, which taken as a whole produced glimpses of a life narrative. The display included collages of newspaper cuttings, and charred documents taken from a house fire from which Helen, too, had been rescued. The overall impression was of the artist setting acute distress within a shared framework of meaning, and in addition piecing together the disparate fragments of a life in order to produce and communicate a meaningful narrative. Similarly, Sue chose to represent aspects of her life using storyboards which represented the story of her career, marriage, and distress, using collages of images arranged into timelines.[9] As with Helen's work, the overall impression was of an ongoing negotiation in which understandings of meaning, cause, and effect were being formed.

Some participants included only passing reference to their experience of distress, and with these framed within creative renditions of the broad contexts of their lives and histories. For instance, working with Dawn, a long-course student, Harold produced an installation entitled 'Where I Live' which communicated a moving and whimsical sense of his life, his history, and neighbourhood using audio, household objects, images and text.[10] In his audio and handwritten text narrative Harold speaks of the street on which

---

7. http://www.storyingsheffield.com/video-fragments
8. http://www.storyingsheffield.com/helen
9. http://www.storyingsheffield.com/sue
10. http://www.storyingsheffield.com/more-prose

he lives and the other people who have also lived there. Included in the narrative is this brief mention of distress:

> Our next-door neighbours were the Halls. Anne is a school teacher and Chris was a mechanic. We get on fine. They had two children, Victoria and Richard. In the year 1989 I had a breakdown, and Anne used to counsel me for a good two years, and I will always be grateful to her for that. We get on fine. Anne used to live in Ecclesfield before she was married. Her father used to own a butcher's shop.

Roy, a short-course student, who worked with Nicola, produced a book entitled *Memory Man*, containing several vignettes from his life.[11] These included an amusing and brilliantly rendered account of an encounter with a psychiatrist, and also passages which evinced his involvement in trade unionism and labour politics, and his interests in sport and poetry. Introducing the section titled 'A Visit to the Psychiatrist', the text firmly locates this encounter within a socio-cultural context:

> Now eighteen months on, with another employer, I was last in and would be first out. To cap it all, my daughter was knocked over on Christmas Eve. I believed it to be my fault – if my wife had not become a market trader to help us out financially, they would never have been crossing the road, and it would never have happened. Under these circumstances, I asked my doctor to refer me to a psychiatrist.

Readers are recommended to read Roy's witty account of his subsequent encounter with 'Dr Parkin' which subtly lampoons clinical authority and expertise. But my point here is that both Roy and Harold choose to frame and situate their experiences of distress within detailed and textured renditions of their lives. By doing so, in different ways they delineate distress as connected to their histories, and the contexts of their lives and cultures.

The range of works produced by participants included many which were of an obviously autoethnographic nature, some of which I have commented on above. It is interesting to reflect on where this critical impulse emerged from, and also why, and by what means, short-course students felt confident and secure enough to explore themes of distress within unfamiliar, large, university workshop environments, collaborating with people with very different backgrounds and experiences. My own sense is that these particular stories were at least in part able to emerge because of the structures and principles of the project. One reason, ironically in my view, is that this

---

11. http://www.storyingsheffield.com/memory-man

happened precisely because the course did not attempt to define participants by categorising them as anything other than residents of the city, and as much as possible avoiding constructing a set narrative frame within which participants were authorised to speak and signify. The fact of participants' service use was not hidden (a key worker accompanied several of them each week), but neither was it emphasised. Moreover, in introductory meetings with short-course students I discussed my reasoning (and the arguments set out in this chapter) and whether this was a helpful or unhelpful strategy, and all students were aware of my long history of service use and distress. The ultimate aim was to create an environment in which short-course students were treated as students of the university and residents of the city, while at the same time acknowledging and allowing distress and the use of services to be discussed and represented freely as *aspects* of a life. It was notable that both groups of students were quickly able to accept and work within this model without difficulty.

Short-course students' work which did not mention distress, or did so only fleetingly such as in Harold's installation, itself may implicitly testify to an autoethnographic impulse. After all, when given free rein to represent their lives and experiences, that short-course students framed distress as either a minor aspect or one not even worth mentioning, and did so in a context where their service use was not hidden but not emphasised either, would seem itself to be a powerful statement about the ways in which people with very long histories of using services view what is important to them. The exhibition, at which all the work was collected and displayed, made this very tangible to those who attended. The overall effect was one of rich diversity, a multi-layered fabric woven from participants' representations, in which stories were told of holidays, families, dancing, and gardening alongside those which spoke of distress.

In conclusion, *Storying Sheffield* has the notion of narrative representation as an important theme. I was concerned to emphasise throughout the course that 'fragments' can be more valuable and revelatory than 'complete' or 'coherent' stories. In part this emphasis emerged from an engagement with the work of 'narrative sceptics' such as Galen Strawson (2004), who have argued that contrary to the fashionable academic view that human life and experience is somehow intrinsically narrative in nature, many individuals do not experience themselves in this way, but rather relate to life in an 'episodic', more fragmented, or image-based manner. In a related vein, Judith Butler has argued in her important work, *Giving an Account of Oneself*, that what she calls 'enigmatic articulations' may be more likely to produce 'the truth of the person' than a seamless, coherent autobiography. She contends that such articulations are characterised by 'moments of interruption, stoppage, open-endedness', and 'cannot easily be translated into narrative form' (Butler, 2005: 71).

For some, and I count myself in this group, the notion of selfhood as being bound to the story of a life may be a deeply unappealing prospect. Thus I tried to avoid any implication that subjectivity needed to be conceptualised as 'whole' or 'complete' – or wholly 'known' and 'understood' – before it could be represented. Indeed, in line with Butler's argument, the emphasis in *Storying Sheffield* on valuing and collecting fragments and images led to many powerful artefacts being produced, sometimes through a sustained engagement with one such fragment, and at others simply through the presentation of the fragment itself. In line with what I have argued for here, participants were encouraged to study and engage with the fine grain of their experience, their everyday lives, and the city in which they lived. This permission to select a moment, or episode, or a taken-for-granted aspect of a life, and to spend time and attention on mining its significance and aesthetic potential not only was an implicit corrective to an over-concentration on the concept of the 'story', but also tacitly asserted that the fabric and minutiae of everyday life is valuable and can form the basis of artistic work with merit and interest. While this idea is, I would argue, an important one in itself, it may have a particular importance and significance for individuals whose lives and identities have in greater or lesser part been defined as lacking value, or been subsumed within a powerful narrative of failure and deficit.

References

Beresford, P (2005) Social approaches to madness and distress: User perspectives and user knowledges. In J Tew (Ed), *Social Perspectives in Mental Health: Developing social models to understand and work with mental distress* (pp. 32–52). London: Jessica Kingsley.

Brison, S (2002) *Aftermath: Violence and the remaking of a self*. Princeton, NJ: Princeton University Press.

Butler, J (2005) *Giving an Account of Oneself*. New York: Fordham University Press.

De Certeau, M (1984) *The Practice of Everyday Life*. Berkeley, CA: University of California Press.

Denzin, NK (1997) *Interpretive Ethnographics: Ethnographic practices for the 21st century*. London: Sage.

Herman, J (1992) *Trauma and Recovery*. New York: Basic Books.

Kerby, A (1991) *Narrative and the Self*. Bloomington, IN: Indiana University Press.

Lippuner, R (2004) *Culture, Space and Everyday Life*. Revised manuscript of a speech given to the 30th Congress of the International Geographical Union (IGU), Glasgow, 19.08.2004, available online at http://www.uni-jena.de/Roland_Lippuner.html

Read, J & Haslam, N (2004) Public opinion: Bad things happen and can drive you crazy. In J Read, L Mosher & R Bentall (Eds), *Models of Madness: Psychological, social and biological approaches to schizophrenia* (pp. 133–46). Hove: Brunner-Routledge.

Ricoeur, P (1984) *Time and Narrative, Vol 3* (Trans, K McLaughlin & D Pellauer). Chicago: University of Chicago Press.

Ricoeur, P (1991) Life in quest of narrative. In D Wood (Ed), *On Paul Ricoeur* (pp. 20–33). London: Routledge.

Ricoeur, P (1992) *Oneself as Another* (Trans, K Blamey). Chicago: University of Chicago Press.

Stone, B (2010) An anti-discriminatory approach to therapy with seriously distressed clients. In C Lago & B Smith (Eds), *Anti-discriminatory Counselling and Psychotherapy Practice* (2nd ed, pp. 75–85) London: Sage.

Storying Sheffield (2011) University of Sheffield. Online: http://www.storyingsheffield.com/

Strawson, G (2004) Against narrativity. *Ratio, 17*(4), 428–52.

CHAPTER TEN

Film, Fractals, and Emergent Themes

Shaun & Marian Naidoo

Working across and alongside Arts, Health and Education has been something that we have been doing for longer than we can remember. In this time we have helped with and developed pioneering methods and encouraged people and organisations to embrace creativity, to develop critical and inquiring capabilities, and to find ways to improve what they do. In particular, work involving those who use and deliver mental health services has brought additional key challenges and issues to address. Here are some examples:

- to address the profound negative influence of the stigma attached to mental illness and in particular amongst younger and older people
- to ensure that healthcare professionals show respect for and treat with dignity those who experience mental health problems while delivering an inclusive and responsive approach to care and wellbeing
- to encourage the growing recognition by healthcare professionals of the positive value that creative participation has on the lives of people who are constantly engaged in the process of well-becoming
- to develop new ways in which a sustainable approach to improvement can be achieved that has critical co-creative inquiry at its core, to encourage learning and the confidence to put that learning into practice.

In this chapter we shall attempt to show how on our journey as researchers we have developed our own way of using video to contribute towards achieving this. Today, as film and video use become more accessible, increasing numbers of researchers are beginning to recognise the potential for its use within qualitative research. We will discuss how our use of film and video in qualitative research has developed from our initial recognition of the importance of video as a data collection tool to its relevance within different research methodologies and its place in the presentation of research outcomes.

Our recent work has been within healthcare, with people who use services and those providing services, but its roots go back beyond that.

Video has long been used as a tool by media journalists to evidence their journalistic inquiries. The power of the medium of video is evident in everything from vox pops to full-blown documentaries crafted by editors in order to communicate the relevant 'angle', and hammer home their discourses to maximise impact on the viewer.

We started using video over 30 years ago (1979) when as theatre practitioner/researchers we wanted to capture as much as possible of the human dynamic contained in the communication of the individual narrative. Using video then wasn't easy; the equipment was cumbersome and required much effort to carry long distances on public transport. Our research involved filming the stories and perceptions of young people who were first-, second- and third-generation Asians living in Southall in London. The research explored their perceptions and struggles with the cultural conflict that helped to both inform and confuse their identities as British-born Asians, living in a British culture while dealing with strong South Asian cultural values that they and their predominantly nuclear families retained. We asked them: '*What is it like being a British Asian in today's society?*'

We wanted to both capture their stories as individuals and groups and also record the context in which they lived. The effort, however, was worth it as we were able to capture on tape the rich depth of their lived experience and perceptions. We were also able to capture what they felt was important to them within the community in which they lived. We would often 'hand the camera over' so that they could take it away and record from their perspective and to add their own commentary as they recorded.

For us, as very young and raw researchers, video was the best way in which we could evidence our research. The intention was to then '*decodify and then recodify*' this evidence (Freire, 1970) by devising and performing a theatre piece based on the process.

As we set about reviewing and analysing the data it became clear that much of it should and could be used in the theatre in its raw state. The 'data' was real; there was something in its rawness that didn't need art to reflect life, but as a slice of life itself it held its own robustness and validity. This was used both as part of and supporting the theatre content using a mixed-media approach to presentation and performance. We applied Freire's educational philosophy to inform the relationship between form and content, based on the authentic footage, and the outputs of the process of research became embedded in the outcome/report/performance. This was, at that time, both innovative and groundbreaking.

It was this experience that started a long journey in refining and developing the use of video within the research process and the presentation of research outcomes. Over the years we have developed new insights into ways of using different methodologies in our exploration of how this can be done.

Film is a valuable asset to qualitative researchers. On an individual level it can record the richness of individual stories and across a larger project it can be used to evidence emergent themes and patterns while remaining authentic to its primary source.

In the process of communicating the narrative of the individual, the written word cannot fully convey what is happening, particularly within a creative environment. The written word can be restrictive; we miss the subtleties of seeing the relationships being played out before us. So much of what we communicate is through body language: how we respond with gestures and glances, silence, pauses and how we place ourselves in relation to each other and within space. Even how we enter and leave a space can speak volumes. Watching how people react and interact can also communicate the nature of any relational dynamic that is present in the moment. Sometimes these are fleeting moments where a particular spark or connection can be profoundly evident. Eisner (1995) also placed emphasis on the potential for achieving greater understanding that may be difficult to express in words.

Film, therefore, plays a major role in our practice as researchers. It is an alternative way to communicate, collect and record our data, and share our experience of the relational dynamics and the subtleties of the individual narrative within the 'present' context. It uncovers the multifaceted identities that people play within their roles and interactions, while at the same time identifying the authenticity behind the values that drive people.

Our personal journey as research practitioners has been one of self-inquiry, as we hold ourselves to account for living our values in our practice. This can be equated to our work in the theatre. Theatre is many things artistically but it is also a means by which we are connected to our living values through our practice, engaged in constant self-inquiry.

As theatre practitioners it was a natural step for us to create a performance piece as a way of communicating. The performance of texts developed from research data can also be used as part of the inquiry itself. Since 1979 we have used this process as part of our developing research methodology. When we talk about theatre we mean what theatre is to us. Theatre is play, learning, drama, dance, music, singing, visual arts, and video, which can be included in its raw form or shaped, for passive engagement. It can even be crafted in a design to help others engage actively in the process of creative endeavour and/or to communicate self and self in relation to other. The permutations that theatre can adopt make it both a flexible and responsive medium that is empathic, compassionate, and a critical catalyst. This sentiment has been illustrated by McIntyre and Cole (2001):

> Performance of the research text is an embodiment and representation of the inquiry process as well as a new process of active learning. The possibility of active learning in each performance or recreation of the text exists through our ongoing commitment to maintaining the conditions of our relationship. Each performance is an experiential basis for reflection, analysis, and learning because in relationship we are 'participants-as-collaborators' (Lincoln, 1993, p. 42). Together we were able to draw out each other's knowledge and strength. (McIntyre & Cole, 2001: 43)

When we research we talk to people. We always start by having a conversation; it is in the conversation that much of the knowing and indeed much of the knowledge is created (Shaw, 2002). With traditional research methods the researcher stands outside the research and views the subject of the research from a distance as an object. We do this and in doing so develop methods of formulating questions to ask people. Often the questions can be open-ended or propositional; they already have a value embedded within that may reflect the thinking of the researcher or the designer of the questionnaire. Once the questions are asked and piloted we can go back and reformulate them in order to hone the questions and focus in a more accurate way. All of this is an accepted methodology. It can be both qualitative and quantitative. Some answers to the questions will be coded. This provides a statistically based picture and breakdown of the responses. When statistical analysis rules are applied in order to interpret the data, we create a summative analysis of these statistical patterns of opinions. At each stage a robust methodology is adopted in design and delivery. The design is led by the researcher, driven by the need to achieve an objective delivery of results. The researcher and the people involved have been reduced to objects in statistical conversions with added supporting statements.

When using video the researcher is able to capture much richer data, from the dynamics of a relationship through to perceptions and attitudes. Video records the way we move, how we look and also the very subtle nuances of personal behaviour and characteristics. It can show us not only how we 'perform' but also how we may feel about it. When analysing video data the researcher looks for similar patterns and these patterns can also be reflected statistically. The difference is that there are more layers to read as we witness the complexity involved in how people engage in developing and communicating their relational dynamics and demonstrate their living values in the moment. Video captures the richness of this complexity.

As theatre practitioners, we know well the value of this. We are trained to replicate behaviours and identify the subjective motivations that are behind certain behaviours and how they manifest themselves. We also seek to utilise our own values that are embedded in our practice to relate compassionately and responsively in an 'alongside way' with the subjects of the research. We constantly seek to understand both cognitively and emotionally how and why behaviours change and what personal process the individual engages in to effect changes in how they relate and what they learn from this. We seek also to embrace a multi-dimensional understanding of how they colour their perceptions in the moment. Video can pick this up and by doing so it will capture the life-affirming energy embodied within the individual and demonstrate how both individual and collaborative energy are used to contribute toward a relational dynamic with others.

We know that video will not capture everything and like the written word it is a 'restricted' medium. Video can, however, bring a richness and provide a portal in which we can witness the complex and multi-dimensional narrative of people.

The importance of the narrative/fractals

As we engage in qualitative research we acknowledge the profound impact that systems have on our personal and professional lives. Theories of organisations and management within organisations are traditionally based on organisational structure and systems. Over recent years, however, there has been a move towards recognising that organisations are made up of people and that theories of organisations are theories of people. It is people who create the systems that manage and control many aspects of our behavioural thinking, feeling and life in general (McNiff, 2000). Organisations rely on the behaviour of people to run effectively and efficiently in a way that is productive.

The behaviour of people is something that contributes to the culture of an organisation, and, as such, will also demonstrate the values underpinning that organisation. When change is needed, organisations usually create plans to help formulate the structure upon which this change can occur; they create a new system. Project planning is a perfect example of how organisations can lay down a strategy, structure and appropriate systems for change. As a consequence we live in a highly complex world of interacting systems that objectify us, manage our behaviours and erode our authentic identities. Long-term project plans do not usually focus on individual narratives and their contribution to the collective culture. These narratives are the bridges between the personal and the professional and depend on the fuel of living one's values in a relational dynamic in order to enable the emergence of change and growth of self and self in relation to others. They represent the profound nuances that exist in personal and professional relationships and inform the needs of people in ways that structure and systems cannot affect. It is often our behaviours and how we practise that reveal our deeply embedded living values. Each of us has individual narratives that we are aware of (and some that we try to forget). These narratives affect how we behave, perceive our selves and perceive our self in relation to others. Often we will engage in an interesting contra-dynamic between our professional and personal identity, as we seek that within ourselves that is authentic and real. This is a living narrative that is continually changing. It informs how we relate and communicate with everyone around us; it informs the choices that we make and the actions that we take. In researching with video within a particular culture/s we often find patterns emerging from the data. These patterns (or fractals) reinforce the values we live by. So when we develop our analysis we not only identify the fractals but also retain the primary evidence to support the research report.

Video as evidence: Video as a real-time research tool

One of the most important aspects of video is its capability to gather real-time evidence of what people think and how people 'are' in the context of what they do. Video can record in real time, i.e., in the moment. For researchers this is an invaluable opportunity to log not only the perceptions of people but also their actions. These actions can often throw up new data that do not rely on recalled narratives or 'after the event' analysis of experience. So why should this be so valuable to the researcher? Our belief is that video applied in this context is able to demonstrate how people develop their actions, reactions and interactions within a relational dynamic. Use of video allows the researcher to irrefutably *capture* the application of living values while enabling them to track and capture the changes and development of both values and practice as the projects being researched progress, i.e., it can capture the learning, growth and transformation in relational dynamic capability. In many ways this requires very different skills to both interpretation and analysis of data. This is because video can record the points in the dynamic interface where discourses (usually absolute and based on systemic thinking and management) that sometimes occupy the behaviours and direction of an interaction, merge with relational dynamics. This is based on living values that are less absolute but nevertheless profoundly influential. In these circumstances the individual experiences themselves as a *'living contradiction'* (Whitehead, 1989); we are able to see and record this on video. It is also possible to record how effective the individual is in engaging self and others in developing new perceptions based on authentic living values in the relational dynamic that exists between those involved. This is creative living/learning in action. Video will capture behaviours that can be themed as enabling rather than disabling, harnessing rather than controlling, including rather than excluding. Video in this context provides real-time research data that is rich, multi-dimensional and is a reliable resource for researchers.

Video as a constructed medium/Video as a means of communicating research outcomes

When we use video in real-time contexts the camera will capture the subtleties of one's practice. If a researcher records video evidence/data, the researcher can develop, through analysis, the ability to identify patterns of behaviour and or perceptions. These patterns, as discussed earlier, when found to be repeated become themes. Themes when they emerge frequently enough become fractals. The term *fractal* is used in complexity theory to describe the repeated nature of a discourse or a discourse in practice. Over the years we have developed a system to log these fractals. In this way, within an organisation, for example, we can review the fractals in order to gauge the cultural signifiers within them.

When we are at the point where we need to report back the findings of our research we can use video to reconstruct these fractals to represent the research outcomes. Since the research outcomes are derived from a real-time primary resource, the authenticity of the data is self-evident. Video is also a powerful and effective way to communicate the research findings in a condensed form.

There remain some issues surrounding this process and in particular those of interpretation and quality of analysis. We recommend that other research tools are used to help triangulate the video evidence that has been developed. This serves to maintain a degree of reliability and robustness in the methodologies which include the use of video material. Recent developments have involved the concept of reconstruction. Reconstruction is where the video-maker uses the same robust approach to identify key themes and fractals that emerge in the analysis of the research data which are further represented via interpretation through the medium of video.

Using real-time video research material together with other data derived using traditional methods, the researcher can develop enough material to artistically construct the findings of the research through the medium of video. This method allows the researcher to merge analysis with interpretation. The creation of composite characters, for instance, is used by many performative social science researchers. Using the fractals from the primary research resource, researchers can create compositions of fractals within the one character. This model is based on the research approaches first developed in the 1960s by Theatre-in-Education and community theatre companies. The actor/citizen/researcher engages in a process of bringing together research material for the purpose of devising a theatre piece for performance with a specific community. Such theatre would often use video as well as participation as part of its delivery, using real-time video evidence or constructed video, based on real-time evidence.

Living theory action research

The development of living theory action research over recent years has brought about new opportunities for using video in research. This is an approach that involves researchers engaging in their own process of inquiry. Researchers record their progress using video, placing the researcher and the subject together as one, bringing together a robustness of critical self-inquiry designed to improve practice. This process includes sections about who they are and what they do. What is significant about this approach is that researchers can also use video to record and evidence their progression as they engage in a process of improving what they do. In living theory action research, the researcher can record their own narrative and demonstrate their practice while discussing what they are learning and discovering about the relationship between the researcher and the ways in which they develop their own practice.

We have detailed below a number of examples that describe how video in research can be used in creative ways as well as being a robust evidence-gathering methodology in the field of research.

Living theory

In the following extract from 2005, Marian described how video was used to help focus her practice and insights into her learning while studying for her Ph.D. She described how she was able to tap the richness of her learning via the video captured in order to help transform her values into living standards of judgement.

> *Throughout the period of this inquiry I have kept a video record of much of my work as part of my process of data collection. The more I looked at the video recordings the clearer I became about my practice, my embodied knowledge and the values I was living as part of my practice. I believed that creating a DVD of my practice that included insights into my values would help the process of transforming my values into living standards of judgement by which I would be more able to hold myself accountable. I also believed that engaging in this process in a transparent way would enable the validity of my work to be judged. Any claims I make within the writing of my thesis could be validated by seeing me living my values in practice.*
>
> *As I began the process of editing my material and creating a DVD, a process that lasted for a period of about four weeks in November 2003, I was at first almost overwhelmed by the amount of material I had amassed.*
>
> *I was initially daunted by the prospect of first of all watching all of this material and then creating something, in an artful way, that would have the potential to be informative and also would be able to communicate what I needed it to communicate. Not only was I overwhelmed by the material but also by the technology involved in this kind of editing process.*
>
> *We decided to approach the making of a DVD in the same creative and disciplined way I would begin a devising process. When devising we immerse ourselves in all the research material we have amassed and then apply ourselves to a process of dialectically engaging with the material. In this process we are not only aware of ourselves as 'living contradictions' (Whitehead, 1989) we are also able to create characters and scenarios where these contradictions are re-enacted in a creative form in order to engage and influence an audience. (Naidoo, 2005)*

Breaking Down the Walls of Silence

The project 'Breaking Down the Walls of Silence' was established to improve the quality of services provided to patients with dementia. As the project lead I wanted to develop a more inclusive way of working that placed the patients and their carers at the centre of the project. In our walk-talk discussions with each other in the opening clip we are expressing our delight at the way in which some of the patients and carers embraced this project and the welcome they gave us in accepting us into their homes and into their lives. In three clips Marian is interviewing patients with dementia and their carers in their homes. These particular clips have been selected because we believe that they are able to clearly communicate to those watching how Marian is living her values in her practice. The first clip communicates Marian's compassion by showing how she strives to live her embodied values of trust and love and respect for self and for others and that this is being communicated through the loving and trusting relationship that has been established.

The second clip shows Charlie reading a letter he had prepared for Marian. Charlie cares for his wife, (also called Marion, note the spelling), at home. Marion has Alzheimer's disease which is quite progressed and her ability to converse is limited. Charlie was anxious that he might leave something important out about his experience as a carer and how he had had to change in order to look after his wife. He was reading this letter out loud and Marian was listening to him and filming at the same time. Marian was very aware of Marion's body language. Marian was worried that she was losing Marion who was unable to take part in the conversation; it appeared that she was feeling excluded and as a consequence had become disengaged. Marion then catches Marian's eye and in a very beautiful moment of connection she makes a grand gesture behind Charlie's back. This moment captured on video communicates the trust and respect and the responsive and inclusional nature of the relationship. (Naidoo, 2005)

Changing role of nursing

In this research we were asked by the Welsh National Assembly to look at the role of the nurse and the impact that changes in nurse training have had on the profession. We amassed a great deal of material in our literature search for this project. We wanted to capture both the feelings of those working in the profession and the feelings of the members of the public who used health services as raw grass-root data. This qualitative evidence was captured on video. Semi-structured interviews were used and emergent themes and fractals were identified. A selection of videos was kept for use in the delivery of the project report. The main evidence, once triangulated with the reports and literature, was offered as the primary data source for a devising process in the creation of three characters.

> In some of the work involved in the research project 'I Am Because We Are', we interwove selected clips from the interviews we conducted as part of the research for this project with clips from the characters in the game show we devised to communicate the research findings. These video clips have again been chosen because of the significance we placed on them in relation to their specific contribution to our learning and our growing understanding of our practice and the values that inform our practice. In this context we feel we are able to demonstrate the importance we place on working in an inclusional and responsive way. We do this by including the voices of those contributing to the research captured on video and also by the construction of a theatre form that allows the audience to participate in the theatre itself. The performance of these three characters also enables us to communicate the empathic relationship we have developed with those we are portraying.
>
> The first character, April, communicates the stereotypes with which many people we talked to still see nursing and nurses. This was often in conflict with what those interviewed said was their experience when they were patients. The question of identity was a big issue for nurses, patients and those responsible for the development of nurse education.
>
> The character of May, a newly graduated nurse, is grappling with the decision of whether to stay working as a nurse, a job she feels passionate about, or to take up the offer of a lucrative position with a pharmaceutical company.
>
> The initial response from the audience to the character June was laughter as they recognised her from their own experience. The laughter of recognition is very important as it allows me as an actor playing the character to engage with the audience and the character I am portraying and to fully express my empathy with the character. June's voice represents the voices of many nurses who we interviewed who expressed their frustration at not being able to do what they felt intuitively they wanted to do. They expressed their frustration at being locked into a system that only seemed to value outcome in the form of waiting times, delays, waiting lists and discharges.
>
> People we talked to about their experience as patients talked about the need to be cared for while in hospital. They needed to be supported and their expectation was that that was the nurse's role, but their experience was that the nurses were often too busy to tend to their needs. What this event was able to do was to create an environment where, stimulated by the characters and the research, nurses could engage in a relationship where the issues that were raised could be discussed and challenged in an open, honest and meaningful way. (Naidoo, 2005)

Sing Your Heart Out

In 2009 we were asked to evaluate an Arts in Health group in Norwich called Sing Your Heart Out (SYHO). This group was started by a psychotherapist based in a mental health hospital in Norwich. She felt that singing was not only a therapeutic activity but she also felt that singing could contribute significantly towards enriching the lives of people involved. As part of the evaluation we decided to:

- record on video the perceptions of SYHO participants
- take part in SYHO meetings to understand more fully the impact of SYHO
- record the singing sessions in order to capture the way in which the group members interacted with each other
- record how the skill and expertise of the SYHO workshop facilitator lent itself to the delivery of an inclusional and responsive approach to SYHO members.

The research produced a lot of video material that included individual narratives and footage of the meetings. Themes began to emerge from many of the interviews conducted. This was supported by the footage of the group singing together. We were able to capture moments where the act of singing together produced the mutual joy of celebrating through voice – without stigma – in communion.

As the fractals became clearly identifiable, we were able to triangulate narratives, participant statements, and choir footage to produce a filmed evaluation of SYHO. This was supported by a written report but the essence and richness of the research was contained on the video evaluation.

Ladder to the Moon

Ladder to the Moon (LTTM) is a small theatre company operating in South East England. The company works mainly in care homes and nursing homes for older people. The company takes versions of well-known Hollywood movies and re-enacts scenes, scenarios and storylines from these movies in a participative way with staff and residents in care homes. Residents and staff get to play alongside the actors as the company employ Relationship Theatre[TM]. They video the event and hand an edited version back to the care homes so that they can show participants what they did – to remind them of the time spent together in a shared experience that was as far from routine care home culture as could be.

Our research of LTTM involved looking at the effectiveness of their Studio Programme. This programme was run along the same lines as described above, however it was contextualised within a staff-development framework where care home staff were trained by LLTM staff to creatively engage with residents as part of their routine work as well as when the company visits 'The Care Home Studio' to film the programme. We used video in this research to record the activity and gather individual narratives through semi-structured interviews from staff members, residents, and carers/family members about how their skills and behaviours may have changed as a result of LTTM interventions in the care home.

The evidence gathered was pivotal in the development of a robust evidence base that demonstrated how effective the LTTM programme has been. We clearly saw residents and staff engage in novel ways to provide a creative and stimulating environment where creative play is possible. The impact on the energy of the home was also recorded as were the reactions of staff about their new learning and development. Furthermore, video was used to record the reflections of participants in the programme about their experience.

Conclusion

Using video can provide the researcher, the practitioner and the academic with a rich means by which they can hold their living values and therefore their authentic selves to account. This is especially true in the context of learning and self-inquiry where passion and compassion in inclusional and relational practice is embraced. The use of video has come a long way since we first started using it in 1979. Video capability is now accessible to us all in some form. It is both a tool and an art form, but its capacity to show us the richness of our existence and the complexity in our lives is of paramount importance. It is also important to remember that its influence, at its most powerful, is based on three principles: story, practice and context. By combining its creative and educational potential many healthcare service users and providers can gain much.

References

Eisner, E (1995) What artistically crafted research can help us to understand about schools. *Educational Theory, 45*(1), 1–6.

Freire, P (1970) *Pedagogy of the Oppressed*. London: Penguin.

McIntyre, M & Cole, A (2001) Dance me to an understanding of teaching: A performative text. *Journal of Curriculum Theorizing*, *17*(2), 43–60.

McNiff, J (2000) (with Jack Whitehead) *Action Research in Organisations*. London: Routledge.

Naidoo, MJ (2005) *I Am Because We Are: A never ending story: The emergence of a living theory of inclusional and responsive practice*. PhD thesis, University of Bath. Available online at www.actionresearch.net/living/naidoo.shtml

Shaw, P (2002) *Changing Conversations in Organisations: A complexity approach to change*. London: Routledge.

Whitehead, J (1989) Creating a living educational theory from questions of the kind, 'How do I improve my practice?' *Cambridge Journal of Education*, *19*(1), 41–52.

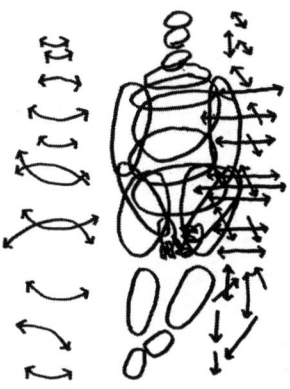

CHAPTER ELEVEN

Catching Life: The contribution of arts initiatives to recovery approaches in mental health

Helen Spandler, Jenny Secker, Lyn Kent, Suzanne Hacking & Jo Shenton

Introduction: Recovery and mental health

It is increasingly recognised that with appropriate support, people with even the most severe and enduring mental health problems can recover. In some cases this refers to a clinical sense of an absence of symptoms, and in others in the more social sense of recovering a fulfilling life, regardless of mental health diagnosis. Indeed, the so-called chronicity of mental health problems is not necessarily connected to the inherent course of a defined category of illness, but rather to the quality of a person's life in society. Thus, recovery is not necessarily predicated on a biomedical notion of 'recovery *from* illness' or 'remission *of* symptoms' (although this is often how it is interpreted). Notions of recovery have been inspired by services users' accounts of their own recovery journeys that have occurred with, without or sometimes despite, specific mental health interventions (Deegan, 1990; Coleman, 1999; Soteria Network, http://www.soterianetwork.org.uk).

In this context, we have seen the emergence in the last 15 years of what has been called a recovery approach to mental health in the UK, North America, Australia and New Zealand. This notion of 'recovery' has been embraced by some sections of the service user movement and, to some degree, practitioners and policy drivers. However, recovery has been increasingly contested and its conflation – in policy and practice – with paid employment and social inclusion has raised some concerns (Spandler, 2007). In addition, the study of recovery can be problematic because there is no agreed-upon conceptual model to guide research design and methodology. There is, for example, no clear consensus within the mental health community about what people are recovering from, what the process of recovery is, nor what the outcomes of recovery should be.

Notwithstanding these difficulties, we use the notion of recovery in this chapter to refer to a user-centred and primarily social ideal. This may, or may not, involve symptom reduction, use of services, diagnosis or medication, but *does* involve the individual moving towards being able to live the kind of life she or he wants to live. In this sense, recovery can be seen as the long-overdue emergence of a 'social model' within mental health (Beresford; 2000; Ramon, 2003). This is because it challenges the traditional way of providing mental health support and instead focuses on social conditions and the importance of having the necessary assistance to be able to pursue one's own self-defined goals and aims. Arguably, this approach circumvents sterile arguments between competing intervention and treatment models by working within the service user's own frameworks, definitions and understandings of their difficulties and aspirations (Repper & Perkins, 2003).

Key components of recovery

A user-centred ideal of recovery, by definition, should not impose particular norms of what recovery means for people, but should where possible, prioritise individually defined accounts and goals (within their particular social context). Having said that, there are a number of commonly agreed components which seem to be necessary for processes of recovery and which are subjective enough to keep this individuated notion at its core.

Feelings of despair and hopelessness are often key features of long-term mental health difficulties and use of mental health services. Hopelessness is a predictor of poor long-term outcomes (Aguilar et al., 1997) and suicide (Drake & Cotton, 1986; Beck et al., 1990). This hopelessness is often exacerbated by the low expectations and therapeutic pessimism of services as well as by the stigma and discrimination frequently associated with mental health difficulties (Dunn, 1999). In this context, hope is viewed as a 'life-saving force' (Russinova, 1999) and recovery can be viewed as a reawakening of hope after despair (Ridgway, 2001). The importance of having a sense of hope for the future has, therefore, been identified as an essential factor across the literature (Adams & Partree, 1998; Pitt et al., 2007).

Hope is often seen to involve the anticipation of a future based upon mutuality, a sense of personal competence, coping ability, psychological wellbeing, purpose and meaning in life, as well as a sense of 'the possible'. In this way, hope could be an overarching theme in recovery as these factors relate to other components commonly referred to in the literature. For example, having a sense of purpose and meaning is frequently considered central to recovery (Turner-Crowson & Wallcraft, 2002). In addition, the development of coping strategies and self-management of mental health problems are also viewed as important (Ridgway, 2001; Onken et al., 2002). Finally, the importance of social support and the rebuilding of identities beyond mental ill health have also been recognised (Repper & Perkins, 2003).

Art participation and creativity often feature in anecdotal and individual recovery journeys, and research suggests that participatory art does have a range of positive therapeutic benefits for people with mental health needs (Heenan, 2006). However, there has been limited research which explores the importance of arts activities as contributing to notions of a social model of recovery, at least in the sense described above. Therefore, the rest of this chapter draws on the qualitative findings from a recent national research study which was conducted by the authors (Secker et al., 2007). We use this to explore how arts and mental health projects can facilitate some of these key elements in a recovery approach to mental health.

National arts and mental health study

This national study was jointly funded by two government bodies in England, the Department for Culture, Media and Sport and the Department of Health. The study comprised a number of strands of research, including a survey of arts projects that resulted in a 'mapping' of arts and mental health activity in England (Hacking et al., 2006); a six-month follow-up survey of arts participants using standardised outcomes measures relating to mental health, social inclusion and empowerment (Secker et al., 2008); and a series of qualitative case studies. The qualitative case studies are the focus of this chapter.

For the case studies, we selected six diverse arts and mental health projects to explore the processes though which arts projects achieved benefits for participants. These included an 'arts on prescription' project, which offers short art courses to people experiencing mainly depression and anxiety associated with distressing life events or pressures (Project 1); a studio-based project in which people with severe and enduring needs, often related to experiences of abuse, are able to work together to develop their creativity and develop and exhibit their art work (Project 2); a rural community organisation facilitating workshops and projects for vulnerable, isolated groups, including people with a range of mental health needs (Project 3); an arts project which is part of an Asian women's mental health organisation providing culturally relevant opportunities, including arts and crafts, through which women can gain support from each other (Project 4); a Mind day centre offering art as part of a range of activities aimed at providing a structure for developing social interaction with others for people with severe mental health needs (Project 5); and a college-based project offering flexible arts-based courses for people with mental health needs at the college and in local mental health facilities (Project 6).

We carried out individual in-depth interviews with 34 arts project participants. The interviewees were between the ages of 35 and 78 years and had been involved with the projects for between four months and five years. Twenty-nine were of white British ethnicity and five were South Asian women. The interview questions focused on participants' expectations of their project, what they saw as the benefits, how they thought any benefits had come about and specifically whether participation in arts (rather than other activities) was important in achieving them. The interviews lasted between an hour and an hour and a half and were all recorded and transcribed. Interview data were analysed by two members of the research team working independently and then comparing notes in an iterative process to agree and refine an account of 'what worked' for participants and the mechanisms involved in achieving any benefits. The data were then reviewed and subjected to a further thematic content analysis to identify key themes from participants' accounts of the impact of arts participation in relation to the key features of 'recovery' as defined above.

Themes from the case studies

Most participants across all six projects reported how arts participation had increased their motivation by enabling them to gain inspiration to engage with their art work. It was clear that this process, alongside developing their artistic abilities and belief in themselves, helped participants to gain a sense of purpose and meaning in their lives:

> *Eventually over time doing a little bit and a little bit and being able to come in here and getting that little bit better, there's a slow progression of being able to do things and it gives you some kind of positive purpose in life ... that little something has a positive effect on me, mentally ... it presses my creative button I suppose. (Project 5, participant 5)*

> *Before I didn't think I could do it, whereas now I know I can, I'm a completely different person ... now I want to go and do things ... Focusing on creativity means you've got like a little reason for doing things. (Project 6, participant 3)*

This sense of purpose was not confined to their art work but often enabled participants to have more purpose and direction in the rest of their lives:

> *I feel when I come that I have got some purpose ... Coming here gives me impetus to make the rest of my time more important ... It gives me something to look forward to. (Project 6, participant 1)*

For participants who did not have a background in art, this was often related to arts participation enabling them to becoming aware of their latent abilities, especially around their awareness and sensory perception. Some of these participants reported being able to use their new artistic abilities to find meaning in the local and natural environment:

> *It was a nice spring day and I picked up my pad and I took my little fold-up garden chair and I just ... went down with a drink and a sandwich and I drew. I was on my own and I did it and that was just brilliant so I think I will do more of that now ... I am getting more confident now to actually sit on my own and do this because and this is where it is helping me ... I am going to actually take it out of what I am doing in the class. (Project 1, participant 4)*

For the following participant, having a greater sense of purpose and meaning in her life was especially important in the context of having taken early retirement as a result of her mental health difficulties:

> *Feeling and doing these small things, [I get a] a kind of excitement that my life at whatever level can have meaning ... and it's important as you get older that you feel you have value. (Project 1, participant 2)*

It is perhaps not surprising that art has the potential to enable people to find purpose and meaning in their lives because of the way that arts projects are often able to support participants to discover individual sources of meaning and value through their art work and through the active creation of something unique and new:

> *It doesn't matter if your leaf or a flower doesn't look like a leaf or a flower, it's your leaf and your flower and it's your expression of what's inside you, and I think that's a good thing, because all of us can only get better by facing ourselves and what's inside and working on our own stuff, and not judging ourselves either and truly saying to ourselves, 'well this is where I am, this is what I've been through, this is where I'll start'. And I can do something with my life. (Project 1, participant 2)*

Having a sense of purpose and meaning also enhanced participants' ability to engage in other aspects of their lives. For many participants, art had become an activity that they were able to pursue elsewhere, usually at home. For some, increased motivation had led to an expansion of their creative repertoire though the taking up of additional new interests outside the project, such as music lessons, creative writing or computers. Several participants also reported taking their art with them on holiday or doing creative activities at home with their family. Many participants made an explicit link between the growing hope and aspirations inspired by their creative activities and decreased levels of hopelessness, which, as we have seen, is an important factor in 'recovery':

> *It gives me a destination ... Without it I would be very depressed, it gives something to aim for and stay in touch and keep going on for ... It enthuses me where I wouldn't otherwise have, I know I wouldn't. (Project 6, participant 6)*

> *It's an ignition, it's a spark ... What happens is when they've ignited me a little bit here I go home and I stay on that creation. If you are creating things you don't get depressed. (Project 3, participant 2)*

Many participants referred to their engagement in arts activities as improving their motivation and inspiration. At one of the projects, all six participants reported having increased the days they attended the project, even though it meant having to pay for themselves. They explicitly related this to their growing motivation to develop their art work, which was particularly striking as all had clearly described how unmotivated and pessimistic they had been, both about the project and the future, before they started attending the project.

> *It's actually given me back in my life some ambition to do something. Which is something that had been absent for a very long time. (Project 2, participant 3)*

Only a minority of participants actually reported taking up new formal opportunities in the world (what may be seen as 'hard outcomes' in relation to, for example, social inclusion or employment). However, most participants did describe often quite profound increases in their personal aspirations. Widening aspirations should not be underestimated because a broadening of the horizons of people's lives beyond the world of mental health services is such an important aspect of the journey towards recovery. The aspirations described by participants revolved around the world of art, work and education:

> *It does spur you on to consider that, either it's a hobby that you take up and you can use that in a positive way, or you can decide that perhaps you're good enough to want to go and work in that sort of field ... This art project I must admit has inspired me to think that perhaps I could do something in textiles and things like that. (Project 5, participant 5)*

> *Gradually, it's through this, gradually I'm starting to get back into the big wide world again. I don't find it so scary ... I don't know what it is, it gives you something. It gives you a reason to get up in the morning, it makes you think, 'well if I can do this two days a week, maybe I can do a job'. (Project 2, participant 2)*

Another important aspect of recovery is often the development of coping strategies. There were three different ways in which arts participants reported being able to use art projects to help them develop new or alternative coping strategies. These related to three processes we identified as being important for individuals in gaining benefits from the projects. First, most of the participants reported how arts activities enabled them to relax and 'ground' themselves by focusing on something specific and absorbing. This seemed to enable them to develop ways of dealing with distress, by focusing on something outside of themselves. A small number of participants across different projects described how concentrating on art helped reduce the distressing impact of voices or visions:

> *While I'm painting I'm not listening to the voices I'm hearing, I'm not trying to reply to them, they're forced into the background almost as a distraction because you're involved with something ... and I think also when I'm painting I find a rhythm to it. (Project 2, participant 1)*

A number of participants also reported that the focus and concentration involved in art had a positive impact in relation to their self-harm. Many people who self-harm describe this as a need to focus their emotional pain onto something physical and tangible which gives them a break from difficult thoughts, feelings and memories. Some participants were able to transfer this onto their art, which gave them an alternative way of dealing with distress:

> *It was a 'stopgap' in a way but it kept me going, it took my mind off doing more harmful things [to myself] and that eased off how bad I felt, the intensity sort of eased off. So it's a preventative sort of measure in a way and it helped me for a period of time. (Project 2, participant 5)*

Another participant recalled how she was able to recreate the memory of the effect gained from focusing on art, suggesting that the more she was able to achieve this effect the easier it was to recreate:

> *You can only do it for so long and you are bound to come back to it but at least it can give you a break ... sometimes it stops it just building up into that, you know, 'I can't escape' feeling, if you can just break it. Once you have been there it is easier to get back to it. (Project 1, participant 5)*

The lasting effect of focusing on art described by participants was linked for several people with the 'portability' of their art. This was particularly the case for people who were beginning to use art in the rest of their lives as a way of deflecting or focusing them away from problems. The following participant was able to use art at home to help him cope with the distress of hearing voices, which in the past he had coped with through self-harm:

> *Once I've lost myself in the art work the problems in my head just disappear, they just alleviate and just leave me feeling better ... I can use it as a good distraction now to free me up from my head ... I used to be distracted by voices. Even though I was on medication to stop it sometimes they'd still come through and distract my days or bring me just right down to the point where I'd cut [myself]. Now, as a distraction, if I feel I'm getting like that, I'll try and draw what I'm feeling on paper so that I can actually visualise it and see it, and then I'll set fire to it and then I've got rid of it, I've killed it, it's gone. (Project 5, participant 2)*

Some of the arts projects enabled participants to find new ways of coping with distress, through self-expression, for example, by recreating painful images, creating more positive images, or expressing difficult feelings directly into their art work and/or through the process of making art. The art projects enabled them to make their difficulties more visible to themselves and others, and gave them a way of relating to their experiences in new and different ways. This helped to make their difficulties easier to cope with and also gave them an alternative means of coping with their distress. Self-expression seemed to be particularly beneficial for individuals who were struggling with issues such as self-harm and hearing voices that were related to past experiences, for example, of abuse and bullying:

> *If you've got lots of crap going on in your head and you're thinking 'god I can't cope with this', the voices are strong or something or you just can't cope. It's just good to get it out on paper ... the voices ... its a way of saying 'I'm not going to cope with you today' ... It helps you get shit out of your head when you feel you can't cope ... Even if you chuck it away afterwards you know at least you've got it out on a piece of paper and you can look at it and say 'well that's that piece of shit!' And then you've got it all on a piece of paper and you can sort it all out in your head and get it in some sort of order. You can sort it all out in your head seeing it on paper just makes sense of it. (Project 3, participant 1)*

> *If I have a vision like that, I can put it straight into my art work, so a lot of the things I am seeing or experiencing are coming out in my painting ... So I have found it easier to deal with the things I'm seeing ... It has given me an emotional, visualistic and creative outlet ... It takes the edge off any bad visions ... Sometimes if I find if I'm in a bit of a state ... then I find it easier to draw that out and exorcise my demons so to speak. (Project 6, participant 5)*

For many participants, the self-expression facilitated by their arts project contrasted with experiences of feeling out of control, of being controlled by others or by circumstances:

> *I think it's because my life is so restricted now ... Because you know, that's a good word, control. I feel like my life is controlled through no fault of my own, so much that to suddenly have that freedom, it just released something inside of me. (Project 1, participant 4)*

Arts participation was related for some participants with the process of rediscovering or rebuilding an identity within and beyond that of someone with mental health difficulties, again an important element of recovery. Because building identities is in large part a social process, involving internalisation of the perceptions of others (Howarth, 2003), the process was especially associated with opportunities to create and display a finished art work. Creating a finished work of art made participants' achievements visible to themselves, in turn enabling them to see themselves as someone who *could* achieve something. This was frequently mentioned across all six projects. Participants often referred to the importance of feeling valuable and worthwhile, especially in relation to others.

Arts participation helped some participants strengthen or realign their self-image in relation to others, including family, friends and the local community, because they felt people began to see them as having artistic talents and viewed them differently as a result. Manifestations of this change included participants' art work being welcomed by their families and friends. Other participants spoke of requests for art work to be displayed in community venues, of being able to teach art skills to others, and of families or friends making great efforts to support their arts activity. In addition, eight participants described an even more profound change, above and beyond being seen as someone with some artistic ability, in that the production of art work enabled them to develop or consolidate a renewed identity in the world, challenging their identity as being primarily highly valued for their involvement in their mental-health-specific arts projects.

If we take a user-centred view of recovery, it is important to recognise the important part that the safety and mutual support offered by such projects can play in individual recovery journeys. As a number of service users have pointed out, people with mental health difficulties (or indeed other oppressed groups) do not *necessarily* want to be part of a mainstream society that has rejected them (Spandler, 2007). Indeed, some participants appeared to be in the process of establishing a confident renewed identity that did not involve subscribing to mainstream social norms, but enabled them to accept and value themselves for who they were. It is important to recognise that social inclusion, in terms of integration into mainstream society, may not be lacking for some arts project participants, and may not be desirable for others.

While the participants in the Asian women's project did report a number of benefits of arts participation, there was less emphasis on elements that directly related to notions of recovery as discussed here. In general, we should avoid drawing any simplistic conclusions from this observation, but there are a variety of possible interpretations. First, our interviews with these participants were primarily carried out with the aid of an interpreter and there may have been some issues in interpretation of keywords and phrases that did not resonate with our own understandings of these concepts.

Thus, we may have 'missed' references to these themes in these women's accounts. Second, it may not have been a key process for women using this project. Indeed, most of these participants specifically referred to the importance of their arts sessions as being 'time out' from the stresses and strains of their everyday lives and familial caring responsibilities. They often used art as a 'distraction' to focus themselves *away* from their lives, rather than *rebuilding* their lives. While they enjoyed the art sessions, the women often valued learning something new and gaining mutual support from each other. Finally, it could mean that these aspects of recovery are less important to South Asian women, although we would be especially cautious about this interpretation. More generally, it raises important issues regarding the importance of art and creativity in diverse communities, the applicability of what are currently primarily white Western notions of recovery to minoritised or diverse ethnic populations and the specific role and impact of cultural or gender-specific initiatives.

D.W. Winnicott argued that it is the inability to be creative and the living of one's life according to others' demands and requirements which often results in psychiatric problems as 'compliance carries with it a sense of futility ... and is associated with the idea that nothing really matters and that life is not worth living' (Winnicott, 1991: 65).

> [T]he link can be made ... between creative living and living itself, and the reasons can be studied why it is that creative living can be lost and why the individual's feeling that life is real or meaningful can disappear. (Winnicott, 1991: 69)

Conversely, he argued that the ability to be creative instils a greater sense of the meaningfulness of life and this gives an individual greater individual agency and hope. It seems to be this sense of 'life worth living' that was one of the most important contributions made by the arts projects in our study. While we could debate the universality of creativity, or our understanding of 'recovery', the ability to have some control over one's actions does seem to be an important human requirement and was also an important facet in the reported benefits of arts participation.

While there was less evidence of 'recovery talk' among participants in some of the projects, the sense of freedom and control offered by their involvement in art was important, especially for women, whose lives were often dominated by caring responsibilities and the expectations and demands of others. In the context of a growing international recovery movement and increasing interest in the importance of hope and health (Parse, 1999), it may be that arts initiatives have an important role to play.

However, the evidence-based practice agenda clearly poses a number of challenges for arts initiatives. For example, despite general agreement about the common features of 'recovery', there remain qualities that are particularly hard to standardise, define and measure (Bracken & Thomas, 2004; Wallcraft, 2005). Although there have been attempts to measure some of these components, for example 'hope' (e.g., Miller & Powers, 1988; Herth, 1991), research has tended to focus on clinical or 'hard' outcomes rather than on these more nebulous and elusive concepts which are highly subjective and do not in themselves have to relate to specific outcomes in order to be extremely important and beneficial to the individual.

In addition, it is clear that recovery, however defined, should be seen as an ongoing process, not as an outcome (Ralph & Corrigan, 2005). In this way, the understanding of various aspects of 'distance travelled' towards individual service user-defined outcomes should be among the criteria in evaluating the impact of arts projects. However, these should be flexible enough both to take into account the individuals' changing aspirations and to prioritise the aspects of life that they may particularly value.

Conclusion

While creativity might be viewed as an essential human need, not everyone will find a route to recovery through arts participation. Despite the importance of arts participation for many of the individuals involved in our case studies, we cannot necessarily assume this is a universal facet of recovery. Art may be important for some people, but arts participation (or for that matter involvement in any other activities) should not be predetermined as 'good for' people with mental health needs and thereby imposed on them (Repper & Perkins, 2003).

However, our study suggests that arts participation may be one important element of recovery for mental health service users who have found their lives caught up in a cycle of hopelessness and despair. For many of our interviewees, engaging in creative activities helped to reverse an enduring sense of hopelessness, despair and futility about the future, which can be common in people who are long-term users of mental health services. Therefore, we suggest that a recovery approach to mental health must recognise the potential contribution of arts and creativity. Moreover, specific arts and mental health provision may have an important role to play in the future of mental health and social care provision.

Acknowledgments

The research was jointly commissioned and funded by the Department for Culture, Media and Sport and the Department of Health. The views expressed are the authors' and do not necessarily reflect those of the funders.

A version of this chapter was first published as a journal article in *Journal of Psychiatric and Mental Health Nursing* (2007), *14,* 791–9, and is reprinted here with the permission of the publishers, Wiley-Blackwell.

References

Adams, SA & Partree, DJ (1998) Hope: The critical factor in recovery. *Journal of Psychosocial Nursing, 36,* 29–32.

Aguilar, EJ, Haas, G & Manzanera, FJ (1997) Hopelessness and first episode psychosis: A longitudinal study. *Acta Psychiatrica Scandinavica, 96,* 25–30.

Beck, AT, Brown, G, Berchick, RJ, et al. (1990) Relationship between hopelessness and ultimate suicide: A replication with psychiatric outpatients. *American Journal of Psychiatry, 147,* 190–5.

Beresford, P (2000) What have madness and psychiatric system survivors got to do with disability and disability studies? *Disability and Society, 15,* 167–72.

Bracken, P & Thomas, P (2004) Hope. *Openmind, 130,* 10.

Coleman, R (1999) *Recovery: An alien concept?* Gloucester: Handsell.

Deegan, P (1990) *Spirit Breaking: When the helping profession hurts.* New York: Routledge.

Drake, R & Cotton, P (1986) Depression, hopelessness, and suicide in chronic schizophrenia. *British Journal of Psychiatry, 148,* 554–9.

Dunn, S (1999) *Creating Accepting Communities – Report of the MIND Inquiry into Social Exclusion and Mental Health Problems.* London: MIND.

Hacking, S, Secker J, Kent L, et al. (2006) Mental health and arts participation: The state of the art in England. *The Journal of the Royal Society for the Promotion of Health, 126,* 121–7.

Heenan, D (2006) Art as therapy: An effective way of promoting positive mental health? *Disability and Society, 21,* 179–91.

Herth, K (1991) Development and refinement of an instrument to measure hope. *Scholarly Inquiry for Nursing Practice, 5,* 39–51.

Howarth, C (2003) Identity in whose eyes? The role of representations in identity construction. *Journal for the Theory of Social Behaviour, 32,* 145–62.

Miller, JF & Powers, MJ (1988) Development of an instrument to measure hope. *Nursing Research, 37,* 6–10.

Onken, S, Dumont, J, Ridgway, P et al. (2002) *Mental Health Recovery: What helps and what hinders?* Alexandria, VA: National Technical Assistance Center for State Mental Health Planning.

Parse, RR (1999) *Hope: An international human becoming perspective.* Sudbury, MA: Jones and Bartlett Publishers.

Pitt, L, Kilbride, M, Nothard, S et al. (2007) Researching recovery from psychosis: A user-led project. *Psychiatric Bulletin, 31,* 55–60.

Ralph, RO & Corrigan, PW (Eds) (2005) *Recovery in Mental Illness: Broadening our understanding of wellness.* Washington, DC: American Psychological Association.

Ramon, S (2003) *Users Researching Health and Social Care: An empowering agenda?* Birmingham: Venture Press.

Repper, J & Perkins, R (2003) *Social Inclusion and Recovery: A model for mental health practice.* London: Bailliere Tindall.

Ridgway, P (2001) Re-storying psychiatric disability: Learning from first person recovery narratives. *Psychiatric Rehabilitation Journal, 34,* 335–43.

Russinova, Z (1999) Providers' hope-inspiring competence as a factor optimizing psychiatric rehabilitation outcomes. *Journal of Psychiatric Rehabilitation, 16,* 50–7.

Secker, J, Hacking, S, Spandler, H, et al. (2007) *Mental Health, Social Inclusion and Arts: Developing the evidence base.* London: National Social Inclusion Programme, Care Services Improvement Partnership.

Secker, J, Spandler, H, Kent, L, Hacking, S & Shenton, J (2008) Empowerment and arts participation for people with mental health needs. *Journal of Public Mental Health, 6*(4), 14–23.

Spandler, H (2007) From social exclusion to inclusion? A critique of the inclusion imperative in mental health. *Medical Sociology online, 2*(2), 3–16.

Turner-Crowson, J & Wallcraft, J (2002) The recovery vision for mental health services and research: A British perspective. *Psychiatric Rehabilitation Journal, 25,* 245–54.

Wallcraft, J (2005) Recovery from mental breakdown. In J Tew (Ed), *Social Perspectives in Mental Health* (pp. 200–15). London: Jessica Kingsley.

Winnicott, DW (1991) *Playing and Reality.* London: Routledge.

Final Thoughts

Theo Stickley

This book has presented 11 examples of arts-based research projects that have used various qualitative methods to capture the contexts and meanings of arts practice that in their own and varied ways, have sought to promote mental health. The methods are varied, but most have endeavoured to reflect the voice of the participant, whether through narratives, ethnography or participatory action research. There is a growing demand for the use of standardised outcome measures for the assessment of the health benefits of arts activities to people who use mental health services. However, the very nature of art demands that the focus of research inquiry be more upon the individual's personal experiences, perceptions and unique expression of their inner world. Creativity and mental health have been linked in one way or another throughout history. The last 200 years have seen the medicalisation of mental distress and although it is evident that people want services that are more hopeful and creative (recovery-focused), the notion of providing mental healthcare that focuses less upon medical interventions and more upon creativity is complex. Those who hold the purse strings in statutory healthcare often look for scientific evidence. While mental healthcare remains dominated by reductionist science, researching the arts creatively will continue to be largely ignored by many in the healthcare sector.

There is also the tendency to 'commodify' the use of arts approaches to fit in with the health agenda and justify the benefits of the arts and creativity to conform to the language of statutory services provision. Thus, what develops is an articulation of the relevance of the arts and creativity to public health and health promotion. This commodification of the arts for 'good health' or 'wellbeing' may strengthen the argument for public funding of the arts in health promotion but further entrenches control of the 'product' in the hands of those who manage public spending. In mental healthcare, sadly, much of the resources in the statutory sector are used to contain, coerce and medicate people. Ultimately, the power to commission services remains with healthcare providers, who have the duty to protect the public, not to invest in artists.

It is sad to hear of the arts being used in purely instrumental ways for the fulfilment of the funders' agenda. What is clear from the chapters in this book, however, is that participation in the arts can have transformational effects. An approach that trusts in the intrinsic benefit of the arts delivered in a health-promoting context can significantly affect people's lives. Some of the findings of the research published in this book relate to highly important concepts of identity and belonging, not the kinds of concepts usually present in mental healthcare policy, which focuses more upon risk and containment. The emerging recovery approach, however, supports these kinds of outcomes and perhaps artists working in mental healthcare should embrace the recovery agenda.

To research the arts in mental health practice, perhaps researchers of the future need to be prepared to experiment with creative methodologies and have the faith that the imagination can inform us, that art is not non-cognitive, but that it binds together both feeling and form in a way that can reveal the truth of the individual's expression. Attempting to understand the essence of researching participatory arts requires the capability of being open not only to scientific cognition but also to artistic imagination. While it is recognised that offering evidence for the need for the arts and the efficacy of creative expression for wellbeing is essential, it may be better to adopt more sociocultural approaches that emphasise the user's voice, for this needs to become central to our research and evaluation. Research of this nature will involve sophisticated assessment of qualitative evidence rather than short-cut analysis of cost efficiency alone.

For those services that are committed to promoting mental health through the arts, there is the need for enough flexibility to work in genuine partnerships with those who are already succeeding in this field of work. Although statutory services may provide limited creative therapy, the voluntary sector, freer from statutory policy directives, has provided many examples of excellent work, largely based in the community. One of the shifts in recent years in UK politics is the focus upon unlocking the potential of communities. Participatory arts are well placed to contribute to this political development in the future and to develop recovery-orientated approaches. This book has provided examples of research approaches that can be developed in the future to complement recovery-focused community development.

In closing, I sincerely hope that the coming decades will see mental healthcare and mental health promotion transformed to become something that is creative and more meaningful to our society. Arts-based approaches can make unique and life-transforming contributions to mental healthcare in the UK and it is only by rigorous evaluation and research that this work will be adequately documented for practitioners of the future.

If you would like to contact me about anything at all, please email me: theo.stickley@nottingham.ac.uk

Theo Stickley
University of Nottingham
UK

Contributors

Helen Brooks is a Research Associate in the Health Sciences Primary Care group within the School of Community Based Medicine at the University of Manchester.

Langley Brown is Arts for Health Visiting Research Fellow at Manchester Metropolitan University, where he is establishing the Arts for Health Archive. He has worked in Arts and Health since 1978.

Alma Cunliffe is Creative Programmes Officer at City Arts, Nottingham. She specialises in working with groups of people with mental health needs and also working within schools.

Julie Hanna works in education, health and the arts. She uses strength-based approaches to help realise potential to live as fully and sustainably as possible in all kinds of weather.

Mick McKeown is the first author of Chapter 7 although it is written by a collective of authors who have been involved in both the mental health Film Festival and associated teaching and learning at the University of Central Lancashire (UCLan) and the Bradton e-learning project, which was a collaboration with the University of Bradford. Russell Hogarth, John Lunt and Keith Holt are all members of the Comensus service user and carer involvement initiative at UCLan, Lisa Malihi-Shoja is the Comensus co-ordinator, and Fiona Jones is employed as a researcher with service-user experience. Mark Edwards is a student mental health nurse and Mick McKeown, Garry Watkins and Sarah Traill are academic staff, all at UCLan. Jane Priestley and Michael Hellawell were academic staff at Bradford at the time of writing, with Jane now having moved to the Higher Education Academy.

Polly Moseley is an Arts Consultant working for Culture Liverpool and Royal de Luxe. Her career spans work supporting digital media businesses and brokering Franco-British exchange. Since 2003, she has been responsible for developing cultural programmes and partnerships designed to tackle health and social inequalities.

Contributors

Marian Naidoo works with Naidoo & Associates. She has a research and development background in Health, Education and Arts and is visiting research fellow at the University of Bath and Associate of Liverpool Hope University.

Shaun Naidoo works with Naidoo & Associates and is involved in research, evaluation, service improvement and developing inclusional and responsive methods that embrace creative approaches in the development of relational dynamics within organisations.

Hester Parr is a Reader in Human Geography at Glasgow University. She has researched social dimensions of mental health issues for 20 years, and her book *Mental Health and Social Space: Geographies of inclusion?* was published by Blackwell in 2008.

David Pilgrim is Professor of Mental Health Policy in the School of Social Work at the University of Central Lancashire and Visiting Professor of Clinical Psychology, University of Liverpool.

Edward Sellman is a lecturer in Education (Special Educational Needs) at the University of Nottingham, where he researches children's behaviour, student voice, inclusion and the arts/creativity. He is also an artist (see www.megaumbrella.co.uk), winning the Djanogly Prize at the Lakeside Arts Centre, Nottingham in 2010.

Helen Spandler is a Senior Research Fellow at the University of Central Lancashire (UCLan). She is part of the editorial collective of *ASYLUM: The magazine for democratic psychiatry* (www.asylumonline.net) and co-editor of *Beyond Fear and Control: Working with young people who self-harm* – both also published by PCCS Books. Helen led the qualitative aspect of a national research project looking at the 'evidence base' of arts and mental health projects – with colleagues from Anglia Ruskin University (Jenny Secker), UCLan (Sue Hacking) and service-user researchers and artists (Lyn Kent and Jo Shenton).

Theo Stickley is Associate Professor of Mental Health at the University of Nottingham. Having firstly trained as a nurse and therapist, over the last ten years he has concentrated on developing and researching arts and mental health practice. He is also a non-executive director for City Arts (Nottingham) Ltd and leads on the innovative Art in Mind programme of work, promoting mental health through community arts. Theo is a member of the Nottingham Society of Artists and attends evening workshops every week. He is an international speaker and is known widely for his work on narrative research in the arts and mental health. He is a keen gardener and takes pride in the quality of the compost he produces!

Brendan Stone is an academic in the School of English at the University of Sheffield where he leads the *Storying Sheffield* project (www.storyingsheffield.com). His research interests include the study of narrative in the representation of trauma and distress.

Index

3bisf (centre for arts practice) 100
   website 100

A

abuse (DVD production project) 44 (*see* projects)
action research 98
   living theory 192–3
   participatory methods 118, 124–6, 213
   projects 30, 37, 123, 125
Adams, SA 201, 211
Aguilar, EJ 200, 211
Aked, J 110, 111, 113, 116, 143, 166
Akram, A 123, 136
Alder Hey Children's Hospital 101
Angus, J 28, 40
animation project 44 (*see* projects)
Arnstein, S 119, 136
art/s
   and academia 134–5
   -based mental health projects x
      motivations 72–3, 133
      recommendations for 56–7
      (*see also* projects)
   effects on mental health 33
   for mental health projects in Scotland 4–5, 10
   impacts of participation in 35–8, 65
   and insiderness 1, 3–4, 5, 20
   mainstreamed in healthcare ix
   and mental health study (*See* National Arts and Mental Health Study)
   and mental wellbeing in schools (*see* schools)
   and outsider 'madness' 2–3 (*see also* 'outsider art')
   project/s (*see also* community arts projects)
      promoting equality and dialogue 112–3
      spaces 10–14 (*see also* creative spaces)
   therapy vii, 3, 22*ff*, 37
      and non-therapy art x, 9, 13, 19, 25, 27, 28–30, 37, 38
      evolution of 3, 34–5
Art Angel, Dundee 5*ff*
   website 6
'art brut' 2 (*see also* 'outsider art')
Art Extraordinary Gallery, website 15
Art in Mind, Nottingham 58, 65, 66, 69, 70, 73, 75, 76, 83, 84, 87, 90, 93, 96, 218
Arthur, A 167
artistic
   communities 14, 16, 17, 18, 19
   development 11, 13
   endeavour x, 4, 174
   geographies 5–6, 7, 19
   integrity 27, 52, 54, 57
   outputs, high quality 49, 55, 56
   practice 5, 7, 9, 19, 30, 100
artist-led research 98, 107
'Arts Advocacy' 6
Arts and Health programme, Liverpool 98*ff*
Arts Council for England 142, 149, 167
Arts in Health, Norwich 196
Arts for Health Archive, Manchester Metropolitan University 40, 217
Arts Partnership Nottinghamshire (APN) 149, 152, 166
Asylum magazine 218
Atkinson, M 141, 167
Atkinson, R 123, 136
autobiography 37, 182
autoethnography ix, x, 22*ff*, 24, 28, 170*ff*

B

Bain, A 17, 20
Bakhtin, MM 99, 116
Barthes, R 60, 73
Basset, T 136
Beck, AT 200, 211
behaviour management 165
belonging 1, 4, 5, 7, 8, 10–14, 16, 17, 18, 19, 20, 35, 67, 75*ff*, 93–6, 214
Beresford, P 119, 136, 171, 183, 200, 211
Berger, R 162, 167
Bethlem Royal Hospital 2
Beuys, J 33, 35, 38, 41
Bhugra, D 122, 123, 136
bias ix, 107
Bloom, T 4, 21

Index

Blundell, P 120
Boardman, C 167
Bocock, R 33, 38, 40
Bohm, D 115, 116
Bondi, L 9, 20
Bourdieu, P 140, 167
Boyce, S 113, 116
Boyd, M 139
Bracken, P 210, 211
Bradbury, H 124, 139
Bradford University 124
Bradton e-learning project 124, 126, 130, 217
Branfield, F 136
'Breaking Down the Walls of Silence' (project) 194
Breeze, J 119, 139
Bridgehead Arts 28, 40
Bridges, K 41
Brison, S 173, 183
British Association of Art Therapists (BAAT) 34, 37
Brockmeier, J 61, 73
Brooks, H x, 217
Brown, G 211
Brown, K 119, 136
Brown, L x, 25, 40, 217
Brown, P 119, 133, 136
Burgess, A 138
Butler, J 170, 172, 182, 183
Butler, T 32

C

Calman, K 29, 40
Cameron, J 162, 167
Campbell, P 136
Cape, G 122, 123, 136
Care Services Improvement Partnership 43, 55, 57
Carey, J 58, 73
Carlin, H 116
Carter Park, D 2, 20
case studies 1, 28, 29, 36, 37, 38, 143, 146, 148, 149, 202–10
Chadwick, S 166
Challenge Programme 42*ff*
Chandler, A 166
Chapman, B 23
Chase, SE 60, 74
children, vulnerable (animation project) 44 (*see* projects)
Chung, B 122, 136
Church, K 119, 136
City Arts, Nottingham 73, 149, 152, 166, 217, 218
  website 166
Clancy, B 122, 138
Clift, S viii, xi
cognitive fluidity, concept of 31
Coholic, D 144, 167
Cole, A 188, 198
Coleman, R 199, 211
Colgan, S 35, 41
collaboration
  effective 50, 64, 69–71, 72, 140
collaborative
  commissioning 112, 149, 152
  working relationships 26, 34, 50, 54, 55, 145, 147, 178, 179, 189
collective narrative 71–2, 92–6
Comensus initiative 118*ff*
community arts projects 4, 11, 14, 59
  belief in the work 68
  concepts and philosophy 66–7
  effective collaboration 67–71
  personal experiences 67–8
  personal motivation 72–3
  researching the project developers 59
  and spaciality 14–16
Community Involvement Team (CIT) (Comensus) 125
confidentiality 30–1
conflict resolution 9, 143, 144–8
Connors, A 166
context–mechanism–outcome configurations 48, 54, 55
Corbett, C 136
Corrigan, PW 123, 136, 212, 210
Cotton, P 200, 211
Couanet, C 105
Cowie, H 141, 167
creative arts, health and practitioner education 120–1
  partnerships 142, 144
  spaces 6–10 (*see also* art project spaces)
Creative Personalities 120
creativity *passim*
  benefits of 64–5
  and inclusion 1*ff*
Cresswell, M 135, 136
Crossley, N 119, 133, 136
Crouch, D 7, 20
Csíkszentmihályi, M 25, 35, 41, 146, 167

Index

Cunliffe, A x, 217
Czarniawska, B 62, 74

D

dancer, listening to the voice of 99, 103, 109–12
Daniels, H 148, 149, 166, 167
Datta, V 123, 136
De Carlo, K 122, 136
De Certeau, M 177, 178, 183
Deacon, L 101, 116
Deegan, P 199, 211
Denholm, A 149, 167
Denzin, NK 62, 74, 174, 183
Department for Culture, Media and Sport 201, 211
Department of Education (DoE) 142, 167
Department of Health (DH) 44, 57, 101, 119, 137, 142, 167, 201, 211
Dewson, S 153, 167
dialogical process 102–3
Dissanayake, E 31, 32, 34, 41
Dixon, A 166
Dorling, D 116
Downe, S 119, 125, 133, 137
Drake, R 200, 211
Dubuffet, J 2
Dudhope Arts Centre 5
Dumont, J 211
Duncan, K 59, 73, 74, 144, 149, 166, 168
Duncan, WH 101
Dunn, S 201, 211
DVD production project 44 (*see* projects)

E

Eccles, J 167
education 141 (*see also* Bradton e-learning project)
 arts and 142 (*see also* schools)
 practitioner 118, 119, 120–1
Edwards, D 9, 20, 61, 74
Edwards, M 217
Eisner, E 187, 197
e-learning (*see* Bradton e-learning project)
Ellis, C 28, 41
Erikson, EH 95, 96
Essler, V 146, 167
ethnography 5, 29, 154
evaluation, planning for meaningful 153–5
Every Child Matters 142
evidence viii, 145

-base for Arts and Health work viii–ix
 randomised controlled trials viii, 153
 right kind for the NHS viii
exhibition spaces identifiers for 'outsider art' 14
experiences and beliefs 64, 67–8

F

Fairclough, N 96
families, vulnerable (animation project) 44 (*see* projects)
Felton, A 119, 137
Fewell, J 9, 20
film 118, 185 (*see also* video)
 festivals (*see* mental health film festivals)
 website (psychflix) 123
filmmaking 6, 45, 118*ff* (*see also* video)
 motivations for involvement 126–8
 and qualitative research 187
Flowers, P 110, 117
Foresight Mental Capital and Wellbeing project 111, 116
Forestry Commission and School A 152, 161, 162, 166
Foucault, M 96, 141, 167
Fouts, G 122, 138
fractals 189, 190, 191, 192
Frankham, J 119, 124, 132, 137
Freire, P 124, 134, 137, 186, 187, 197
Fritz, G 123, 137
Fromm, E 33, 38, 41, 93, 94, 96, 97

G

Gabbard, G 122, 137
Gabbard, K 122, 137
Gablik, S 33, 41
Gelkopf, M 122, 137
Gell, C 139
geographies, artistic 5–6
Gergen, KJ 60, 74
Gergen, MM 74
Gillett, G 61, 74
Gilroy, A 28, 41
Giving an Account of Oneself 172, 182, 183
Glasgow Art Fair 17, 18
Glasgow City Council 16, 20
Gleeson, K 122, 137
Goffman, E 94, 95, 97
Gonen, B 137
Gould, H 35, 41
Gramsci, A 135

Green, A 136
Greenberg, H 122, 123, 124, 137
Greenpeace 146
Griffiths, S 146, 167
Guardian, The 120, 137
Gubrium, JF 60, 62, 74

H
Haas, G 211
Hacking, S viii, xi, 201, 211, 212, 218
Hadfield, M 154, 167
Hadland, R 144, 165, 167
Hall, C 165, 167, 168
Hall, S 150, 167
Hancox, G viii, xi
Hanley, B 119, 137
Hanna, J x, 101, 116, 117, 217
Harber, C 141, 167
Harré, R 61, 74
Haslam, N 171, 184
Haw, K 154, 167
Haywood Gallery, Manchester 2, 20
Health Development Agency 36, 41
Health is Wealth Commission, Liverpool 101, 116
Heenan, D 144, 165, 167, 201, 211
Hellawell, M 217
Herman, J 173, 183
Herth, K 210, 211
Hesse, M 122, 137
HM Government 119, 137
Hogan, S 3, 20
Hogarth, R 217
Holliday, A 126, 137
Holstein, JA 60, 62, 74
Holt, K 21
homelessness and mental illness collaborative arts project 44 (*see also* projects)
Hopkins, EJ 31, 41
Hornby, G 141, 167
Houghton, N 144, 168
Howarth, C 207, 211
Hyler, S 122, 123, 137

I
identity
    changing 77, 79, 86, 96, 131
    collective 92, 95, 96, 160
    integration of 82
    and mental health 94, 214
    narrative, an 87–92
    narrative model of 172–3
    necessity of 33, 83
    rebuilding 79, 81, 87–92, 207, 208
    social 75*ff*, 93–6
    storying selfhood 131–2
'illness narrative' 60, 76–8, 92
Improbable Theatre 108
Inclusive Learning and Teaching Project (Sheffield University) 176
innovation-based projects 42
'insane art' 2, 3 (*see also* 'outsider art')
insider positions 3, 18, 93
insiderness, art and 1, 3–4, 5, 20
Institute Dentamental 180
interview/s 98, 202
    analysis 48–9, 63, 109, 202
    etymology of 99
    as generative practice 98*ff*
    method 62–3
    narrative x, 59, 63
    psychiatrists, by young patients 103, 106–7
    research 62, 73, 87, 99
'Involve' 119, 137

J
Jadi, I 9, 20
Jensen, J 111, 113, 116
Jones, F 217
Jorgenson, MW 96, 97
Jung, CG 73, 74

K
Kaplan, F 34, 35, 41
Kaprow, A 33, 38, 41
Kelly, B 122, 137
Kelly, D 119, 139
Kemmis, S 124, 138
Kent, L 218
Kerby, A 172, 183
Keyes, CLM 111, 116
Kilbride, M 212
King's Fund, The 114
    website 114
Krizek, RL 28, 41

L
Labov, W 62, 74
Ladder to the Moon (research evaluation) 196–7
Laing, J 2, 3, 20
Lathlean, J 119, 138

Lawson, A 122, 138
Lefkowits, J 122, 139
Lewin, K 124, 138
Lewis, S 101, 116
Liebmann, M 146, 168
Life at Liff Exhibition, McManus Galleries, Dundee 15
Liff Hospital 6, 11, 15
Lime 37
    website 37
Lippuner, R 177, 183
Liverpool
    Arts and Health programme 98
    Capital of Culture Waiting Programme 102
    context, the 101–2
    health inequalities in 100
    Health is Wealth Commission 116
    Primary Care Trust 98, 112, 114, 116
    Year of Health and Wellbeing 100, 113
living theory 193–7
    action research 192
Loach, K 124
Lombroso, C 2, 20
Long, I 155, 166, 169
Lost Artists Club (LAC) x, 73, 75*ff*
LUNA (a next-step arts organisation) 6, 14
Lunt, J 217

M
Mad History curriculum 123
Maddern, C 4, 21
Magos, T 122, 123, 138
Maison de Solenn (Maison des Adolescents) 103, 104, 105, 107, 108
Malchiodi, C 3, 21
Malihi-Shoja, L 138, 217
Mangala, R 122, 138
Marcuse, H 134, 135, 138
Marks, N 166
Marsden, S 145, 147, 160, 168
Masson, J 32, 41
Matarasso, F 35, 41, 100, 117
McAndrew, S 120, 139
McCollum, D 124
McCourt, A 166
McDermott, P 108
McDonald, A 122, 138
McIntyre, M 188, 198
McKeown, M x, 119, 122, 125, 134, 137, 138, 217

McLaughlin, M 124, 132, 138
McManus Galleries, Dundee 15
McNiff, S 146, 168, 189, 198
McTaggart, R 124, 138
mechanisms
    context–mechanism–outcome configurations 48, 54, 55
    outcome producing xi, 48, 54, 85, 202
    art and research as 114
media
    mass 122
    negative impact 15, 51, 107
Memory Man 181
Menon, K 122, 138
mental health *passim*
    film festivals
        'One in Four' 118, 120, 121, 135
        Scottish (SMHAFF) 120, 123
        website 120
    in the movies 122–3
        website (psychflix) 123
    politics of 11, 135
Mental Health in Higher Education (mhhe) 121, 138
mental health services
    modernisation ethos 43
    risk-averse culture 43
    transformational change in 43
Mental Wellbeing Impact Assessment, Liverpool 101
Merryweather, W 74
mhhe 121, 138
Miller, JF 210, 211
Mindell, A 114, 117
Mirza, M 143, 168
Mishler, EG 62, 74
Mithen, S 31, 41
Moseley, P x, 103, 116, 117, 217
movies (*see also* film, video)
    making sense of making 126–32
    mental health in the 122
    as teaching mechanism 123
music ix

N
Naidoo, MJ xi, 193, 194, 195, 198, 218
Naidoo, S xi, 218
narrative/s
    co-constructed 72–3
    collective 60, 71–2, 92–6
    definition of 61–2

Index

and discourse 71–2
'illness' 60, 92
importance of 189–90
research 62
theory 60–1
turn 60–2
National Arts and Mental Health Study 200–2
  themes from case studies 202–10
  conclusions 210
National Endowment for Science Technology and the Arts (NESTA) 42, 44, 53
  projects funded by 44
National Health Service (NHS) viii, 5, 6, 24, 27, 43
National Service Framework (NSF) for Mental Health 44
Neighbourhood Renewal scheme 37
New Deal for Communities 59, 72, 73
non-therapy artists 34
non-therapy arts
  comparison of art therapy and 25, 37, 38
  practice 25, 38
Nottingham Society of Artists 218
nursing
  impact of training changes (project research) 194–5
  education 120, 121
NVivo software 5, 64

O

O'Brien, A 136, 144, 168
Obeyesekere, G 32, 41
'One in Four' Mental Health Film Festival 118, 120, 121, 135
Onken, S 201, 211
ontological depth 48
'Oor Mad History' group, Scotland 123
open systems 49
Orchowski, L 122, 138
Ordinary House, The 179
outcome/s viii, 1, 145
  context–mechanism–outcome configurations 48, 54, 55
'outsider'
  art 1, 2–3, 5
    exhibition space signifiers for 14
    forms of 9
    history of 2
    not sufficiently 18
  artists 17, 92

'madness', arts and 2–3
  positions 3
'outsiderness' ix, 1, 3, 4

P

Parr, H ix, 6, 7, 10, 20, 21, 32, 41, 134, 138, 218
Parry, W 123, 138
Parse, RR 209, 211
partnerships
  creative 142, 144
  organisations 112, 161, 214
  research 119
  supportive of innovation 115
Partree, DJ 201, 211
Passeron, JC 140, 167
Pathways Pilot project 37
patients
  dementia 194
  general hospital 195
  psychiatric 2, 3, 4, 24, 58, 103
    marginalised 4
  young, interviewing psychiatrists 103, 106–7
Pawson, R 46, 56, 57
Performing Medicine programme 108
  website 108
Perkins, R 44, 57, 200, 201, 210, 212
Phillips, L 96, 97
Philo, C 2, 11, 21
Philo, G 122, 138
Pilgrim, D x, 43, 44, 55, 57, 141, 168, 218
Pinder, D 17, 21
Pink, S 154, 168
Pitt, L 201, 212
Poe, R 123, 137
Poivre d'Arvor, V 108
Potter, J 61, 74
Powell, L 123, 138
Powers, MJ 210, 211
practitioner education 118, 119, 120–1
Priestley, J 217
Prinzhorn, H 2
Project Ability 6, 17
  funding 6
projects, four innovative arts-based
  artistic integrity in 52, 54
  descriptions 45
  discussion 54–7
  findings 49–54
  funded by NESTA 44

224

Index

methodology 46–9
   project champion 48, 50, 51, 55, 56
   staff resistance to 51, 53
   structural instability of 50
Psychopolitics 135
psychiatric unit arts activities project 44
psychiatrists 103, 108, 181
   early collectors of 'insane art' 2
   young patients interviewing 103, 106–8
'psychotic' art 2, 32
Putnam, R 145, 168

Q

qualitative research *passim*
   and the NHS viii–ix
   and bias ix, 107
   film and xi, 186, 187
   interview method 62–3
quantitative research viii, 28, 115, 188 (*see also* randomised controlled trials)
Quinn, N 120, 123, 138

R

Raingruber, B 123, 124, 39
Ralph, RO 210, 212
Ramon, S 43, 55, 57, 200, 212
randomised controlled trials viii, 153
Ranjith, G 122, 138
Read, J 171, 184
Reason, P 124, 139
recovery
   approach
      in mental health xi, 199*ff*, 213, 214, 215
      to mental distress, arts and 9, 209
   key components of 200–1, 204, 205, 207, 210
   notions of 43, 121, 199, 200, 201
   potential for 73
   strategy for 7
   through identity establishment 83–7
   user-centred view of 208
Reitz, C 134, 139
relationships
   art and mental health ix, 1, x, 143
   in schools 140
   art and outsiderness/insiderness 3, 4
   art therapy and non-art therapy 25, 28
   benefits of 73, 111
   identity and mental health 94
   improved 47
   need for 61, 96, 143
   therapeutic 121
Relationship Theatre 196
Repper, J 44, 57, 119, 139, 200, 201, 210, 212
research (*see also* action research, autoethnography, narrative, qualitative, quantitative research)
   artist-led 98
   bias ix, 107
   connecting, referencing and contributing to 114
   difficulties 200
   evaluation 153–4
   evidence vii, ix, 36
   and imagination 214
   interview methodology 62–3
   journals viii
   methodology 29
   partnerships 119
   studies 35
   tools (*see* films, interview, video)
   transparency ix, 112
resilience, developing 163–4
Reville, D 123
Rexer, L 2, 21
Reynolds, C 101, 117
Rhodes, C 2, 3, 9, 21
Ricoeur, P 62, 74, 172, 173, 178, 179, 184
Ridgway, P 201, 212
Riessman, CK 60, 61, 62, 74
risk-averse culture 43, 44, 56
Roberts, R 122, 139
Robinson, D 122, 123, 139
Rogers, A 141, 168
Rogers, CR 83, 97
Rose, G 4, 14, 21
Rosenstock, J 122, 139
Rufo, M 108, 117
Russinova, Z 201, 212
Ryerson University, Mad History curriculum 123
Ryerson University, Toronto 124

S

Sacks, S 35, 41
Sainsbury Centre for Mental Health 44, 57
SCH!ZO 174, 175, 180
Schön, D 30, 41
school/s 140
   arts projects in
      behaviour management 165
      case studies 148

Index

difficulties 165
evaluation planning 153–5
impact on wellbeing 156–8
partnerships 161–2
responsible management 147–8
resiliance development 163–4
selection of groups 164–5
social benefits 144–6, 160–1
sustainability 165
nature of 140–2
pupils'
comments about mental wellbeing 151
ideas for arts projects 151
social regulation in 148
sustainability 165
Scott, M 165, 168
Scottish Arts Council 6
Scottish Collection of Extraordinary Art 2
Scottish Mental Health Arts and Film Festival (SMHAFF) 120, 123
website 120
Secker, J xi, 201, 211, 212, 218
Sedgwick, P 135, 139
Seligman, M 141, 146, 164, 168
Sellman, E x, 144, 146, 150, 165, 168, 218
Senior, P 23
sense of place, importance of 152
Servan-Schreibner, D 143, 146, 168
service user involvement in universities 119, 124, 125, 135
Shaw, P 188, 198
Sheaff, R 43, 57
Shearman, Z 113
Shenton, J 218
Shingler, A 40
Shulman, A 138
Sierles, F 123, 139
Silverman, D 62, 74
Simpson-Housley, P 20
Sing Your Heart Out (research evaluation) 196
Slee, R 142, 168
Smail, D 32, 41
Smith, JA 110, 117
social capital 4, 10, 66, 144, 145, 153, 160–1
social change 132–5
social exclusion 143, 176
Social Exclusion Unit 143, 168
social identity 75*ff*, 93, 94, 95
and belonging 93–6
social science research
narrative turn 60–2

video in 154 (*see also* video)
Soteria Network 199
website 199
Spandler, H xi, 218, 119, 135, 136, 139, 200, 208, 212, 218
Spickard, B 138
Staricoff, R viii, xi, 120, 139, 142, 168
START (Manchester) 30
Stickley, T 59, 73, 74, 96, 119, 137, 144, 149, 165, 166, 167, 168, 218
Stone, B x, 171, 184, 218
stories ix, 28, 59, 126, 127, 129 (*see also* narrative)
storytelling 126–32, 179
Storor, M 107
Storr, A 94, 95, 97
Story, R 37
storying 171
selfhood 131–2, 172
Storying Sheffield 170*ff*, 184, 218
Stowell-Smith, M 122, 138
Strawson, G 182, 184
Sutton, J 166
systems, organisational 189

T

Tajfel, H 93, 96, 97
Targeted Mental Health Services in Schools (TaMHS) (Notts) 149, 166
Taylor, B 144, 168
Telling Stories: The Arts and Wellbeing in North Liverpool 100
Tew, J 119, 139
Thara, R 122, 138
Thatcher, M 95
theatre practitioner/researchers 186, 188, 192
Thiele, M 145, 147, 160, 168
Thomas, P 210, 211
Thompson, S 110, 111, 113, 116
Thomson, P 143, 145, 153, 165, 167, 168
Thornton, K 166
Tilly, N 46, 56, 57
Tomlinson, S 168
Torrey, E 122, 139
Trafford (Manchester) 37
Traill, S 217
transformational change within mental health services 43
Trongate Studios, Glasgow (Trongate 103) 4, 5, 6, 16, 17, 18
website 16

Turner, JC 93, 97
Turner-Crowson, J 201, 212

U
University of Bradford 124
University of Central Lancashire (UCLan) 43, 118, 120, 124
University of Nottingham 149, 166
University of Sheffield initiative 176

V
video (*see also* film, movies)
    communicating research outcome 191–2
    as educational tool 118, 120
        concern about control 129–31
    as research tool xi, 153, 171, 174, 186, 187, 189, 190–2
    in social science research 154, 192

W
Wahl, O 122, 139
Waletzky, J 62, 74
Wallcraft, J 201, 210, 212
Walsh, A 107, 117
Walter, G 122, 138
Warne, T 120, 139
Watkins, G 217
Wedding, D 123, 139
Welsh National Assembly 194
West, H 101, 117
White, M 4, 21, 142, 143, 144, 152, 153, 169
Whitehead, J 191, 193, 198
Williamson, C 119, 133, 139
Willis, J 3, 21
Wilson, P 155, 166, 169
Winnicott, DW 209, 212
Winship, G 122, 139
Woolf, F 153, 169
World Health Organization (WHO) 31, 41
Wykurz, G 119, 139

Y
Young, N 119, 136

Z
Zavetoski, S 119, 133, 136

First Steps in Practitioner Research
a guide to understanding and doing research in counselling and health and social care

Pete Sanders & Paul Wilkins

ISBN 978 1 898059 73 8

First Steps in Practitioner Research provides a much-needed, reliable and accessible introduction by two trusted and well-known authors. It builds confidence by not only outlining contemporary methodologies in everyday language, but also by explaining how to approach, understand and evaluate a range of published research.

This is Survivor Research

Angela Sweeney, Peter Beresford, Alison Faulkner, Mary Nettle & Diana Rose (eds)

ISBN 978 1 906254 14 8

This is Survivor Research is a groundbreaking book for policy makers, researchers, educators, students, service users and practitioners in the mental health field and beyond.

This first overview of the state of service user research in Britain today explores the theory and practice of service user research, provides practical examples of service user research, and offers guidance for people wishing to carry out such research themselves.

This book marks the coming of age of user- and survivor-led research. It maps out the why, what and how of an important strand of research whose influence is growing in strength. It needs to be read by researchers, policy makers and the wider mental health community to increase understanding of the impact and integrity of user- and survivor-led research.
Paul Farmer, Chief Executive, MIND

Discounts and free UK p&p from www.pccs-books.co.uk +44(0)1600 891509